INSIGHT GUIDES

HONG KONG
smart guide

APA PUBLICATIONS

Part of the Langenscheidt Publishing Group

Contents

Areas

Below: the Po Lin Monastery.

A–Z

Left: the harbour at night, the best way to arrive.

Atlas

Below: traffic jams, a common sight in Central.

Hong Kong

Exciting, mysterious, glamorous: these words have described Hong Kong for a century. With its vibrant feel and night-and-day activity, Hong Kong is an intoxicating city. Chaotic, intriguing, puzzling, endlessly exciting, in parts possessed of astounding natural beauty, it is a place that sparks strong emotions. Many say this must be one of the earth's acupressure points.

Hong Kong Facts and Figures

Population: 6.9 million (95 per cent Chinese)
Area: 1,098sq km, divided between the four main areas of Hong Kong Island, Kowloon, the New Territories and the Outlying Islands
Location: Just inside the Tropic of Cancer, on the same latitude as Havana and Calcutta.
Official languages: English and Cantonese, a southern dialect of Chinese. The use of Putonghua (Mandarin Chinese) is growing.
Climate: subtropical, with high temperatures and high humidity. Late Sept–late Dec is the driest, most pleasant time to visit. July–Sept is typhoon season, but direct hits on Hong Kong are rare.

Atmosphere

Fuelled and inspired by constant immigration, Hong Kong has nearly 7 million souls simultaneously focused on top dollar and the bottom line in an area smaller than the English county of Berkshire, or less than half the size of the US State of Rhode Island. But although it is crowded – it has one of the world's greatest population densities – it is also efficient, with one of the best transport systems anywhere, and for such a crowded place, it is often surprisingly quiet: you rarely hear voices raised in anger, or motorists sitting on their horns.

Cosmopolitan, yet integrally Chinese, Hong Kong's inhabitants are defined by what is written on their business cards. Hong Kong has long been China's handiest window on the West, and the city is unrivalled in its commercial know-how and managerial expertise.

The Handover and Other Challenges

Around the time of the Handover in July 1997 there was much speculation about how things would change. When Prince Charles and Chris Patten, the last colonial governor, sailed off into the sunset aboard the royal yacht Britannia, it marked the end of a colony, an era and an empire.

A decade on, what little has changed post-Handover has changed for the better. It has a world-class airport, its economy is booming and its excellent stock of hotels continues to upgrade, refurbish and expand. The post-Sars Hong Kong is also a visibly cleaner and friendlier place. Now officially known as Hong Kong Special Administrative Region, it is as vibrant and exciting as ever. As an SAR, Hong Kong has a key role to play in the spectacular growth of the Chinese economy, yet it remains markedly different from the mainland. Hong Kong maintains its own identity, a mix of Chinese parentage with the flamboyance and style of the west. It is anyone's guess what may happen in future, but for now Hong Kong bristles with energy and ambition.

The Lie of the Land

Sightseeing in Hong Kong starts at sea level with the enthralling water traffic against a background of the sci-fi cityscape of spec-

Below: vintage trams still serve the city.

tacular tower blocks climbing up steep hills. From The Peak, Hong Kong Island's highest point, or from its skyscraper-hotels, the views are especially exciting at night, when the harbour comes alive in a blaze of lights.

The business and financial centre and the most eye-popping architecture are on Hong Kong Island. Across Victoria Harbour, connected by ferry and the MTR railway, is the Kowloon peninsula with its hotels, nightlife, and almost non-stop shopping. Beyond, in the New Territories, is a mixture of high-rise suburban towns, ancient temples and walled villages, nature parks and farms with ducks and fish ponds. Hong Kong's other islands, Lantau, Lamma and Cheung Chau, provide tranquil getaways. You can also take a ferry to Macau to find an entirely different city, a rare blend of Chinese and Iberian culture.

Inspiring Mainland China

In spite of increasing competition from its neighbours – the economic revolution in the Pearl River region has catapulted whole new cities like Shenzhen onto the world map, and Macau's lackadaisical ambience has been given a makeover with the arrival of a clutch of casinos and major new developments – Hong Kong remains one of Asia's must-see cities, and looks sure to hold its own for many more decades to come.

Highlights

▲ the **Skyline at night** is a fantastic backdrop for a romantic boat ride.
▶ **Calligraphy** and other uniquely Chinese crafts make exotic souvenirs and the markets are an experience in themselves.

▲ **Dining** in Hong Kong covers all bases, from chic and cheerful fusion cuisine to traditional tripe and chicken feet recipes.

▶ **Beaches** on the southern side of Hong Kong Island and those on outlying islands make for a tranquil retreat from the busy centre.

▲ **Nightlife** is as urgent and frenetic as the business day. SoHo and Lan Kwai Fong are favorites.
▶ **Temples** preserve the people's Buddhist and other religious traditions.

Central and the Peak

When the British arrived on Hong Kong Island in 1841 they settled on its north coast, naming its capital Victoria after their queen. Her Foreign Secretary Lord Palmerston, though, dismissed Hong Kong as only a 'barren island'. The area now known as Central grew around the original colonial capital. Today, with its iconic skyscrapers looming over Victoria Harbour, this is the beating commercial heart of Hong Kong, as well as the backdrop for a trillion postcards. Visit on a weekday lunchtime, when Asia's powerhouse heads for lunch, and you will begin to understand what it is like to share just over 1,200sq km with 6.9 million people.

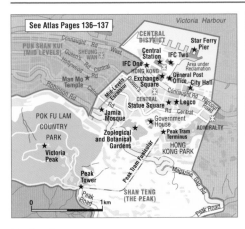

Housing a central business district that is *feng shui'*d within an inch of its life, Central is a good area in which to observe this ancient system of Chinese divination. Dragons, water and lions all play a part in ensuring prosperity, and in guarding the welfare of its inhabitants. The HSBC bank's doors are guarded by a pair of bronze lions, while the Bank of China building purposely flies in the face of *feng shui*, and so is considered to be an untamed 'dragon's den'.

The Star Ferry

Nothing stops progress in Hong Kong – not even its beloved icon, the Star Ferry. The Hong Kong Island pier, its famous clock tower and its small parade of shops were all unceremoniously bulldozed in 2006 and the ferry pier moved a kilometre further west into the ever-shrinking harbour.

The Star Ferry Terminal is now merely Pier One in a string of piers serving Hong Kong's outlying islands. The ferry journey – albeit shorter – still takes in magnificent harbour views, and remains Hong Kong's greatest cheap thrill.

SEE ALSO TRANSPORT, P.125–6

Left: catch one of Hong Kong's iconic trams, which rattle on a loop from Western to Happy Valley via Sheung Wan, Central, Wan Chai and Causeway Bay from De Voeux Road.

climbs up into the narrow lanes of **Lan Kwai Fong**. 'The Fong' is one of Hong Kong's great nightlife hubs, even though the trendier now prefer SoHo next door *(see p.9)*.

Just west you will find one of Hong Kong's curiosities, the 800m-long outdoor **Mid-Levels Escalator**, built to help commuters down (until 10.20am daily) and then up (for the rest of the day) between their Mid-Levels apartment blocks and their workplaces in Central. The Escalator serves as a rough boundary between the Central and Western districts.
SEE ALSO NIGHTLIFE, P.74; SHOPPING, P.100–1

The Peak

Pick your day and you may never see a better city vista anywhere in the world than from the top of Hong Kong Island's mighty mountain. The trick is to head up a bit before dusk at around 4pm so that you enjoy the day and night-time views. Part of the Peak's appeal lies in the getting there: for more than a century the most exhilarating way up has been via the **Peak Tram** funicular, which takes in dizzying glimpses of the harbour below.

Recently re-vamped, the **Peak Tower** now houses more shops, a wider choice of restaurants, a 360-degree rooftop observation deck and an expanded Madame Tussauds waxwork show.
SEE ALSO CHILDREN, P.29; TRANSPORT, P.125; WALKS AND VIEWS, P.128–9

Central Business District

Soaring up around and behind the old Ferry Pier, Hong Kong's steel and glass paeans to commercialism are a must-see. Key landmarks include the cloud-piercing **IFC** towers, which are connected by walkways to the rest of Central via **Exchange Square**, home of the **Hong Kong Stock Exchange** and the **General Post Office**. A few streets further inland is the city's colonial hub, **Statue Square**, where throngs of Filipina maids congregate on a Sunday. Around and near the square are the **Cenotaph** war memorial, the recently refurbished **Mandarin Oriental Hotel**; Norman Foster's **Hongkong and Shanghai Bank Building**; the **Bank of China** tower and the colonial-style former **Supreme**

Opposite: Victoria Harbour during the rainy season.

Court Building, now occupied by the SAR's Legislative Council (Legco).
SEE ALSO ARCHITECTURE, P.23; HOTELS, P.53–4; TEMPLES AND HISTORIC SIGHTS, P.116

Lan Kwai Fong and the Mid-Levels Escalator

Uphill from Statue Square the emphasis changes from making money to spending it, in the glitzy shopping area around the huge **Landmark** mall. Across Queen's Road Central, D'Aguilar Street

---

Time for Tea

On Queen's Road Central there are many Chinese tea shops selling 'cakes' of Chinese teas and fine teaware. Pop in for a demonstration. Just off the Escalator in Stanley Street you can enjoy piping hot tea and *dim sum* at the legendary **Luk Yu Tea House** *(see p.86)*, one of few genuinely old-styled tea houses around Hong Kong.

Western

The Western District contains many of Hong Kong's oldest neighbourhoods, making this one of the most fascinating parts of the city to explore. A few minutes' tram ride from the glass office-obelisks and luxury shopping malls of the Central business district, the traditional shops and distinctly Chinese atmosphere of Sheung Wan represent a classic example of the city's unique East-meets-West culture. Herb and medicine shops, paper shops, rice merchants, makers of incense and *chops* (traditional Chinese carved seals) and some of the city's best antiques dealers can all be found within its warren of side streets.

Sheung Wan

A good point of entry is **Western Market**, opposite the Macau Ferry Terminal. It is a very English-looking four-storey building from 1906 in an otherwise very Chinese district. Here market traders now sell a mix of memorabilia, handicrafts, toys and other gift items on the ground floor, while fabric merchants proffering everything from Chinese silk to Harris tweed occupy **Cloth Alley**, on the upper level. The restaurant on the same floor serves *dim sum* by day and often hosts dances in the evenings.

Visitors can orientate themselves to the many traditional trades and shopping streets in Sheung Wan at the neighbouring compass-style piazza, **Sheung Wan Fong**.
SEE ALSO SHOPPING, P.103

CHOP ALLEY

Man Wa Lane, just east of Sheung Wan MTR, is better known as Chop Alley, due to the dozens of *chop* makers located here. A *chop* is a Chinese seal, carved from natural materials like jade, soapstone, bone or ivory, with the owner's name engraved in Chinese characters; they are still used on contracts today.

There have been *chop* makers in this area since the 1920s; the art itself is 3,000 years old. Ask the maker to translate your name for a custom-made seal; it takes one to four hours to carve. Man Wa Lane is also a good place to pick up fine calligraphy brushes and name cards.

Visit a Chinese medicine shop in Sheung Wan. It is a treat to watch the bizarre and exotic ingredients being chopped, weighed (with hand scales) and calculated (sometimes with an abacus). Among oddities like dried bull's penises, shark's fin and sliced antler you may find a surprise remedy for a problem.

FUNERAL SHOPPING

Queen's Road West is a popular haunt for those in search of floral wreaths, joss sticks, paper money and brass urns. Boutiques sell everything one could possibly need for a traditional Chinese funeral, and coffin shops are conveniently located just around the corner on Hollywood Road. Keeping up with the times, paper items for the afterlife now include speedboats, microwave ovens, mobile phones and karaoke players.

ANTIQUES

Around the western end of **Hollywood Road** and Upper

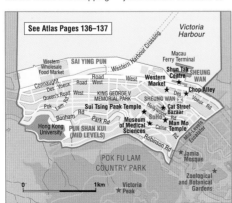

See Atlas Pages 136–137

Victoria Harbour

Western Wholesale Food Market
SAI YING PUN
Macau Ferry Terminal
Shun Tak Centre
Western Harbour Crossing
Connaught Road West
Des Voeux Road West
Western Market
SHEUNG WAN
Queen's Road West
KING GEORGE V MEMORIAL PARK
Des Voeux Rd
Chop Alley
SHEUNG WAN
Pok Lam Rd
Sui Tsing Paak Temple
Hollywood Rd
Cat Street Bazaar
Bonham Rd
Park Rd
Museum of Medical Sciences
SoHo
Man Mo Temple
Hong Kong University
PUN SHAN KUI (MID LEVELS)
Caine Rd
Mid Levels Escalator
Robinson Rd
Jamia Mosque
POK FU LAM COUNTRY PARK
Zoological and Botanical Gardens
0   1km
Victoria Peak

Left: the latest fashions, made to order.

Western District was the first part of Hong Kong to be settled by the British in 1841. However, the prevalence of malaria soon scared them away towards Government Hill and Happy Valley, leaving this part of Hong Kong Island to be occupied by the Chinese migrants who began to arrive in the early 1850s.

where one of the founders of modern China, Dr Sun Yat-sen, worked and trained, and so form the focus of the **Dr Sun Yat-sen Historical Trail**. Maps of the trail are available at the **Sun Yat-sen Museum** on Castle Road.

Returning to modern Hong Kong, a short way eastwards you can wander into one of the most fashionable areas for socialising, **SoHo** (South of Hollywood Road), running across into Central either side of the Mid-Levels Escalator *(see p.7)*. What began as a handful of restaurants and cafés on **Staunton Street** has spread like a rash, with a diverse mix of bars, cafés, restaurants, clubs, boutiques and designer shops nudging old Chinese shopfronts.

SEE ALSO MUSEUMS AND GALLERIES, P.64, 67; NIGHTLIFE, P.74

Lascar Row (also known as **Cat Street Bazaar**) is a fascinating, pedestrian-friendly area known for its antiques and curios. Shop windows and open doors reveal an alluring selection of Asian furniture, carpets, carvings, porcelain and bronze. Among the junk you will find real bargains, as well as a healthy line in Mao memorabilia.

Man Mo Temple

Man Mo is the island's oldest house of worship (though the date of its foundation is disputed), and a photogenic tribute to the gods of literature and martial arts. The temple is often crowded with worshippers and, on entering, visitors are confronted by a dense pall of smoke from scores of burning joss sticks and the incense coils that hang from the ceiling. The

gold-plated sedan chairs on one side of the temple were once used for transporting the statues of the temple's gods in processions.

Mid-Levels and SoHo

The quieter streets on the slopes above Man Mo form an area rich in historical resonances. Along Caine Lane you will find the rather quirky **Hong Kong Museum of Medical Sciences**. Hong Kong's first medical institutions were also the places

Right: Sheung Wan street scene.

Wan Chai and Causeway Bay

T he vibrant neighbourhoods of Wan Chai and Causeway Bay are some of the most populated and fascinating in Hong Kong, with the 'movie-reel' strip of road – Johnston and Hennessy roads – that links the two is best viewed from the top deck of a tram. Once the haunt of off-duty servicemen and wayward women, Wan Chai will forever be associated with *The World of Suzy Wong*, but a rash of new shops, bars and restaurants and luxury flat developments has given the area a new lease of life.

Wan Chai Waterfront

The **Hong Kong Convention and Exhibition Centre** or 'big bird', as this gull-like structure has been dubbed, dominates the spectacular harbourside development in Wan Chai. Built on reclaimed land just in time for the Handover ceremony in 1997, it affords stunning views.

Behind it soars **Central Plaza**, Hong Kong's second tallest building and the world's 10th, at 374m tall. Just west is another modern highlight, the **Hong Kong Academy for Performing Arts** on Gloucester Road, opposite which is the black-brick **Hong Kong Arts Centre**, a thriving hub for the city's arts scene with theatres, cinemas and art galleries.

SEE ALSO MUSIC, DANCE
AND THEATRE, P.72

BAR SCENE

The busy MTR exits of **Lockhart Road** and **Hennessy Road** form the epicentre of Wan Chai, and heading westwards you will find a lively neighbourhood that is home to furniture shops, office blocks and plentiful bars and restaurants, tucked beneath the office towers. Some of Hong Kong's trendiest bars are here, leaving the diehard girly bars on Lockhart Road fighting for customers.

Hong Kong's newest corner of culinary excellence can be found on **Star Street**, a stylish enclave of restaurants (a couple with roof gardens), cafés and shops on Wan Chai's south-western edge. Do not miss the freshly contemporary **Ming Cha** tea shop (7 Star Street), offering a modern, more accessible take on the traditional Chinese tea shop with a tea bar, over 40 varieties of loose-leaf tea and pleasant, friendly staff to boot.

Victoria Harbour

See Atlas Pages 138–139

Below: the Hong Kong Convention and Exhibition Centre.

Left: Wan Chai has left its notorious past behind.

Happy Valley racecourse is a state-of-the-art tribute to sport and gamling. Gigantic 20- by 5.8-m video screens show the races in progress, as well as the state of the betting, racing forms and other relevant data. The total amount bet every season is the highest of any racecourse in the world, with much of the profits donated to charity. *See also Sport, p.114.*

CRAFTS AND TEMPLES

Three blocks south of Lockhart Road, **Queen's Road East** and the narrow streets around it are remarkable for their rattan and rosewood furniture shops. It is worth taking a look also at two traditional temples that stand in stark contrast to their modern surroundings. Tiny, dark **Hung Shing Temple** on Queen's Road East (by Tai Wing Street) was named after a Tang-dynasty official who was renowned for his ability to make valuable predictions for traders.

The impressive **Pak Tai Temple** at the top of Stone Nullah Lane is a triple-halled building noted for its 400-year-old, 3m statue of the deity Pak Tai, who assures harmony on earth. There are usually elderly locals pottering around in the dark recesses of the temple, lighting incense sticks or laying out offerings.

Causeway Bay Shopping

Nowhere is the relationship between the Hong Kong dollar and the shopping bag more visible than in the retail forest that is Causeway Bay. Known locally as 'Little Japan', it is packed with designer boutiques, cosmetics shops and Japanese department stores, and is nothing short of a shopper's heaven, albeit a polluted one. If you can not find it here, it probably does not exist.

Fans of Muji and all things minimalist should pop into the landmark **Sogo** on Hennessy Road, for a Japanese style fix or a healthy bowl of noodle soup. Every kind of shop can be found in megamalls such as **Times Square**, while yet more Japanese brands and some interesting local designers can be found around **Great George Street** in mini-malls such as **Island Beverley** and the **Fashion Walk**. For a rest, just to the west there is the green space of **Victoria Park**.

SEE ALSO SHOPPING, P.99–101; PARKS AND GARDENS, P.85

Happy Valley

Continue eastwards on a Happy Valley-bound tram for another 15 min or so and you will arrive at **Happy Valley Racecourse**. A visit to the Wednesday-night races during the September to June racing season is a must, but during the day it is worth calling in at the **Hong Kong Racing Museum**, at the Happy Valley Stand inside the racecourse, which tells the story of horseracing in the colony with plenty of colourful background on the equestrian obsession that, twice a week, holds much of Hong Kong to ransom.

SEE ALSO MUSEUMS AND GALLERIES, P.64; SPORT, P.113–14

Venture beyond Happy Valley to several panoramic lookouts. One of the most popular is the **Stubbs Road Lookout** (bus 15), which offers vistas of the harbour, the Kowloon waterfront and the Central Plaza building, with the racecourse down to the right.

11

The Southside

In contrast to the northern coast of Hong Kong Island, which has changed almost beyond recognition in the last 20 to 30 years, the rocky southern shore remains more or less as nature intended. The character of this relatively unspoilt part of Hong Kong is in complete contrast to the heavily urbanized strip on the other side of the mountains. The rides and dolphins at Ocean Park are a major draw, while elsewhere there are some fine beaches for swimming, surfing or just sunbathing; engaging water-front towns with relaxed streetlife; pleasant villages; and challenging walks through remarkably empty forests with wonderful vistas.

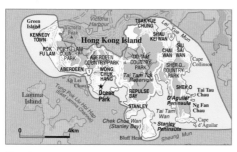

On your way to Stanley look out for a large blue apartment building called The Repulse Bay, with a big square hole in the middle. Some say the hole is a passageway for the heavenly dragon to come down from the mountains; others that it was put there to generate good *feng shui*; others that it was simply the architect's attempt at being funky.

Aberdeen

The harbour town of Aberdeen has a character unlike any other part of Hong Kong, and is immediately recognisable for its flotilla of bobbing junks and sampans housing what remains of Hong Kong's 'boat people'. This waterside community resides in one of the island's few natural typhoon shelters, and consists of two main groups: the *Tanka* (literally, 'the egg people', because they used to pay taxes with eggs rather than cash) and the *Hoklo*.

Tourists often get a ring-side view of life on the harbour during the boat shuttle journey to one of the world's largest floating restaurants, the **Jumbo Kingdom**. These famous boats recently underwent a multi-million dollar refurbishment, and now include shops, a museum and even a Chinese culinary academy. Aberdeen's commercial attractions do not only relate to eating, either, for on the offshore island of Ap Lei Chau is the hugely popular **Horizon Plaza** discount warehouse and factory store.

SEE ALSO RESTAURANTS, P.93; SHOPPING, P.105

TIN HAU TEMPLE

A trip to Aberdeen is not complete without a visit to the island's Tin Hau Temple on Aberdeen Main Road, and particularly during the **Tin Hau Festival** in April or May.

Tin Hau is the goddess of the sea and a traditionally important figure in the fishing community, and there are temples honouring her all over Hong Kong. At festival time thousands of boats converge on Aberdeen's shores, and the temple is decorated with paper shrines and lanterns. Highly charged and photogenic lion dances are performed outside.

Left: Stanley Beach.

Left: boarding a boat at Aberdeen harbour.

contains the **Hong Kong Maritime Museum**. The **Old Stanley Police Station** is one of only 30 protected historic buildings in Hong Kong, and the quirky **Correctional Services Museum** relates the history of Hong Kong's prisons. Near the prison is **Stanley Military Cemetery**, with tombstones dating to early colonial times.

Around the coast from Stanley, in the south-east corner of the island, **Shek O** is one of its most laidback villages. It is best known for adjacent **Big Wave Bay**, the haunt of Hong Kong surfers.
SEE ALSO MUSEUMS AND GALLERIES, P.62–3; SHOPPING, P.103

Ocean Park

Ocean Park celebrated its 30th anniversary in 2007, making it relatively ancient by Hong Kong standards. But thanks to a combination of its seaside setting on a headland overlooking the South China Sea and continual investment, the theme park remains perennially popular with locals and a must-see for visiting families. A cablecar ride with spectacular views is a highlight, and the 200-acre park houses rides, an aquarium with 2,000 sea creatures and two giant pandas. The latest attraction is South-east Asia's first jellyfish aquarium.
SEE ALSO CHILDREN, P.28–9

Repulse Bay

Primarily an upmarket residential area, sun-drenched **Repulse Bay** (named after the British battleship HMS *Repulse*), has a relaxed resort-like atmosphere. The wide, wave-lapped beach is great for sandy strolls in the early morning, when the sun is up and the sunbathers are starting to come out in force, or at sunset when all is at peace. This crescent-shaped stretch of sand is one of the most beautiful beaches in Hong Kong, and picturesque gardens lead down to it. The nearby colonial-style Repulse Bay development houses designer shops and award-winning restaurants.

Stanley and Shek O

With its relaxed seaside ambience and sprawling cluster of market stalls, **Stanley Market** is a great place to stock up on bargains. Stanley is also now home to **Murray House**, a former British Army barracks built in 1848, moved stone by stone from the site now filled by the Bank of China in Central, and which now

Beyond Ocean Park to the east is a region of rocky coasts and white sand that contains 14 of Hong Kong's 36 beaches. A few locations, such as **Rocky Bay** on the road to **Shek O**, have virtually no public facilities but offer unparalleled views and uncrowded stretches of sand and sea. Others, like **Repulse Bay**, attract bus loads of tourists and, at weekends, offer about as much peace and quiet as a carnival.

Deep Water Bay 5, the first beach east of Ocean Park, has some beautiful mansions, and is reputed to enjoy some of the best *feng shui* in Hong Kong. It also has a nine-hole golf course managed by the Hong Kong Golf Club (open weekdays to the public). Further along the road towards Stanley is the exclusive Hong Kong Country Club. The long stretch of beach here offers a quiet place to soak up the sun or go for a swim. *See also Sport, p.115.*

Kowloon

Though not short of the malls and hotels Hong Kong is known for, sprawling Kowloon is in many ways the Chinese alter ego of bold, modern Central. Its waterfront has some of Hong Kong's biggest recent constructions, in the mall-space of Harbour City or the giant tower of One Peking Road, while along the great snake of Nathan Road is the gaudy array of discount electronics stores that has become a new Hong Kong landmark. Leave commercial Kowloon behind, however, and you will find in its streets and markets genuine pockets of Chinese-ness that will transport you far from the glamour of 21st-century Hong Kong.

The Waterfront

The **Star Ferry Pier**, with its adjacent **Railway Clock Tower**, the sweeping curve of the **Hong Kong Cultural Centre** and the igloo-like **Hong Kong Space Museum** are the Kowloon harbourside's most prominent landmarks. Plenty more have sprouted up around them, such as the five malls of **Harbour City** and massive new hotels.

Above: the high-rise flats on the coast of Kowloon.

Dating from 1915, the railway tower is the last vestige of the historic **Kowloon-Canton Railway (KCR) Station**, once the final stop in a system that ran all the way to Europe. The waterfront promenade offers unparalleled views of the harbour and Hong Kong Island, and is now also known for its **Avenue of Stars** along Salisbury Road, a star-studded path honouring the city's film glitterati.

SEE ALSO FILM, P.43; MUSEUMS AND GALLERIES, P.65; MUSIC, DANCE AND THEATRE, P.72–3; SHOPPING, P.100; TEMPLES AND HISTORIC SITES, P.117; TRANSPORT, P.125–6.

Tsim Sha Tsui

TST, as this southern tip of Kowloon is known, is the commercial honeypot that attracts the tourist bees. The heart of Tsim Sha Tsui is known as the 'Golden Mile', its central axis, which actually rolls on for far more than a mile (1.6km) of **Nathan Road**. Tsim Sha Tsui's southern tip is also the location of the majority of Hong Kong's tourist hotels.

Lacking the steep mountainsides that hem in the north shore of Hong Kong Island, Kowloon sprawls in every sense of the word. But with Nathan Road as its spine, and peppered with MTR stations, it is very easy to navigate.

SEE ALSO SHOPPING, P.100

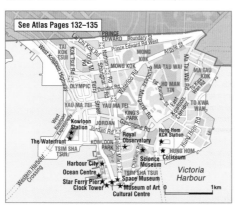

See Atlas Pages 132–135

Left: the Kowloon Bird Market.

towers, the **Hong Kong History** and **Science** museums and the new main railway station, in **Hung Hom**. With all this building there has naturally been a growth of shops, bars and restaurants, especially around **Mody Road**.
SEE ALSO MUSEUMS AND GALLERIES, P.64–5

Yau Ma Tei and Mong Kok

Street markets and old buildings have escaped demolition in these areas further north along Nathan Road, making them great places to explore. The **Flower**, **Goldfish** and **Bird** markets, the **Temple Street Night Market** and the famous **Jade Market** are all here. These areas can provide fascinating vignettes of local life, and are home to a clutch of Hong Kong's most interesting temples, such as the **Tin Hau Temple** in Yau Ma Tei.
SEE ALSO SHOPPING, P.102–3; TEMPLES AND HISTORIC SITES, P.117

ALONG NATHAN ROAD
Named after former Governor Sir Matthew Nathan, whose central urban planning and reconstruction policy led to the development of several major thoroughfares on the Kowloon peninsula, these days Nathan Road is fast being usurped by newer and more stylish shopping options. Host to the Hong Kong image of gaudy neon signs and hundreds of small electronics shops, it is not an attractive place, but few can deny the electricity of life here, especially at night.

SHOPPING AND DINING
The main shopping and entertainment area of Tsim Sha Tsui extends either side of the MTR station: around **Peking**, **Hankow** and **Haiphong** roads on the western side, and **Carnarvon** and **Kimberley** roads to the east. There are some excellent shopping and dining pockets here, with hundreds of restaurants from five-star haute cuisine to inexpensive *dai pai dongs* dishing out noodles and sticky rice balls. The Kowloon renaissance is particularly evident in and around **Minden Avenue**, which some say is Kowloon's answer to Lan Kwai Fong.

The latest focus for modernisation is further on in the area labelled **Tsim Sha Tsui East**, with more gleaming

Left: neon signs, Nathan Road.

Kowloon's Changing Face
Until Kai Tak Airport closed in the late 1990s, regulations restricted Kowloon's buildings to a modest height. Now, they shoot skywards as never before, a process most obvious in the 'West Kowloon Reclamation' above Kowloon MTR station, where the Union Square development is to include a 484-m skyscraper, set to be the city's tallest. The Hong Kong government has also earmarked the land around the cross-harbour tunnel's mouth as the site of a new 'cultural district'. Among the buildings that have already pierced the Kowloon sky are One Peking on Peking Road, and Langham Place, a multi-use mall, hotel and office complex, (*see p.57*).

New Kowloon

Officially part of the New Territories, the districts such as Sham Shui Po, Kowloon Tong, Wong Tai Sin, Kowloon City, Kwun Tong and Yau Tsim Mong that spread north of Boundary Street – so-called because it marks the boundary between Hong Kong Colony and the territory leased from China in 1898 – have long been integrated into the city, and are known as New Kowloon. The urban forest that characterises these areas is juxtaposed with historic architecture, temples and archaeological ruins and – if you know where to look, among the densely populated housing estates and shopping malls – it is possible to find some real Hong Kong gems.

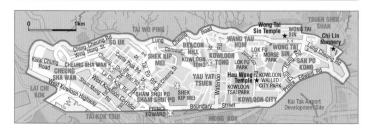

Sham Shui Po

To the northwest of Mong Kok, the old districts of Sham Shui Po and **Cheung Sha Wan** are easily accessed by MTR. Sham Shui Po is the place to head (as locals do) for computers and related merchandise, with a huge assortment of arcades and stalls around the junction of **Yen Chow**

The **Chi Lin Nunnery** (close to Diamond Hill MTR) is the largest Buddhist nunnery in Southeast Asia, and a living museum of the Tang dynasty (618–907). The nunnery comprises a number of Buddhist halls serving various functions, and a tranquil garden with lotus ponds flanks the main entrance. A dining hall, open on Sundays, serves decent vegetarian food. *See also Temples and Historic Sites, p.117*

Right: Wong Tai Sin Temple.

and **Fuk Wa** streets. All along **Apliu Street** there is an open-air market selling cheap electrical goods, and many of the latest gizmos, from iPods to DVD players, are *sui foh*: imported directly from Japan, and so available at very low prices. Be prepared, though, because the service style is often hectic and high-pressure, and rip-offs do occur. Check items carefully before parting with your cash.
SEE ALSO SHOPPING, P.107

Wong Tai Sin

Probably the liveliest and most colourful place of worship in Hong Kong, and one of the most rewarding for outsiders to visit, is **Wong Tai Sin Temple**, sitting opposite the MTR station of the same name, and easily recognisable by its bright-

yellow roof tiling. Backed by the formidable Lion Rock and facing the sea, this shrine to the Taoist god of healing has *feng shui* in spades. The rear of the main altar is carved to show, both pictorially and in calligraphy, the story of this great god. There are two gardens surrounding the temple and a Confucian hall next door, and

Kowloon City is known for cheap, rough-and-ready restaurants that serve dishes within minutes of ordering. If you don't mind high-decibel dining, or sharing a table with strangers, then the area has an enormous range of inexpensive and highly rated Chinese, Vietnamese, and especially Thai restaurants.

English-speaking fortune-tellers are on hand to predict your future.

SEE ALSO TEMPLES AND HISTORIC SITES, P.118

Kowloon City

Within New Kowloon, just south of Wong Tai Sin, this area's name commemorates the once-famous **Kowloon Walled City**, a place with a unique history within Hong Kong. A fortress was built here by the Chinese government in the 19th century, governed by a Manchu magistrate; hence, it was excluded from the treaty that granted Britain the New Territories on a 99-year lease in 1898. The Walled City was thus outside the laws of the British colony, from criminal laws to building regulations, and by the 1950s the area had become a notorious slum, a centre of criminality with some of Hong Kong's worst housing.

Any change was complicated, since governments in both Beijing and Taiwan demanded their say, but eventually, in 1992, the Walled City was demolished and much of its former site landscaped as an attractive city park. Kowloon City is easily explored on foot, starting at Lok Fu MTR station. As well as the park, other sites include the **Chinese Christian Cemetery**, with its graves stacked up like sardines on concrete terraces, and the tiny **Hau Wong Temple**.

KOWLOON WALLED CITY PARK

Laid out like a classic garden of southern China, the park seeks to preserve something of the heritage of Kowloon's fabled Walled City. Several remnants – the foundation of

Right: the Chinese Christian Cemetery.

the former wall, large parts of the Walled City's south and east gates, and a flagstone path next to the drainage ditch along the foot of the inner wall – have been preserved. Other attractions include a chess garden, the **Mountain View Pavilion**, from which Lion Rock (495m) can be seen looming in the distance, sculptures, pavilions and attractive pathways lined with trees and flower borders. Near the southern gate an information centre houses a photographic exhibition detailing the history of the Walled City and the construction of the park, as well as many relics used or found within the Walled City.

The New Territories

Hong Kong's northern hinterland is well off the tourist trail, which seems surprising given its calm beaches, lofty mountains, forests and ancient walled villages. Many visitors seem so used to thinking of Hong Kong as a city that they never look beyond its urban core, or realise just how much countryside the Territory possesses. Acting as a buffer between Kowloon and the boundary with Mainland China, the towns and villages of the New Territories are an odd mix of the traditional and the very modern. Exploring is easy, with access on the KCR railway lines from Kowloon up to the Chinese border at Lo Wu, and northwest to Tuen Mun.

Left: Hakka woman wearing a traditional fringed hat and a rare smile.

Sha Tin Racecourse

Hong Kong's first and largest 'new town', **Sha Tin** is home to a handful of attractions, notably the **Hong Kong Heritage Museum** and the racecourse. Happy Valley tends to steal Sha Tin's thunder on the international stage, but to overlook this magnificent course is a great shame: it is a bigger course, it has racing all weekend rather than just one night a week, and it now hosts all local racing's blueriband events, such as the Hong Kong Derby.

Sha Tin Racecourse can hold some 78,000 spectators, and has the world's largest Diamond Vision Video Screen (70.4m high). Betting pools regularly reach into the hundreds of millions of dollars. In terms of sheer pageantry Chinese New Year is possibly the best time to come here, but race days are never short of excitement – or crowds.

SEE ALSO MUSEUMS AND GALLERIES, P.63; SPORT, P.113–14

SHA TIN'S TEMPLES

The Sha Tin Valley has several places of worship, but first and foremost is the **Temple of 10,000 Buddhas**, reached by climbing 431 steps flanked by gold-painted effigies of enlightened beings up the hillside above Sha Tin station. The temple's main altar room actually has 12,800 Buddha statues along its walls. A further 69 steps up the hill is the Temple of **Man Fat**, containing the preserved remains of the monk who created this temple-pagoda complex, Yuet Kai.

From the Temple of 10,000 Buddhas you can look across the valley at **Amah Rock**, said to resemble an *amah*, or nanny, with a baby on her back. A place of

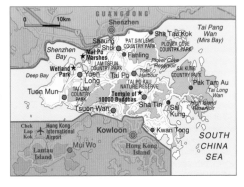

The Walled Villages of the New Territories trace their roots to the 10th century, when the 'five clans' moved here from further north, near Guangzhou, and built these fortified settlements to protect themselves from marauding outsiders, and each other. Later villages were occupied by the *Hakka*, North Chinese migrants settled here by government decree in the 17th–18th centuries, and who lived apart from the Cantonese. The way of life in the walled villages remains fairly traditional, so it is worth paying the small donation to enter. The price for taking a picture of a *Hakka* woman wearing a traditional fringed hat will vary depending on your bargaining skills, and do not expect a smile. *See also Temples and Historic Sites, p.118.*

worship for Chinese women, it stands as a symbol of women's loyalty and fidelity. SEE ALSO TEMPLES AND HISTORIC SITES, P.118.

Plover Cove and Sai Kung Peninsula

The northeast corner of the New Territories is one of Hong Kong's least-developed areas, and a good place to observe the traditional lifestyles of farmers and fishing communities in the surrounding countryside. It also includes large stretches of remarkably wild countryside, coast and mountain, excellent for hiking and bird watching. At **Plover Cove** visitors can obtain information on walks and nature trails around the nearby **Plover Cove Reservoir**.

Just to the south, the **Sai Kung Peninsula** is a designated recreational area and a popular destination for local walkers, picnickers, swimmers and sailors.

SAI KUNG COUNTRY PARK
The convoluted coastline of the New Territories includes some fine stretches of beach – nowhere more so than at **Tai Long Wan** on the eastern edge of Sai Kung, where powdery white sands meet some relatively decent surf. Kill two birds with one stone and get here (it takes about an hour's hike) along part of the **MacLehose Trail,** which starts in Sai Kung Country Park and stretches for 100km through mostly open country. Join the trail at **Pak Tam Au**.

Some of Hong Kong's most enjoyable outer islands sit in the inner Port Shelter, offshore from Sai Kung Village. Sampan owners will make a 1hr trip for around HK$100 to whichever island you wish, or charge around HK$300 to drop you at your destination and collect you later. Whichever you decide to do, bargain hard!

Sai Kung town itself is known for its string of seaside restaurants, which line the busy quayside. You can also take a sampan from here to some of Hong Kong's outlying islands *(see box, left)*. SEE ALSO SPORTS, P.115

Other Nature Reserves

Tolo Harbour north of Sai Kung, the **Mirs Bay** islands to the east, and the new **Hong Kong Wetland Park** in the Mai Po marshes in Deep Bay are all worth exploring. But one of the best places to escape urban Hong Kong is the **Tai Po Kau Nature Reserve**, a short taxi ride from Tai Po Market KCR station. Planting began here in 1926, and today the 450-hectare forest shelters a good proportion of Hong Kong's flora and fauna. SEE ALSO CHILDREN, P.28

The Outer Islands

Hong Kong's outlying islands are quite literally a breath of fresh air in what can sometimes be a stifling city. But as well as being good for the constitution, a visit to laid-back Lantau, Cheung Chau, Lamma, tiny Peng Chau or – with a bit more exploration – some of the smallest and more remote islands can offer an insight into a way of life that is fast disappearing in Hong Kong. The islands are also home to some of the Territory's most beautiful temples and most vibrant festivals. Take at least half a day and if possible a bit longer to explore, adapt to the pace, and you will be rewarded with memories far removed from the hurly-burly of the city.

Above: Tai O fishing harbour, Lantau.

Each year Cheung Chau hosts its four-day **Bun Festival** when giant bamboo towers covered with edible buns are erected in the courtyard of Pak Tai Temple. In the past, local boys climbed the towers to pluck their lucky buns, and the higher the bun, the more luck it would bring. These days, it is trained athletes who risk their necks.
See also Festivals, p.38

Lantau

Majestic and ruggedly mountainous, Lantau is often referred to as Hong Kong's green lung. More than twice the size of Hong Kong Island, it has country parks, beaches and coastal villages that make it a popular retreat for day-trippers and weekenders. Lantau remains largely rural, but inevitably the peace and seclusion of much of the island, typified by the Buddhist monasteries dotted around the mountain slopes, is steadily being eroded. Hong Kong International Airport lies on its north-western coast, while **Hong Kong Disneyland** now occupies a giant site on the island's eastern tip at Penny's Bay. Lantau's main sights can be covered in a day, but avoid

Sundays and public holidays, when the ferries are packed.
SEE ALSO CHILDREN, P.28

TEMPLE IN THE CLOUDS
Lantau's main draw is its bronze 202-tonne Big Buddha, which peers down over the **Po Lin Monastery** complex. Po Lin is the largest of Hong Kong's Buddhist temples, a sprawling complex of

temples, gateways and gardens, and a major point of pilgrimage for Hong Kong's Buddhists. Founded in 1905 by three humble monks who wanted a quiet retreat away from the hustle and bustle of Hong Kong, it also has an excellent vegetarian restaurant for its visitors.
SEE ALSO TEMPLES AND HISTORIC SITES, P.119; WALKS AND VIEWS, P.131

Left: the Big Buddha at Po Lin Monastery.

have their ways of getting round this, with noisy little 'tractor-trucks'. It is also an island of two halves. The small village of **Yung Shue Wan** is where the majority of the island's residents live, including a large number of expats. Despite a frequent ferry service to Central, this road-free island remains slow-paced, and Yung Shue Wan clings to the last vestiges of Hong Kong's hippy backpacker scene. A handful of restaurants, pubs and cafés line the waterfront, although it is **Sok Kwu Wan**, a 90-minute walk across the island, which is better known for its string of Chinese seafood restaurants.
SEE ALSO WALKS AND VIEWS, P.131

Cheung Chau

Dumbbell-shaped Cheung Chau, just south of Lantau, offers some good walks, fine beaches, a handful of temples dedicated to Tin Hau, goddess of the sea, and is known for throwing some of Hong Kong's most exuberant and colourful festivals, such as the **Bun Festival** *(see opposite)*.

Cheung Chau village has a lively waterfront atmosphere. The waterfront promenade, the **praya**, is one of Hong Kong's most pleasant alfresco dining spots, especially after sunset. Head off in any direction from the ferry terminal and you will find both modern and traditional shops and restaurants. The village, around the ferry dock, is a tangle of interesting alleyways best explored at leisure; if you get lost, simply steer yourself back downhill. Cheung Chau also offers excellent **windsurfing**, centred on **Afternoon Beach**.
SEE ALSO SPORT, P.115

Peng Chau

About a third of the size of Cheung Chau, and linked to it by an inter-island ferry service as well as to the main Hong Kong ferry piers, Peng Chau has many of the larger island's charms but on a more intimate scale. It is so small that you can walk around the island in an hour. There is an attractive little fishing harbour, 200-year-old **Tin Hau** temple and the **Kum Fa Temple**, dedicated to Lady Kum Fa, who is said to help fertility.

Lamma

Characterised by grassy hills, picturesque bays and small inland patches of farmland, Lamma is famously the island where no motor vehicles are allowed, although locals

For information on island ferries, *see Transport, p.126*. The three key islands are accessible in under 1hr (or as quickly as 25 min on the faster ferries) from the Central Ferry Piers. Services are frequent and inexpensive. Alternatively, the Island Hopping Pass allows unlimited daytime travel to Cheung Chau, Lantau and Peng Chau, and comes with a handy guidebook. Another time-saving option is the HKTB's Lantau Island tour, which takes in the monastery and Big Buddha, Cheung Sha beach and the stilted fishing village of Tai O, home to the Tanka boat people. More adventurous island-hoppers can find various ferry and *kaido* services that will enable them to explore more of Hong Kong's backwater villages, such as the fishing communities of Tap Mun, (accessible via Tolo Harbour or Sai Kung) or Po Toi (via Stanley or Aberdeen).

21

Architecture

A forest of gleaming towers, Hong Kong's cityscape is a dazzling emblem of its energy, and one of the most astonishing things about it is that it is a very recent creation. As Hong Kong's economy has picked up from its stumbles by launching into ever-bigger booms since the 1980s, the world's star architects have come here to realise some of their most ambitious ideas, in glass, steel and rarer materials. The buildings of an older Hong Kong – despite campaigns to save them – are given scant respect when their sites are wanted for something newer and bigger, but a few still poke through among the towers.

Colonial Hong Kong

The British administrators of Hong Kong began putting up buildings in styles to their taste soon after the foundation of the colony in 1841. The first settlement was around Possession Street in Sheung Wan, but the centre of administration was on higher, more salubrious ground further south, which became known as **Government Hill**.

The city's first Anglican church, the neo-Gothic **St John's Cathedral**, was inaugurated there in 1849. The army headquarters, **Flagstaff House** (1846), and **Government House**, the official residence of Hong Kong's governors (1851–5), on the other hand, were both built in Georgian neoclassical style.

SEE ALSO MUSEUMS AND GALLERIES, P.62, TEMPLES AND HISTORIC SITES, P.116

1920s–1930s

Hong Kong experienced its first big burst of growth after World War I, but few major buildings from that era remain. The most distinguished survivor is the **Peninsula Hotel**,

from 1928, though its 30-storey central tower was only added in the 1990s. Hong Kong's first skyscraper came in 1935 at **Chater Garden**, on Statue Square (Central). The sombre granite building has been demolished, leaving a pair of bronze lions marking the spot at the foot of its replacement, the HSBC headquarters (*see opposite*).

SEE ALSO HOTELS, P.58

1945–1980

The growth of Hong Kong really soared with the massive population influx from mainland China after the Communist takeover in 1949. In 1953 the Housing Authority was formed in reaction to a disastrous fire that made 50,000 squatters homeless. The anonymous blocks thrown up in the next 20 years set sadly low architectural standards, but are characteristic of modern Hong Kong. A spate of demolitions also followed, removing colonial landmarks such as the original 1920s Repulse Bay Hotel.

In 1973 Hong Kong's first modern office tower,

When Hong Kong's airport was at nearby Kai Tak, official restrictions limited the height of all buildings in Kowloon. Since the new airport opened in 1998, though, Kowloon has become the new area for developers to realize their most ambitious projects. In 2005 the Langham Place shopping mall, hotel and office complex kick-started regeneration in Mong Kok. Kowloon's mushrooming structures also include Hong Kong's first solar-powered skyscraper, One Peking Road, and all Hong Kong's tallest towers will be demoted by Union Square, a vast development being built around Kowloon MTR station.

the 50-storey, aluminium clad **Jardine House**, was built for Jardine Matheson, one of the the colony's oldest companies. Its porthole-like windows prompted one of the city's most enduring nicknames: 'The House of a Thousand Arseholes' (also referring to its occupants).
Jardine House
1 Connaught Place, Central;
MTR: Central; map p.137 D3

Left: steel and glass are the keynotes of Hong Kong's modern skyline.

Post-1997

The pace has not let up since the Handover. The vast new **Hong Kong International Airport**, also by Norman Foster, opened in 1998 at Chek Lap Kok on reclaimed land off Lantau. In the same year the 346-m high **Center** tower rose above Sheung Wan, and still stuns the city with its nightly light display.

In a different direction, in 2000 the **Kadoorie Biological Sciences Building** opened at the University of Hong Kong, winning awards for its energy-efficient design.

More usual for Hong Kong is the 2003 **International Financial Centre Two (Two IFC)** tower, the tallest in Hong Kong (so far) at 415m, capped by a mass of curving spires.

The Center
99 Queen's Road, Western; MTR: Central; map p.137 C3
Two IFC
Finance Street, Central; MTR: Central; map p.137 D4
Kadoorie Biological Sciences Building
University of Hong Kong, Pok Fu Lam Road, Western; bus: 23, 40

1980–1997

Hong Kong surged skywards with a string of emblematic buildings. In 1985 the soaring Norman Foster-designed **Hongkong and Shanghai Bank (HSBC)** was completed. With an atrium open to the public, 'The Bank' is a symbol of modern Hong Kong, featuring on its banknotes. In 1988 it was followed by the **Lippo Centre** at Admiralty. With precariously protruding blocks clinging to the outside of its two towers, it is nicknamed 'The Koala Building'.

In 1990 the HSBC was joined by the equally spectacular, bamboo-inspired **Bank of China** tower by I.M. Pei. To the consternation of locals, Pei ignored *feng shui* and its sharp corners mean bad luck for the building's neighbours, in particular the HSBC.

The last years of British rule saw a constant wave of new building. **Central Plaza** in Wan Chai, Hong Kong's second tallest structure with 78 storeys, opened in 1992, and the bird-like **Peak Tower**, by British architect Terry Farrell, in 1996.

The **Hong Kong Convention and Exhibition Centre**, begun in 1994, was completed just in time to host the Handover ceremony in 1997. The imaginative building, on reclaimed land off Wan Chai, is evocative of a flying gull, or perhaps lotus petals or clam shells. In May 1997 the 2.5km **Tsing Ma Bridge**, linking the city to Lantau and the new airport, opened: a stunning sight when illuminated at night.

Bank of China
1 Garden Road, Central; viewing gallery Mon–Fri 8am–6pm; MTR: Central; map p.137 D2
Central Plaza
18 Harbour Road, Wan Chai; MTR: Wan Chai; map p.138 B3
Hong Kong Convention and Exhibition Centre
Expo Road, Wan Chai; MTR: Wan Chai; map p.137 D2
HSBC Building
1 Queen's Road, Central; MTR: Central; map p.137 D2
Lippo Centre
Queensway, Central; MTR: Admiralty; map p.137 E2
Peak Tower
128 Peak Road, Central; daily 7am–midnight; Peak Tram: Garden Road; map p.136

Below: Bank of China.

Bars

Hong Kong's hard-working populace also likes to play and drink hard as well. With both a large expat community and locals who like to enjoy a tipple or two, there is a huge number of bars, from local drinking dens to stylish wine bars and theme pubs, catering for their needs. The younger crowds mostly head for Lan Kwai Fong and around, SoHo (south of Hollywood Road) above Central, and to Tsim Sha Tsui, along Ashley Road or off Carnarvon Road. Areas to avoid, with sleazy, dressed-up brothels and over-priced 'hostess bars', are Wan Chai and Tsim Sha Tsui East.

Central and the Peak

Agave
33 D'Aguilar Street, Lan Kwai Fong; tel: 2521 2010; Mon–Thur and Sun 5pm–2am, Fri–Sat 5pm–4am; MTR: Central (exit D1, D2), bus: 12M, 13, 23A, 40M; map p.137 C3
Fabulous, lively place, serving margaritas, over 100 varieties of tequila (the biggest range in Asia), and possibly the best Mexican food in town.

Al's Diner
27–39 D'Aguilar Street, Lan Kwai Fong; tel: 2869 1869; Mon–Sat 11.30am–1am, Sun 11.30–midnight; MTR: Central (exit D1, D2), bus: 12M, 13, 23A, 40M; map p.137 C3

A pioneer of the Lan Kwai Fong area. Try their famous Jello shots, made from flavoured gelatin and vodka.

Club Feather Boa
38 Staunton Street, Central; tel: 2857 7156; Mon–Thur and Sun 8pm–midnight, Fri–Sat 5pm–midnight; Mid–Levels Escalator, bus: 12M, 13, 23A, 26, 40M; map p.136 B3
Like a plush Regency drawing room, with two sofas (get here early to nab one), it used to be an antiques shop, which must have supplied the grandiose fittings and furniture; an amazing experience, eclectic and so SoHo. Out-of-this-world drinks are served in ornate glasses.

Dublin Jack
37 Cochrane Street, Central; tel: 2543 0081; daily noon–2am; MTR: Central (Exit D1, D2),

> Cocktails *(left)* are often a better bet in Hong Kong than straight spirits if you are looking for more of a bang for your buck. You get two or three shots per glass for not much extra cost, and in the best Hong Kong bars cocktails are expertly put together.

Mid–Levels Escalator, bus: 12M, 13, 23A, 26, 40M; map p.136 B3
Rowdy but fun Irish bar, serving draught Irish beers and single malt whiskies to cheer the expat clientele. Outside, it looks like an old Dublin post office, with pavement drinking space; inside, there are big screen sports, and comedy. This was the first-ever bar in Hong Kong to go totally smoke–free indoors.

La Dolce Vita
Cosmos Building, 9–11 Lan Kwai Fong, Central; tel: 2973 0642; Mon–Thur noon–2am, Fri noon–3am, Sat 2pm–3am, Sun 2pm–2am; MTR: Central (exit D1, D2), bus: 12M, 12, 23A, 26, 40M; map p.137 C3
Funky, open-fronted Italian café-bar with pulsating post-house music and tasty Italian snacks, and happy hours daily, 4.30–8pm. Popular for people-watching after work, though staff are a bit snooty.

Le Jardin
1/F, 10 Wing Wah Lane, Central; tel: 2526 2717; Mon–Sat 4.30pm–midnight; MTR: Central (exit D1, D2), bus: 12M, 13, 23A, 26, 40M; map p.137 C3

Wine *(left)* is usually imported, and generally pretty expensive, because it is heavily taxed. There is not a huge range of choice in most Hong Kong restaurants, but decent wines are becoming more widely available by the glass.

Top spot for day-time cappuccinos and night-time people watching, right next to the Mid-Levels Escalator. It is busy seven nights a week, and popular with a 20s–30s crowd; food here is expensive, but it is a good place for pre-club drinking.

Wan Chai and Causeway Bay

1/5
Starcrest, 9 Star Street, Wan Chai; tel: 2520 2515; Mon–Fri 6pm–late, Sat 8pm–late; bus: 5, 5A, 10; map p.138 A2
The name of this loft-style bar is pronounced 'One Fifth' by those in the know. The clientele is exclusive and glamorous; get there early to grab a booth, and dress in your finest duds to get in at all.

Carnegies
53–5 Lockhart Road, Wan Chai; tel: 2866 6289; Mon–Tue and Thur 11am–2am, Wed and Fri 11am–4am, Sat noon–4am, Sun noon–1am; MTR: Wan Chai (exit A1, C), bus: Gloucester and Hennessy roads; map p.138 A2

Most Hong Kong bars have long Happy Hours, with discounts of up to 30 per cent, or special promotions, such as two drinks for the price of one. Happy hours usually run during the early evenings, but can be any time of the day, so if you plan ahead you can find somewhere to fit your timetable. Some bars also offer free drinks for women on certain nights. Check with bar staff first before ordering, as some locations have different policies for which drinks are included in their happy hour offers.

The best outdoor bar in the Central and Lan Kwai Fong area, half-hidden up some steps at the end of a winding lane. Isolation from the bustle below encourages a laid-back mood, drawing a pleasant, mixed crowd, and there is great juke box music as well as fine views over the frenzy of pavement restaurants below, all from the comfort of a huge roof terrace.

Right: Central's stylish clientele and surroundings.

Post '97
9 Lan Kwai Fong, Central; tel: 2810 9333; Mon–Thur 9.30am–1am, Fri–Sat 9.30am–3am; MTR: Central (exit D1, D2), bus: 12M, 13, 23A, 40M; map p.137 C3
Comfy, long-standing all-day bar and restaurant, above the Club '97. Set up in anticipation of the Handover, this relaxed place has been the choice of local celebs for more than a decade.
SEE ALSO NIGHTLIFE, P.75

Staunton's
10 Staunton Street, Central; tel: 2973 6611; daily 8am–2am; Mid–Levels Escalator, bus: 12M, 13, 23A, 26, 40M; map p.136 B3

Above: a young set frequents the bars of Hollywood Road.

Friendly, laid back and very popular bar with American and Asian snacks, a lively clientele and plenty of good, old-fashioned American-style fun. Where else can you dance on the bar top?

Karaoke has been serious fun in Hong Kong since the 1990s; any number of bars and even some restaurants have 'karaoke boxes' for crooners' privacy. The boxes are dotted all over town, but are particularly numerous around Causeway Bay. They are very popular at weekends, but rental fees and drinks can be pricey, and booking ahead is advisable at peak times. In some establishments, too, Western visitors who are not accompanied by Chinese people are not usually made welcome. Karaoke bars that are open to everyone, local or not, and are worth trying, include **Big Echo**, Causeway Bay Plaza Phase II, 463-83 Lockhard Road; tel: 2591 1288; MTR: Causeway Bay, exit C; **Green Box**, 8/F, Windsor House, Great George Street, Causeway Bay; tel: 2881 5088; MTR: Causeway Bay, exit E; and **Neway**, 3/F Causeway Bay Plaza Phase I, 489 Hennessy Road; tel: 2559 8989; MTR: Causeway Bay, exit B.

Champagne Bar
Grand Hyatt, 1 Harbour Road, Wan Chai; tel: 2588 1234; www.hongkong.grand.hyatt.com; daily 2pm–2am; MTR: Wan Chai (exit A1, C), bus: A12, 18, 88; map p.138 A3
Intimate, opulent bar for expensive, after-work entertaining.

Delaney's
G–1/F, One Capital Place, 18 Luard Road, Wan Chai; tel: 2804 2880; Mon–Thur and Sun noon–2am, Fri–Sat noon–3am; MTR: Wan Chai (exit A1, C), bus: Gloucester and Hennessy roads; map p.138 A3
Very popular Irish theme pub, serving (very pricey) Guinness and good food, at better-value prices. A giant screen upstairs shows rugby and football matches; there is a less packed bar downstairs. Another branch is at 71–7 Peking Road, Tsim Sha Tsui (tel: 2301 3980).

Dusk till Dawn
74–84 Jaffe Road, Wan Chai; tel: 2527 4689; Mon–Fri noon–6am, Sat–Sun 3pm–6am; MTR: Wan Chai (exit A1, C), bus: Gloucester and Hennessy roads; map p.138 A3
A lively, often-packed fun bar where expats let their hair down to sounds provided by an excellent live Filipino cover band.

East End Brewery
Sunning Plaza, 10 Hysan Avenue, Causeway Bay; tel: 2577 9119; Sun–Thur 11.30am–1am, Fri–Sat 11.30am–1.30am; MTR: Causeway Bay (exit F); map p.139 D2
Casual, patio-style bar with good selection of beers, including some imported from microbreweries. The covered terrace, popular on warm evenings, is shared with adjacent Inn Side Out.

Klong Bar 7 Grill – KBG
The Broadway, 54–62 Lockhart Road, Wan Chai; tel: 2217 8330; daily 6pm–3am; MTR: Wan Chai (exit A1, C), bus: Gloucester and Hennessy roads; map p.138 A2
A little corner of Bangkok, named after the city's canal network. It recreates the authentic ambience well, with imported Thai firewater (at steep prices), as well as optional pole dancing, zebra-patterned pool tables, and cosy nooks hiding faux opium dens. The tasty Thai food is very good value. The monthly full-moon party has a wild reputation, too.

Mes Amis
83 Lockhart Road, Wan Chai; tel: 2527 6680; Sun–Thur noon–1am, Fri–Sat noon–2am; MTR: Wan Chai (exit A1, C), bus: Gloucester and Hennessy roads; map p.138 A2

This French wine bar in the heart of clubland has a good list of wines and Mediterranean-style snacks. Turns into a wild-ish dance joint after 10pm on Friday and Saturday, with DJs.
SEE ALSO NIGHTLIFE, P.77

The Southside

Smuggler's Inn
90A Main Street, Stanley; tel: 2813 8852; Mon–Fri 9am–midnight, Sat–Sun 9am–1am; bus: 6, 260, 973
This British expat pub is a throwback to the pre-97 era, when army boys came here from Stanley Fort to spend half their wages. It still feels like it is stuck back in the days when Britain held all the pink bits on the world map.

On the Rocks
Main Beach, Shek O; tel: 2809 2021; Fri–Sat 9pm–4am; bus: 9
This bar is Shek O's hippest hangout, but do not go expecting too much in this sleepy fishing (and surfing) community. It is a nice place to call in for a drink though, if you are exploring the island's more tranquil side.

Kowloon

Bahama Mama's
4–5 Knutsford Terrace, Tsim Sha Tsui; tel: 2368 2121; Mon–Thur 3.30pm–3am, Fri–Sat 3.30pm–4am, Sun 4pm–2am; MTR: Tsim Sha Tsui (exit B2), bus: Nathan and Chatham roads; map p.134 C3
Long-established Caribbean-inspired theme bar with an unusual mix of front terrace, a dance floor where you can sway to reggae and funk beats, and table football for the non-rhythmic lads.

Chemical Suzy
2 Austin Avenue, Tsim Sha Tsui; tel: 2736 0087; daily 4pm–4am; MTR: Tsim Sha Tsui (exit B2), bus: Chatham Road South; map p.134 A3

> Beer drinking will be more enjoyable if you try locally-brewed labels, such as Chinese Tsing Tao, instead of the more instantly-recognisable worldwide brands (some of which are notorious for giving worse hangovers in the humid tropics)

In-place for a young cosmopolitan set, especially Britpop and Goth fans, this bar is also popular with Japanese residents, as it has the latest computer games. Thursday is ragga night.

Rick's Café
4 Hart Avenue, Tsim Sha Tsui; tel: 2367 2939; Mon–Thur and Sun 5pm–3am, Fri–Sat 5pm–5am; MTR: Tsim Sha Tsui (exit B1, B2), bus: Nathan Road; map p.134 C2
Do not be misled by the Casablanca reference: this is more of a bar-disco, fun and image-free, with dancing to mainstream pop until late. Very popular with expats, and a good meeting place.

Someplace Else
Sheraton Hotel and Towers, 20 Nathan Road, Tsim Sha Tsui; tel: 2369 1111; Mon–Thur noon–midnight, Fri–Sat noon–1am, Sun 11am–midnight; MTR: Tsim Sha Tsui (exit E), bus: Nathan Road; map p.134 C1

Popular and comfortable place for pre-club socialising, as smart as its Sheraton location suggests, with live music late at night.

The New Territories

Cheers Sports Bar & Restaurant
28 Yi Chun Street, Sai Kung; tel: 2791 6789; daily 11.30am–late; MTR: Choi Hung (exit C)
Tons of expats choose to live in Sai Kung, across on the eastern side of Kowloon, and this bar is where the bulk of them hang out after-hours. Go for the rowdy sports bar atmosphere, especially if you are a fan of rugby and football. The atmosphere is always relaxed and friendly, though it is not the place to go for a sleek and stylish Hong Kong night out.

The Outer Islands

Diesel Sports Bar
51 Main Street, Yung Shue Wan, Lamma Island; tel: 2982 4116; daily 9am–late; ferry: Yung Shue Wan
What is it with expat communities and sports bars? This one on quiet Lamma is one of the better ones, thanks to its big screens and permanent party atmosphere.

Below: crowds spill onto the street on sultry summer nights.

Children

Although Hong Kong's family-friendly appeal is not immediately obvious, the city has a surprising amount of affordable and accessible attractions to offer inquisitive and active children. Besides amusement parks, hands-on museums, cable-car rides, nature activities and gadgets galore the city's ferry and tram rides are sure to provide ample entertainment to any youngster, and curious kids should find many hidden treasures in the city's markets. Events and a raft of colourful festivals are held throughout the year, and the annual Hong Kong WinterFest lets kids enjoy the Christmas season in the sun.

Hong Kong Disneyland

Lantau Island; tel: 1-830 830; www.hongkongdisneyland.com; hours vary, usually Apr–Oct: Sun–Thur 10am–8pm, Fri–Sat 10am–9pm, Nov–Mar: Sun–Thur 10am–7pm, Fri–Sat 10am–8pm; entrance charge; MTR: Sunny Bay, then change to special Resort trains

The magic begins on board the dedicated Disney Train (a Disney first), which passengers join at Sunny Bay station. Once inside the park kids will find all the old favourites including Broadway-style shows, white-knuckle rides, Main Street USA, Fantasyland, Adventureland and Tomorrowland, along with fireworks displays and parades. New rides include Autopia, along the highways of the future, and an extraterrestrial aquatic adventure in the UFO Zone.

Hong Kong Wetland Park

Tin Shui Wai, New Territories; tel: 2708 8885; www.wetlandpark.com; Wed–Mon 10am–5pm; entrance charge; LRT: Wetland Park (via change at Tsin Shui Wai)

As well as offering an insight into Hong Kong's wetland reserve, a trip to this major new attraction, in the northwestern New Territories, offers the chance to visit a part of Hong Kong that is a world away from the tourist centres. The park itself borders Mai Po and Deep Bay, and contains extensive wetland habitats. Access to birdwatching hides is provided via an extensive network of boardwalks. An impressive 10,000 sq m visitor centre features interactive exhibits.

Ngong Ping 360

Lantau Island; www.np360.com.hk; Mon–Fri 10am–6pm, Sat–Sun 10am–6.30pm; entrance charge; MTR: Tung Chung

This 5.7km Skyrail ride links Tung Chung with Lantau's **Po Lin Monastery** and takes in spectacular panoramic views of the South China Sea and North Lantau Country Park as well as the monastery and its famous **Big Buddha** statue. On arrival at Ngong Ping village families will find several themed attractions including Walking with Buddha, the Monkey's Tale

Above: Ocean Park's dolphin show.

Theatre and Ngong Ping Tea House. At time of press the cable car was closed for restoration following an accident in June 2007.

SEE ALSO TEMPLES AND HISTORIC SIGHTS, P.119; WALKS AND VIEWS, P.131

Ocean Park

Aberdeen; tel: 2552 0291; www.oceanpark.com.hk; daily 10am–6pm; entrance charge; MTR: Admiralty, then Citybus: 629

One of Hong Kong's oldest

Left: friendly faces at Ocean Park.

The Peak

Hong Kong Island; www.thepeak.com.hk; daily 7am–midnight; Peak Tram: Garden Road; map p.136 B1
EA Experience: tel: 2849 7710; www.ea.com; Mon–Fri noon–8pm, Sat–Sun 10am–10pm; entrance charge
Madame Tussauds: tel: 2849 6966; www.madame-tussauds.com.hk; daily 10am–10pm; entrance charge

Half the fun of The Peak is in the getting there. Kids will love the clanky funicular or Peak Tram (in service since 1888), which climbs 373m at a white-knuckle, see-it-to-believe-it incline. The revamped **Peak Tower** now offers a 360-degree rooftop platform to take in the famously breathtaking view; while an expanded **Madame Tussaud's** features more than 100 wax models that include Hong Kong favourites Bruce Lee and Jackie Chan as well as the more familiar David Beckham. The Peak also houses the **EA Experience**, with utterly state-of-the-art motion simulators and other virtual rides and games, plus acres of retail and dining space.

SEE ALSO TRANSPORT, P.125; WALKS AND VIEWS, P.128

The Pearl River Delta between Hong Kong and Macau is home to an estimated 1,000 Indo-pacific humpback dolphins, known as *sousa chinensis*. **Hong Kong Dolphinwatch** (tel: 2984 1414, www.hkdolphin watch.com) runs trips to see the dolphins in their natural habitat off Lantau Island. If you do not spot one the first time you are entitled to go again free (Wed, Fri and Sun; adults HK$360, children HK$180).

and best–loved family attractions, Ocean Park – one of Southeast Asia's largest aquariums and theme parks – has lost none of its appeal, due partly to its remarkable ability to re-invent itself.

New exhibits include the multi-media **Sea Jelly Aquarium**, another first for the region. As well as its reef-themed aquarium with dramatic shark tunnel and six 'areas' including Kids' World, the Giant Panda Habitat and the Atoll Reef, the park also features a handful of stomach-churning rides including the Abyss Turbo Drop, and the Mine Train and Dragon roller coasters. A must is a ride on the park's much–loved cable car, which hugs the coast of Aberdeen.

Below: fabulous jellyfish illuminate Ocean Park's Sea Jelly Aquarium.

Environment

The outbreak of Sars in 2003 finally led Hong Kong's government to face a topic that should have been on its mind years ago: the state of the local environment. This city of neon and trade made its name from its corporate-friendly business practices, only to find that the incredible boom in industry and finance that brought such astonishing wealth has also introduced secret demons such as pollution and disease-friendly overcrowding. The historic trade in endangered species for use in traditional Chinese medicine is another topic with which most western travellers take issue.

Pollution

SARS

As Sars was a respiratory illness, locals and scientists alike believed that poor air quality and a high population density combined to create the perfect environment for an epidemic of fearful proportions. Could it happen again? Who knows. But, if all bets are on, avian flu could be the next big one.

When Sars hit, the government finally realised that it had to sit up and take notice of the effects its business-friendly laws were having on quality of life. Despite this, it ignored a World Health Organisation guideline on air quality and instead commissioned an 18-month consultation paper that many see as an attempt to put the burning issue on hold for as long as possible.

POOR AIR QUALITY

The government's inactivity and seemingly pro-business practices may now be working against them, as many companies are avoiding the city due to the poor air quality and effects that it would have on the health of their employees. And mainland China, which has seen Hong Kong's success over the past century, is quickly attempting to emulate the city by instituting even fewer air emission standards in order to attract industry, all just a brisk gust of wind away.

With the boom in low-cost air travel bringing even more planes to Hong Kong, worries are also on the rise about aircraft emissions. Low prices bring more tourists, but will they want to come if they experience burning throats and watery eyes? Concerned travellers can offset their carbon footprint by donating to an organization such as Climate Care (www.climatecare.org).

> Consider 'offsetting' the CO_2 from your journey to and around Hong Kong through an organisation like Climate Care (www.climatecare.org). Their on-line calculator will tell you your carbon emissions for your trip and how much you should donate to the scheme.

A LIFESTYLE ISSUE

Ever since Hong Kong was a small fishing and trade port, locals have been treating nature as a convenient toilet that washes away all waste. There are many days in the calendar year when seeing Hong Kong Island from Kowloon – a distance of about 1km – is impossible. Additionally, as there is a distinct lack of parkland in the city centre, children are becoming increasingly obese as there are few outdoor locations where they can be active.

All is not completely bleak, however, as the special administrative region consistently ranks near the top of global life expectancy charts. A group known as Clear the Air is starting to have success as a lobby group, especially when dealing with car and bus emissions. Public transport is switching to electric and hybrid power, a smoking ban went into effect in January 2007 and investment is being made into advertising campaigns that show how locals can conserve energy. Is it

Left: a beautiful morning ruined by an orange haze.

OTHER ENDANGERED SPECIES

Rhinoceros, bear and even shark populations are also rapidly shrinking. Rhinoceros horn is reputed to be an aphrodisiac. Only about 12,500 rhinos remain in the wild and without assistance, the species could soon become extinct.

Also greatly threatened by Chinese demand, bears from as far away as North America are valued for their bile, used to treat a variety of ailments, and paws, which are used to make soup.

Like bear's paw, shark's fin, though not used exclusively for medicine, is a delicacy. It is served most commonly as shark's fin soup, a broth that is believed to benefit the internal organs. Sharks are caught and their top fin sliced off. They are then tossed back into the ocean, alive, to drown.

As endangered animal populations plummet, the use of their parts to supply an ever-growing demand is no longer sustainable. One way or another, the trade in endangered animal parts for medicine must stop. This means finding an alternative to alternative medicine.

enough? Only time, and the lungs of residents, will be able to tell.

The Animals Parts Trade

The Chinese have been using animal parts for medicinal purposes for well over 1,000 years. Yet for all its appeal as an alternative to Western drugs, there is a darker side. Wildlife, under pressure from intensive industrial and economic development in recent decades, is now being pushed to the brink of extinction by the increased demand for body parts.

TIGERS

The demand for tigers, for example, is forcing three of the world's five remaining subspecies ever closer to extinction, threatening the long-term survival of the species as a whole. Various tiger parts are used in Chinese medicine: eyeballs to treat epilepsy; the tail for various skin diseases; bile for convulsions in children; whiskers for toothaches; the penis for male impotence; and the brain to combat laziness and pimples. Yet of all tiger parts, it is the bones that are most valued. Tiger bone is often used to treat rheumatism, but can also be used as a remedy for weakness, stiffness or paralysis.

Recent studies estimate that there are only 30–80 South China tigers, 150–200 Siberian tigers and 600–650 Sumatran tigers left in the wild. Without radical intervention, tigers may disappear altogether in the near future.

Right: the common gecko is freeze dried and flattened to be used in Chinese medicine.

Essentials

Finding your way around an unknown city can be quite daunting, but Hong Kong is so international and geared towards visitors that it is usually easy to find information. Most hotel reception staff are full of information and will usually help with communication problems and bookings. This section gives you the basic, most useful facts, from timing your trip to avoid the summer rainy season to finding the nearest hospital. For specific practical information on getting around Hong Kong see 'Transport'; 'Language' provides some basic phrases for travellers.

Baggage Restrictions

Since March 2007 revised restrictions apply on all flights into and out of Hong Kong (including passengers in transit) to the way in which liquids, gels and aerosols can be carried onto a plane. They must be in containers no bigger than 100ml, and placed in a single (maximum one per passenger) transparent resealable bag, with a capacity not exceeding one litre.

Climate

Hong Kong has a sub-tropical climate divided into four seasons:

Winter: Between late December and February, the weather generally varies from mild to cool, with some fog and rain. Temperatures average between 13°C to 20°C. However, they can occasionally dip down to below 10°C.

Spring: March to mid-May sees plenty of damp, overcast weather, but also pleasant sunny days. Temperatures range from a daytime average of 20°C in March to 28°C in May.

Summer: Temperatures and humidity rise to near-unbearable levels from late May to mid-September. Skies are intermittently clear, but usually hazy. Temperatures usually rise to 32°C in the afternoon, with very high humidity. Thunderstorms are common. July–September is peak typhoon season.

Autumn: The northeast monsoon usually takes over by October, bringing cooler, drier air. From late September to late December expect clear blue skies and pleas-

ant temperatures, dropping from 29°C at the end of September to around 20°C in December. Humidity is generally quite low.

Consulates

Australia
Consulate-General, 23–24/F, Harbour Centre, 25 Harbour Road, Wan Chai; tel: 2827 8881; www.australia.org.hk; MTR: Wan Chai; map p.138 B3

Canada
Consulate-General, Tower 1, Exchange Square, 8 Connaught Place, Central; tel: 2810 4321; www.hongkong.gc.ca; MTR: Central; map p.137 D3

New Zealand
Room 6501, Central Plaza, 18 Harbour Road, Wan Chai; tel: 2525 5044; www.nzembassy. com/hongkong; MTR: Wan Chai; map p.138 B3

Republic of Ireland
Honorary Consul, Heidrick & Struggles, 54/F Bank of China Tower, 1 Garden Road, Central; tel: 2527 4897; www.consulate ofireland.hk; MTR: Central; map p.137 D2

Left: hazy summer skies cover Two IFC.

Left: Hong Kong International Airport.

adapters. When purchasing electronics here check that the system matches your requirements back home.

Emergencies and Police

Members of the Hong Kong Police Force wear navy blue uniforms in winter and olive green uniforms in summer. Many police officers speak English and are generally helpful. The police headquarters is located at Arsenal Street in Wan Chai; there are police stations and reporting centres throughout the territory including in the Airport Express section of Hong Kong station in Central.

In an emergency dial **999**. To report crimes or make complaints against taxi drivers call Hong Kong's Crime Hotline, tel: 2527 7177.

Metric to Imperial Conversions
1 metre = 3.28 feet
1 kilometre = 0.62 mile
1 hectare = 2.47 acres
1 kilogram = 2.2 pounds

items from the list of endangered species that are protected by CITES (Convention on International Trade in Endangered Species of Wild Fauna and Flora).

Electricity

Hong Kong's electrical system is rated at 200/220 volts and 50 cycles AC (alternating current). Most plug sockets take British–style three-pin plugs, but some take other types; usefully, the majority of hotels can supply all-purpose

USEFUL NUMBERS
Emergency: 999 (police, fire, ambulance)
General Police Enquiries
Tel: 2527 7177
Hong Kong Immigration
Tel: 2824 6111 (24 hours)
Hospital Authority Helpline
Tel: 2300 6555

UK
Consulate-General, 1 Supreme Court Road, Central; tel: 2901 3000; www.britishconsulate. org.hk; MTR: Central; map p.137 E1
US
Consulate-General, 26 Garden Road, Central; tel: 2523 9011; http://hongkong.usconsulate.gov; MTR: Central; map p.137 D2

Customs

Hong Kong mostly lives up to its image of being a free port. Visitors aged 18 and above can import almost anything for their personal use (including an unlimited amount of cash), but only 60 cigarettes (or 15 cigars/75g of tobacco) and one litre of wine or spirits.

Firearms must be declared and handed over for safekeeping until you depart. There are also stringent restrictions on the import and export of ivory and other

Below: important directions are usually bilingual.

Above: Hong Kong dollars.

Department of Health
Tel: 2961 8989
Samaritans
Tel: 2896 0000

Health

You will have your temperature taken on arrival when you pass through immigration; this measure was introduced post-Sars. No vaccinations are required to enter Hong Kong, but it is advisable to have up-to-date immunisations against Hepatitis A and B, flu, polio and tetanus; if in doubt, check with a travel health clinic before travelling.

Hong Kong's air quality has deteriorated in recent years, and asthma sufferers may find themselves affected by atmospheric pollution *(see Environment p.30–1).* Parts of the New Territories and most of the outlying islands are less affected. The Department of Health website can be found at: www.dh.gov.hk.

As of January 2007 Hong Kong went smoke-free. Smoking is now prohibited in most enclosed public places, including restaurants, karaoke bars, malls and some bars, as well as some outdoor areas (public beaches and swimming pools, transport interchanges and outside escalators). Some establishments have been allowed to

defer their non-smoking classification until 1 July 2009.

Hong Kong also has strict laws to maintain environmental hygiene, including fixed penalty fines of HK$1,500 for littering or spitting.

MEDICAL TREATMENT AND HOSPITALS

All visitors are strongly advised to take out adequate travel and health insurance before arriving in Hong Kong to cover medical emergencies, hospitalisation and all other possible medical expenses. Hong Kong does not have a free national health care system and visitors are required to pay at least HK$570 if they use the Accident and Emergency services at Hong Kong's public hospitals. Listed below are two of the hospitals that have 24-hour emergency services. For more information on all medical services, call

the efficient Hospital Authority helpline, tel: 2300 6555, or visit www.ha.org.hk.
Queen Mary Hospital
Pok Fu Lam Road, Pok Fu Lam, near Aberdeen, Southside, Hong Kong Island; tel: 2855 3838;
Bus: 3A, 3B, 40M, 91, M49
Caritas Medical Centre
111 Wing Hong Street, Sham Sui Po, Kowloon; tel: 3408 7911;
MTR: Sham Shui Po

PHARMACIES

Conventional pharmacies (identified by a red-cross sign) are abundant in Hong Kong, as are traditional Chinese herbalists. Note that, if you require any prescription drugs, pharmacies will only accept prescriptions issued by a doctor in Hong Kong.

Internet

Nearly all hotels will have Internet access. You can also access the Internet for free at many coffee shops (Pacific Coffee), large shopping malls, major MTR stations and public libraries. Wireless Broadband (WiFi) access is common in major shopping malls and coffee shops. Modem adaptors are supplied at many hotels, or you can buy one; ask for the BT-RJ adaptor.

Money

The currency unit is the Hong Kong dollar, pegged to the US

> ### When to Visit
> Weather-wise the ideal time to visit Hong Kong is October to December: warm, and with blue skies but low humidity. In January or February, Chinese New Year offers a spectacular celebration, but many places will be closed for the holiday. April to August, the rainy season, is generally the least pleasant time to sightsee.

dollar at a rate of roughly US$1: HK$7.80. At time of printing the exchange rate was almost HK$16 to £1 sterling, making Hong Kong's high service standards exceptionally good value for money.

Bank notes are issued by Hongkong Shanghai Bank (HSBC), Standard Chartered Bank and the Bank of China in denominations of HK$1,000 (orange), HK$500 (brown), HK$100 (red), HK$50 (purple), HK$20 (grey–green, except for the Bank of China's, which are blue), and the new plasticised HK$10 (purple). Coins issued include HK$10, HK$5, HK$2, HK$1, 50 cents, 20 cents and 10 cents.

BANKS

Banking hours are Monday to Friday 9am–4.30pm, Saturday 9am–12.30pm. Licensed money-changers and hotels are an alternative option, but they can sting you with a hefty service charge. Money-changers in Tsim Sha Tsui, Causeway Bay and Wan Chai stay open until late at night.

CREDIT CARDS AND CHEQUES

Plastic is used with a vengeance in Hong Kong: Visa, MasterCard, American Express, Diner's Club and other major cards are accepted at most hotels, restaurants and shops. However, be sure to check the cash price in shops; it may be lower than that for card sales. In most street markets only cash is accepted.

Cash machines (ATMs) can also be found everywhere. Visa and MasterCard holders can obtain local currency from Hang Seng Bank and Hongkong Shanghai Bank (HSBC) cash machines (ATMs); American Express cardholders can access Jetco ATMs.

Travellers' cheques are readily accepted by banks, hotels and money changers.

Post

The Hong Kong mail service is fast and efficient. Stamps normally have to be bought at post offices: most are open Monday to Saturday 8am–6pm, and are closed on Sunday and public holidays. The best places to dispatch packages and registered items are the General Post Office, in front of the Mandarin Oriental hotel (2 Connaught Place, Central), and the large Kowloon post office (G/F, Hermes House, 10 Middle Road, Tsim Sha Tsui, Kowloon). Both these larger offices also open Sunday 8am–2pm. For more information on all postal services, tel: 2921 2222; www.hongkongpost.com.

Telephones

Public telephones can still be found all around Hong Kong, but the easiest places to find them are MTR stations, 7–11 stores, and hotel and even bank lobbies, where local calls will be free. Local calls made from your hotel room should also be free, but check for surcharges.

You can make international direct dial (IDD) calls from public card phones with a credit card or stored-value phone card (available at HKTB Information and Gift Centres, 7–11 stores and some bookshops). To make a call outside Hong Kong, first dial the international access code, **001**, followed by the country code and number. To call Hong Kong from abroad or mainland China, the code is **852**.

Below: colonial remnants are still used for the post.

Above: gathering information at the Hong Kong Tourist Board

Within Hong Kong, there are no area codes and all numbers have eight digits, except for toll-free numbers, which begin with **800**, and some public information numbers, which begin with **18** or **10**.

For mobile (cell) users, most of the telephone systems used around the world, including GSM 900, PCS 1800, CDMA and WCDMA, operate in Hong Kong.

USEFUL NUMBERS
Hong Kong Directory Enquiries: 1081
International Directory Enquiries: 10013
International Operator/ Reverse Charge (Collect) calls: 10010
Hong Kong International Airport Information, in English
Tel: 2181 0000 (24 hours)
Weather Information: 187 8066
RTHK's Service Hotline (Newsline)
Tel: 2272 0000

Hong Kong residents are required to carry an identity card, and visitors are advised to carry a similar form of photo identification, such as a passport.

Time

Hong Kong is 8hrs ahead of GMT and 13hrs ahead of US Eastern Standard Time. Unlike Europe and the US, there is no daylight saving time, so from April to October the difference is reduced to 7hrs ahead of London and 12hrs ahead of New York.

Tipping

Most restaurants and hotels automatically add a 10 per cent service charge to the total bill. It is still general practice to round up a restaurant bill to the nearest 10 (larger gratuities are expected when there is no service charge added onto the bill), or a taxi fare to the nearest dollar or two. Toilet attendants and doormen can be tipped one or two dollars. HK$10–20 is good enough for porters and room service in most hotels.

Tourist Information

The Hong Kong Tourist Board (HKTB) is one of the world's most efficient tourism organisations. On arrival collect a free HKTB information bag in the baggage claim area at the airport, which contains a map, current events magazine, brochures and details of day and half-day tours organised by HKTB.

The HKTB also has two large information centres in town, by the Causeway Bay MTR station on Hong Kong Island and by the Star Ferry dock in Kowloon.

There is also an excellent multilingual Visitor Hotline, tel: 2508 1234 (daily 8am–6pm), or for more information in advance visit www.discover hongkong.com.

HONG KONG TOURIST BOARD INFORMATION CENTRES

Hong Kong International Airport

Transfer Area E2 and Buffer Halls A and B, Arrivals Level, Terminal 1; daily 7am–11pm

Hong Kong Island

Causeway Bay MTR station (exit F); daily 8am–8pm; map p.133 D3

Kowloon

Star Ferry Concourse, Tsim Sha Tsui; daily 8am–8pm; MTR: Tsim Sha Tsui; map p.134 B1

Above: final check of passports before departure.

Visas and Passports

Most visitors only need a valid passport to enter Hong Kong. The length of visa-free tourist visit that is allowed varies according to your nationality. British subjects holding full UK passports are granted six months on entry; all other European Union nationals get three months, as do most British dependent passport holders and nationals of Australia, Brazil, Brunei, Chile, Ecuador, Israel, Malaysia, New Zealand, Norway, Japan, Singapore, Switzerland, Turkey and the USA.

Citizens of other countries should consult the Chinese Embassy or Consulate General in their country of origin, or visit the Hong Kong Immigration Department website, www.immd.gov.hk. All visitors should note that when they arrive their passport needs to be valid for at least one month beyond the planned date of departure from Hong Kong, or they may be refused entry.

Visas for travel to **mainland China** can be obtained when you are in Hong Kong. These require two photos and usually take about three working days to process, for around HK$200–300. Visas can be obtained from these offices, or from many Hong Kong travel agents:

Visa Office of the People's Republic of China

7/F, Lower Block, China Resources Centre, 26 Harbour Road, Wan Chai; tel: 3413 2424; MTR: Wan Chai; map p.138 B3

China Travel Service

tel: 2851 1700; www.ctshk.com Has several branches around Hong Kong.

What to Wear

Hong Kong is a much 'smarter' city than say Bangkok, or Manila. Smart-casual attire will see you through most social occasions, outside of business (where suits and dresses are standard) or official functions. Some hotels, restaurants, bars and night-clubs will not admit patrons in trainers (sneakers), flip-flops (thongs), jeans or shorts, or collarless shirts (for men).

Left: tourist friendly signs make Hong Kong easy to navigate.

Festivals

Despite its brash and modern exterior, Hong Kong's population remains firmly rooted in tradition. Temple deities and ancestors are honoured with equal fervour, and barely a month goes by when an ancient tradition or festival is not marked with a colourful pageant or celebratory meal. These traditions are at their most vibrant and visible during the exuberant Chinese New Year festival. It is worth remembering that if a festival falls on a Sunday, or two festivals coincide, the day before or after the main day is usually made a holiday as well. Here is only a sample of the many events through the year.

Chinese New Year

Late Jan or early Feb

Lunar New Year is Hong Kong's major annual event. Family is key to this festival, and this is the only time when Hong Kong effectively shuts down in its entirety, for about a week – so to the outsider, the ghost town that is Hong

Below: the procession up the stairs at the Birthday of Lord Buddha Festival, Lin Po Monastery.

Kong at this time can be a disappointment, with most shops, restaurants and attractions closed and none of the usual buzz and frenetic pace the city is associated with. The upside is in the many colourful events that take place either side of the huge climactic New Year's Day parade. The parade, with its spectacular dragon dances and processions is a sight (and sound) to behold. Tourists can join locals at temples, and there is also a spectacular firework display over Victoria Harbour.

Cheung Chau Bun Festival

One week in late Apr, May or early June

One of Hong Kong's most exciting and well-publicised festivals. During the eight-day spring festival the residents of Cheung Chau island try to dispel what are known as 'hungry ghosts'. Take a ferry to Cheung Chau and make your way along the harbour promenade to the Pak Tai Temple. Here, 18m-high bamboo towers filled with

Want a cut-price designer bag, quality Chinese souvenir or the latest gadget for a knock-down price? Then June to August is the time to come, as Hong Kong hosts its now-annual **'Shopping Festival'**. It is hot and humid outside, but all your bargaining and browsing will be done in air-conditioned shops and malls. As well as bargains galore visitors can expect nightly entertainment and special restaurant promotions across the city's food and shopping districts. The festival also coincides with the summer sales, which offer discounts of up to 70 per cent off major labels and brands. With Harvey Nichols, Chanel and Louis Vuitton recently opening flagship stores in the city, and more designer labels per square metre than you can shake a Fendi Baguette bag at, this is *the* time for label-lovers and fashion addicts to visit the city.

buns are erected as offerings to the ghosts, and a spectacular float procession winds through the streets with children, richly costumed as

Left: Cheung Chau's lucky Buns.

If you are keen to learn more about Hong Kong's festivals, you can join a Festival Tour. These include Dragon Boat Festival Tours, a Chinese New Year Fireworks Cruise, Cheung Chau Bun Festival tours, a mid-Autumn Moonlight Cruise, and Buddha and Tin Hau Festival tours. Tours include such things as reserved seats at processions, meals, martial arts demonstrations and transport, such as ferries. For details of upcoming tours, enquire at tourist offices, or check www.discoverhongkong.com.

figures from Chinese myths, 'floating' above the heads of the adults dressed as Taoist priests, suspended by means of hidden supports.

SEE ALSO OUTER ISLANDS, P.21

Birthday of Lord Buddha
Late May

The devout celebrate the birthday of the Lord Buddha (Fourth Moon) with a ritual bathing of the Buddha on the outlying island of Lantau, where the famous **Big Buddha** is located within **Po Lin Monastery**. But, if you can not make it to Lantau, celebrations take place at all Hong Kong's major temples and monasteries, where worshippers bathe Buddha statues. Interested visitors can also observe special ceremonies at Miu Fat Monastery near Tuen Mun.

SEE ALSO TEMPLES AND HISTORIC SITES, P.119

Dragon Boat Festival
June

The *Tuen Ng* or Dragon Boat Festival is second only to Chinese New Year in terms of pageantry and spectacle,

and, as well as being great fun to watch, is one the few events in which locals and expats get together to have fun and let their hair down. The event combines a traditional celebration with thrilling races, held at various venues around Hong Kong. Teams of paddlers practise in earnest for months before the

Chinese festivals operate according to the lunar calendar, so their dates in the western calendar vary from year to year. Beginning with Chinese New Year in late January or early February, the year is divided into 12 months of 29 days, with an extra month added every two and a half years, similar to our leap years. The calendar operates in 60-year cycles, divided into five smaller cycles of 12 years. Each lunar year is represented by an animal, and, as in western astrology, the permutations – rat, ox, tiger, rabbit, dragon, snake, horse, ram, monkey, rooster, dog and pig – are thought to provide clues into a person's character.

event, when they race in elaborately decorated narrow dragon boats sporting dragon's heads and tails to the beat of loud onboard drums. International dragon-boat races are held in the following week.

SEE ALSO SPORTS, P.112–3

Mid-Autumn Lantern Festival
Late Sept or Oct

This is one of Hong Kong's most popular festivals, and one in which visitors – and particularly families – can easily participate. Also known as the Moon Festival (it celebrates the full harvest moon), it is one of the prettiest of the festivals, as illuminated paper lanterns of all shapes and sizes are taken to public parks and beaches, notably Victoria Park in Causeway Bay and the main beaches of Lamma, Cheung Chau and Lantau. The Fire Dragon Dance that takes place in Causeway Bay is a highlight. The traditional sweet delicacy known as 'mooncakes', though, are an acquired taste!

39

Film

The entertainment capital of East Asia, Hong Kong has pioneered many genres in the Asian movie industry, from kung fu and high-energy Jackie Chan-style comedies to lavish period adventures like *Crouching Tiger, Hidden Dragon* and beautifully crafted art movies. International competition and DVD piracy have been tough challenges, but the city remains a thriving film production centre, and boasts many home-grown stars, directors and producers who have won world recognition. Hong Kong audiences often benefit, too, from the chance to see early-release Hollywood movies and classic art films.

Hollywood of the East

Hong Kong's movie studios churn out dozens of kung fu action films and soppy romantic comedies every year. While the quality does not always match the quantity, local cinema has risen in stature in recent years by its association with the Oscar-winning *Crouching Tiger, Hidden Dragon* (a joint production between Hong Kong, mainland China, Taiwan and the US), giving filmgoers an appetite for leaping kung fu period dramas.

The phenomenal success of *Crouching Tiger* also propelled local stars Michelle Yeow and Chow Yun-fat into the movie-star firmament, where they take a seat alongside Jackie Chan and the late Bruce Lee. Director John Woo meanwhile, is one of the hottest directorial talents in the film world.

Film buffs can find out more about locally-set films by picking up the two volumes of the *Hong Kong Movie Odyssey* guide, which take you on a personal journey with Hong Kong Tourism Ambassador Jackie Chan into the Hollywood of the East, including tours of many of the locations where classic Hong Kong pictures were filmed.

Hong Kong in Pictures

Love is a Many-Splendored Thing (1955)
This classic Hollywood tear-jerker is set in the years after the Communist takeover of the mainland and during the Korean War, and depicts the colonial charm of East-meets-West, 'exotic' China, and the problems of inter-racial romance. The film won three Oscars, and much of the setting still exists. William Holden and Jennifer Jones (Hollywood could not then accept a real Chinese actress) go to The Peak – for shopping, dining and attractions – take a sampan ride from Aberdeen Harbour and visit a floating restaurant for a seafood dinner.
The World of Suzie Wong (1960)
A legendary romance between an American artist (William Holden again) and a beautiful local bar girl (now

Below: the Avenue of the Stars celebrates key figures of the Hong Kong movie industry.

Left: a statue of Bruce Lee on the Avenue of Stars.

locals and tourists throng the bars and restaurants until the wee hours.

Chungking Express (1994)
Director Wong Kar-wai creates two parallel love stories that focus on two ordinary policemen. The first falls in love with a drug dealer, and the second, a beat policeman in Lan Kwai Fong, pines for his ex-girlfriend and misses the advances of a waitress (Faye Wong). The second part of the film follows the world's longest escalator, the Mid-Levels Escalator.

In the Mood for Love (2000)
One of the Hong Kong greats, this visually exquisite film is another Wong Kar-wai production. Set in the 1950s and 1960s, it features Hong Kong favourites Maggie Cheung and Tony Leung. A story of unrequited love, the film reignited a passion for the elegant and body-hugging *qipao* dress, which harks back to the Qing Dynasty. Cheung reportedly went through 46 of them during the making of the film, and wears a different one in every

Who's who?
Mainland director Zhang Yimou, celebrated globally as an art-house director for films such as *Raise the Red Lantern*, made *Hero* in the same mould as *Crouching Tiger, Hidden Dragon*. Look out for Hong Kong's funniest actor-director Stephen Chow *(Shaolin Soccer, Kung Fu Hustle)*, and the movies of critically acclaimed director Wong Kar-wai *(Chungking Express, Happy Together, In the Mood for Love, 2046)*. Hong Kong stars who have made it globally – with a worldwide cult following – include Bruce Lee, Jackie Chan, Chow Yun-fat, Jet Li and Maggie Cheung. Lately, no-holds-barred violent thrillers such as actor-director Andy Lau's *Infernal Affairs* have captured local and international acclaim – to the extent of being remade by Martin Scorsese and Brad Pitt, as the Oscar-winning *The Departed* – and another all-action Hong Kong director, John Woo, has made the move to Hollywood himself with *Face/Off* and *Mission: Impossible 2*.

actually played by a Chinese actress, Nancy Kwan). Filmed extensively on location – beginning with the Star Ferry – *Suzie Wong* is set in a still-colonial Hong Kong that was only just beginning to boom at the end of the 1950s, and centres on the exciting nightlife of Wan Chai. The Wan Chai of old has lost some of its allure, but this is still one of the key districts to head for when night falls. Take the MTR to Wan Chai. Go to Lockhart Road, where

Below: the award-winning *Crouching Tiger, Hidden Dragon*.

Above: adverts for the annual French film festival.

scene. They are available at Chinese department stores and speciality shops and boutiques: head for Pedder Street or Des Voeux Road (Central) and Stanley Market.

***Lara Croft Tomb Raider: The Cradle of Life* (2003)**
Who could forget Angelina Jolie (aka Lara Croft) leaping from the incisor-tooth-like International Finance Centre tower? *Tomb Raider* has Jolie searching for Pandora's Box, taking her from the rainforest to the concrete jungle of Hong Kong. A highlight of the film sees Jolie escaping from the 88-storey-high Two IFC, to be saved by a parachute.

Film Festivals

As well as those listed here various mini film festivals are also held throughout the year. Check the weekly free *HK* and *bc* magazines and the *South China Morning Post* for details.

Hong Kong International Film Festival
Tel: 2970 3300,
www.hkiff.org.hk; late Mar–Apr

Every spring Hong Kong holds this major two-week festival, featuring premieres, retrospectives, local and Asian films and – a growing emphasis – worldwide cinema as well. Movies are shown in many venues around the city. The festival is part of the Entertainment Expo Hong Kong, which includes the Hong Kong Film Awards Ceremony, Hong Kong Independent Short Film and Video Awards and other film-related events. It is advisable to book ahead, online, as tickets sell out fast.

Le French May
Tel: 3196 6200;
www.frenchmay.com; May
Running throughout May, this festival of French culture usually offers a series of classic or new French movies, as well as concerts, exhibitions and many other events.

Hong Kong Lesbian and Gay Film and Video Festival

Tel: 9759 8199,
www.hklgff.hk; Nov
A growing two-week festival featuring screenings, talks and many other events.

Cinemas

There are dozens of cinemas and multiplexes in Hong Kong, which show a mixture of the latest Hollywood releases, local offerings and big-budget Japanese, South Korean or Thai movies. There are also a handful of art-house theatres with European and Asian productions. Almost all non-English films are shown with English subtitles. To find out what is on at any time, check the local English-language press, and especially *HK* and *bc* magazines, or their websites.

Evening shows tend to sell out quickly, so it is best to buy in advance. Tickets cost around HK$70, but discounts of around HK$20–30 are offered on tickets all day Tuesday and for morning and matinée shows. Air conditioning in Hong Kong's cinemas can be fierce – some cinemas loan shawls for a small deposit – and many also have booster seats available for children.

Broadway Circuit
Tel: 2388 0002;
www3.cinema.com.hk
The 11 Broadway movie theatres include **Palace IFC**, in the IFC Mall in Central (MTR

Right: agnès b is the city's leading art-house cinema.

Above: the latest American films are always showing too.

Central/Hong Kong Airport Express station; map p.137 D4), the city's most luxurious cinema, with big comfy armchair seats. Tickets are standard price; it shows art-house movies as well as mainstream films, has a DVD store and café.

Standing out among other Broadway theatres are the **Cinematheque**, 3 Public Square Street, Yau Ma Tei, Kowloon (MTR Yau Ma Tei; map p.132 B1), which shows art-house movies and has a small DVD shop and café, and the luxurious **Windsor**, Windsor House, 311 Gloucester Road, Causeway Bay (MTR Causeway Bay; map p.139 D3), which showcases the latest mainstream films.

Golden Harvest
www.goldenharvest.com
A major force in local film production, the Golden Harvest company also has five comfortable multiplexes around Hong Kong, including

the popular **Golden Gateway** (G/F, The Gateway, 25 Canton Road, Tsim Sha Tsui, Kowloon; tel: 2956 2471; MTR Jordan; map p.134 B2), which shows both first-run English language and Chinese films.

MCL Cinemas
Tel: 3413 6688;
www.mclcinema.com
Operates three large multi-plexes, the **JP Plaza**, Cause-way Bay and the **MCL Kornhillin Quarry Bay** on Hong Kong Island, and the **MCL Cinema Metro** in Tseung Kwan O (MTR Po Lam).

UA Cinemas
Tel: 2314 4228;
www.cityline.com.hk
UA operates 11 multi-screen movie theatres across Hong Kong Island, Kowloon, and the New Territories. Key cinemas include the **UA Times Square** and **UA Windsor**, both in Causeway Bay (MTR: Causeway Bay) and the **UA Langham Place**, Argyle Street, Mong Kok, Kowloon (MTR: Mong Kok).

Art-House Cinema

The Broadway Cinematheque in Yua Ma Tei *(see above)* also shows interesting non-mainstream fare.
Agnès b CINEMA!
Hong Kong Arts Centre,
2 Harbour Road, Wan Chai; tel:
2582 0200; www.hkac.org.hk;
MTR: Wan Chai (exit C);

map p.138 A3
For art-house movies, try this cinema within the Hong Kong Arts Centre, which regularly shows new and classic films and hosts a variety of film-related events.
Hong Kong Film Archive
50 Lei King Road, Sai Wan Ho;
tel: 2739 2139, www.film
archive.gov.hk; MTR: Sai Wan Ho
Whether you are a film buff or just enjoy Hong Kong movies, do not miss this cen-tre in Sai Wan Ho on the east side of Hong Kong Island. Dedicated to the preservation of Hong Kong's rich film her-itage, it offers a fascinating insight into how the industry has developed. There is also a 125-seater cinema, with four wheelchair spaces.

In 2004 Hong Kong made public its affection for its own movie industry with the inauguration of the **Avenue of Stars** along Tsim Sha Tsui harbourside promenade in Kowloon. With an obvious tip of the hat to Hollywood Boulevard, the Avenue captures some of the magic of Hong Kong movies with commemorative plaques (some with handprints of local stars), milestones in Hong Kong's 100-year history of film-making, Film Awards sculp-tures and kiosks selling movie memorabilia. In November 2005, Hong Kong also paid a long-overdue tribute to one of its finest actors when it unveiled a two-metre high statue of Bruce Lee on the Avenue, on what would have been his 65th birthday. For events on the Avenue, check www.avenueofstars.com.hk. It is worth coming here for the panoramic harbour views alone, and the Avenue is an ideal perch from which to enjoy the nightly Symphony of Lights display.

b.
NEMA!
named in recognition
...port given by agnès b

Food and Drink

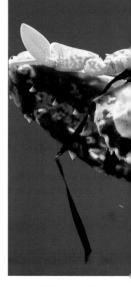

The Cantonese live to eat, and even as a visitor it is impossible to ignore the major role that food and everything around it plays in the lives of locals. The budget-conscious can feast for next to nothing at the scores of local Chinese restaurant chains, or for just a few dollars more on seafood noodles at a seaside restaurant on one of the outer islands; those on a more elastic budget will find literally thousands of restaurants and gourmet hotel dining options to choose from. In Hong Kong one thing is for certain: you are never far from good, enjoyable, enticing food.

Cantonese Cuisine

THE BASICS

Those who are familiar with Chinese food in Western countries soon learn that the authentic cuisine has little to do with what they have been served in Chinese restaurants at home. Sweet-and-sour pork, for example, is said to have been invented by the ever-resourceful inhabitants of Guangzhou solely for sweet-toothed foreigners, while chop suey was reportedly invented in San Francisco when a customer entered a restaurant at closing time and the cooks threw their leftovers into a pot. And, despite the Chinese preoccupation with luck and superstition, American-style fortune cookies do not exist here.

PREPARATION

In the Cantonese system of food preparation, food is cooked quickly and lightly, usually stir-fried in shallow water or an oil base in a wok. Flavours are thus preserved, and not cooked away. Many dishes, particularly vegetables or fish, are steamed. This dis-

Above: dragon fruits.

courages overcooking, and preserves an ingredient's delicate, natural flavours. Sauces are used to enhance flavours rather than overwhelm them, and the sauce usually contains contrasting ingredients such as vinegar and sugar, or ginger and onion.

Communal Dining

The traditional Chinese concept of a meal is very much a communal affair, and one that provides strong sensory impact. Dishes are chosen with both taste and texture in mind, a stomach-pleasing

succession of sweet-sour, sharp-bland, hot-cool and crunchy-smooth. If you are invited to join a group of

Left: live crab for sale, adventurous buyers only.

with a little soy sauce and sesame oil. But beware: Cantonese consider fish eyes and lips to be delicacies. Prawns and crabs – steamed or in a black-bean sauce – are also popular Cantonese dishes.

Meat

Chicken is commonplace, and a single bird is often used to prepare several dishes. Chicken blood is cooked and solidified for soup, and livers are skewered between pieces of pork fat and red-roasted until the fat becomes crisp and the liver soft and succulent. Cantonese chicken dishes can be awkwardly bony for chopsticks beginners, so if in doubt opt for lemon chicken, which is completely boned before cooking and served in a lemon sauce flavoured with onions, ginger and sugar. Cantonese barbecuing methods are unrivalled. Try goose, Peking duck or tender slices of pork, with a golden, honeyed skin and served on a bed of anise-flavoured preserved beans.

Dim Sum

A favourite with visitors, and one of Hong Kong's traditional

Chinese people for lunch or dinner or a celebratory banquet, consider it an honour. Set aside a considerable amount of time for the occasion, and do not eat anything for a while beforehand. A typical meal starts with a cold dish, followed by several main courses. Soup – usually clear, light broth – may be eaten after the heavier courses to aid digestion. If this is a real Chinese banquet, you will be expected to sit through and participate in many courses.

Freshness

Chinese people nearly always insist on fresh food. Many Chinese still shop two or three times a day for fresh meat and vegetables, and not surprisingly Hong Kong is packed with markets, ranging from vegetable and fruit to the lively and pungent 'wet', or fish markets. Not unlike Europe, cooks do not start with a particular dish in mind, but let what is most fresh or in season at the market guide the meal they create. Even if you are not buying, it is worth popping along to the fresh

produce markets and wet market in Wan Chai to see for yourself just how seriously the Chinese take their food.

Fish

Fish and seafood are staples in Cantonese cuisine, hence the popularity of seafood restaurants around Hong Kong, especially on Lamma and Cheung Chau, and in Aberdeen and Sai Kung. At many of these restaurants diners get to select a fish or crustacean from huge tanks.

Fish is typically steamed whole with fresh ginger and spring onions, and sprinkled

Below: fresh greens.

Above: *dim sum.*

Dim sum is one of the most convivial, most informal and sometimes noisiest ways of eating in Hong Kong, as diners talk loudly across tables and chat back and forth with the trolley-pushing waiters. In a traditional *dim sum* restaurant, there is no embarrassment at all in pointing to dishes on the trolley, asking what something is, and if you do not understand the answer just trying it out. Go in a group, so you can share and try as many of the little dishes as possible.

delicacies, *dim sum* literally translates as 'touch the heart', while *yum cha* means 'drink tea'. *Dim sum* snacks – always accompanied by pots of hot tea – were originally served for breakfast, but today are more likely to be eaten around brunch-time.

They take the form of small savoury appetisers, such as *ha gau* (shrimp dumpling), *siu mai* (pork dumpling), *cha siu bau* (barbecued pork bun), *chun gun* (spring roll) and *dun tat* (sweet egg tart). In traditional dim sum restaurants, diners pick from trolleys pushed around by waiters. Each plate taken is marked on a card, and later tallied. But, in many restaurants, menus have replaced the trolleys.

Oddities

To many outsiders, some Chinese foods seem bizarre, if not downright repulsive. The famous 'thousand-year eggs' are duck eggs buried in lime for 60 days, with a resulting cheese-like taste.

The search for rare delicacies is common to all Chinese, but the Cantonese have taken it to the extreme. Monkey's brain, bear's paw, snake, dog, pigeon, frog, sparrow, sharks' fin, birds' nests and lizards are all sought-after delicacies. Many of the rarest are now either illegal or virtually impossible to obtain in Hong Kong, but do not be surprised to see dried sharks fin piled up in the produce shops of Sheung

Tools and Techniques
Many foreigners struggle with chopsticks, and small, loose rice grains are a particular menace. Thankfully, it is perfectly acceptable to raise the rice bowl to your lips and shovel the elusive morsels into your mouth. Scraping and slurping are not considered a faux pas. If chopsticks prove impossible, it is also perfectly acceptable to use the porcelain spoon provided for soups as a scoop for other courses. And no one minds if you make a mess; it is even permissible to wipe your hands on the edge of the tablecloth.

Wan, snake soup on the menu at a five-star hotel or hundreds of baby frogs or 'field chickens' squirming in a tub at the wet market. Here, they are sold live in plastic bags, and chefs serve them in a crunchy batter mixed with crushed almonds, accompanied by a sweet-and-sour sauce.

Drinks

TEA AND COFFEE
The perfect accompaniment to Chinese food is Chinese tea, which is claimed to have digestive properties and helps counteract some of the greasiness in Cantonese

Below: live squid, live frogs and thousand-year eggs.

Above: Temple Street Night Market.

food. The Chinese have been drinking tea for centuries as a thirst-quencher, general reviver, and ceremonial beverage. Tea in China is drunk without sugar or milk, although 'English-style' tea is available and is popular for Afternoon Tea in hotels.

It is worth making the effort to learn to appreciate the many varieties of tea and their histories. Strong black teas are popular, but for a caffeine-free alternative, ask for hot chrysanthemum tea, brewed from the dried petals of the flower.

Tea may have traditionally been first choice in China, but recently younger Hong Kongers in particular have picked up the international taste for coffee in a big way. All the well-known global coffee-house chains have come to Hong Kong to meet the demand, but an excellent local alternative is the Pacific Coffee Company, with branches all around Hong Kong, and which also offers free Internet access.

WINES AND BEERS
Beer is another popular accompaniment, and is more palatable than Chinese wine,

which can be very sweet. Few visitors develop a taste for Chinese wines, despite their 4,000-year history. While some are too sweet, others are too strong. Unlike the Chinese grape and rice wines, the wheat-based wines are notorious for their alcoholic power. *Mao Tai* is a breathtaking case in point.

Due to the high import duty on alcohol, European and New World wines are quite expensive in Hong Kong restaurants, but are widely available nonetheless.

The Chinese are not big drinkers – they have a low tolerance level when it comes to alcohol generally – and tend not to drink for the sake of it. Having said that, alcohol is often used to impress, win a business deal or make a show of wealth. Many locals will have a bottle of their favourite whisky or brandy stored at a hotel for their own personal consumption when dining there. In fact, the Chinese having a dinner party at the table next to you are probably drinking Cognac with their meal. Hong Kong claims the world's highest per capita consumption of brandy, possibly because of a vague belief that it has aphrodisiac qualities.

The best choice for the visitor is beer. The locally

brewed San Miguel is cheap and passable, and Tsing Tao beer from China has a hearty, European taste. You will also find a large selection of European brands, some of them brewed locally under licence.

Below: delicate details in a tea shop.

47

Gay and Lesbian

Hong Kong's gay and lesbian community has been getting more prominent over the past few years, as proud pink residents become more vocal about their demands. Nevertheless, many gay and lesbian locals still set up 'marriages of convenience', to show an outward adherence to society values in line with traditional demands to produce family heirs. While this 'fake marriage' practice is lessening, it is still a last resort option for many. Despite progress, gay and lesbian travellers from North America and Western Europe will find acceptance levels here they would never tolerate at home.

Gay Life in Hong Kong

Sexually, young gays and lesbians have few options when it comes time to try and find a location for moments of intimacy. This is due to the skyrocketing cost of property and the necessity for most young people to live at home with the family until they marry. As a result, saunas and bathhouses have become incredibly popular

getaway spots – especially for young gay men.

The age of consent for men who engage in consensual sex is 16 – the same age as for heterosexuals. This equalisation was only achieved in October 2006, following a challenge by a 20-year-old local in the High Court. Many attribute this change of heart to a more open and accepting local

environment, as evidenced by the development of two local gay lifestyle publications that have recently come on the scene (see box, right).

For gay venues, stick to the areas around Central and Tsim Sha Tsui if you want to party with the local community. Lesbians will be at a distinct disadvantage, as there are few venues catering to them in the city.

Below: in 2006 hundreds of people from around the world came to Hong Kong to protest in favour of Gay rights.

Left: only recently has Hong Kong's gay community felt able to protest against discrimination.

A good resource for finding listings and tips is www.utopia.asia.com

Virus

6th Floor, Allways Centre, 268 Jaffe Road, Causeway Bay, tel: 2904 7207; daily until late; MTR: Causeway Bay; map p.138 B3
This fun karaoke bar is one of the few lesbian-aimed venues in town; gay male friends are also welcome. It's a good place to pick up information on other events around town.

Volume

Lower G/F, 83–85 Hollywood Road, Central; tel: 2857 7683; daily until late; MTR: Sheung Wan; map p.136 B3
After-hours cocktail bar that's high on the kitsch factor – right down to the interiors and 80s-inspired music.

Works

1/F, 30–32 Wyndham Street, Central; tel: 2868 6102; daily 7pm–2am; MTR: Central; map p.136 C2
Formerly home to Propaganda (see left), this dark, maze-like Lan Kwai Fong club is a great place to start a night of cruising and boozing.

Bars and Clubs

SEE ALSO NIGHTLIFE, P.74

New Wally Matt Lounge
Ground Floor, 5A Humphreys Avenue, Tsim Sha Tsui, Kowloon; tel: 2721 2568; www.wally matt.com; daily 5pm–4am; MTR: Tsim Sha Tsui; map p.134 C2
Popular pub-style after work drinking spot, with 5–10pm Happy Hours. A great place to meet mostly-older HK-resident foreigners and the locals who admire them. If you're visiting alone, this is a friendly place to strike up a conversation.

Propaganda
Lower G/F, 1 Hollywood Road, Central; tel: 2868 1316; Tue–Thur 9pm–4am, Fri–Sat 9pm–5am; free Tue–Thur, entrance charge Fri–Sat; MTR: Central; map p.136 C3
The granddaddy of them all is this club – HK's only full-scale gay disco – which welcomes (sort–of) both men and women. Many locals hate this place, yet continue to come back due to its legendary status, and its guaranteed energy. Stay away until at least 1am, as the place will be empty until then.

Above: as recently as 2006, the government still promoted conversion therapy to 'cure' gays and lesbians.

Rice Bar

33 Jervois Street, Sheung Wan, Western District; tel: 2851 4800; www.rice-bar.com; Sun–Thur 7pm–1am, Fri 7pm–late, Sat 8pm–late; MTR: Sheung Wan; map p.136 B4
This intimate gay and lesbian cocktail bar is a popular place for a quiet drink with friends. Go for a delicious drink and mellow vibe.

DS (for *Dim Sum*) magazine is the essential guide to gay life in Hong Kong, with listings, features, classifieds and more. It's distributed free through a wide range of outlets, and has a handy website (www.dim sum-hk.com). The same group also produce the monthly *Q Guide*, with a gay map of Hong Kong. The **Horizons** organization runs a gay help and information line, tel: 2815 9268; www.horizons.org.hk

History

c. 4000 BC	Aboriginal Yue people set up Stone-Age settlements along the coast of South China.
AD 25–220	Han dynasty first extends Chinese imperial rule to the Pearl River area.
969–1279	The Song dynasty. During this time the music and basic styles of Chinese Opera are developed.
12th century	The 'Five Clans', Cantonese migrants from further north, settle in the New Territories.
1277–9	Last Song emperor, overthrown by the Mongols, takes refuge in Lantau and near Kowloon.
1577	Portuguese given permission to establish a permanent trading colony at Macau.
1660s	After revolts in South China the Qing or Manchu dynasty orders the evacuation of many coastal areas. When this is revoked the Hong Kong area is partly resettled by North Chinese migrants called *Hakka*, who form separate communities.
1714	British East India Company establishes trading base in Guangzhou (Canton) to import opium from India. Chinese bans on the trade are ignored.
1839	Commissioner Lin Tse-hsu closes the British Guangzhou factory and confiscates 20,000 chests of opium, sparking the First Opium War.
1841	After China is defeated Britain takes unofficial possession of Hong Kong Island on 26 January, and a year later it is officially ceded to Britain under Treaty of Nanking. Kowloon is added to the colony in 1860, following the Second Opium War.
1865	Hongkong and Shanghai Bank (HSBC) founded.
1898	New Territories and outlying Islands are leased to Britain for 99 years.
1911	Qing dynasty falls; Sun Yat-sen, educated in Hong Kong, forms the Republic of China.
1937–45	Japan invades China. After they take Guangzhou in 1938, some 750,000 refugees flee to Hong Kong. Japanese troops attack Hong Kong itself on 8 December 1941, and after heavy fighting it falls on Christmas Day. Japanese occupation lasts until 30 August 1945.

969–1279: basic tradition of Chinese Opera are laid down.

1714: the British open up trade links with Chinese ports.

1856: early colonial buildings on the harbour.

1911: Sun Yat-sen forms the Republic of China.

1949	Victorious Communists found the People's Republic of China (PRC). The defeated Nationalists flee to Taiwan, and more refugees flood into Hong Kong, where the population swells to 2.2 million.
1966	Pro-Communist riots, inspired by the Cultural Revolution in China, shake Hong Kong.
1979	Mass Transit Railway (MTR) opens.
1984	British Prime Minister Margaret Thatcher and Chinese premier Zhao Ziyang sign 'Joint Declaration' on the future of Hong Kong, agreeing that it will revert to Chinese sovereignty in 1997 as a 'Special Administrative Region' (SAR) of the PRC.
1989	Tiananmen massacre in Beijing leads to large-scale demonstrations in Hong Kong.
1992–7	Chris Patten, last British Governor, seeks to introduce democratic reforms in Hong Kong, including direct elections to the Legislative Council (LegCo).
1997	Handover of sovereignty to China, at midnight on 30 June. Tung Chee-hwa appointed Chief Executive of the SAR, as LegCo is temporarily replaced by a Beijing-appointed Legislature.
1998	New part-elected, part-appointed LegCo established. New airport opens at Chek Lap Kok. Asian economic crisis hits Hong Kong Stock Market.
2003	Sars kills 299, devastates Hong Kong's economy and discredits the Tung administration. Over 500,000 people march against Article 23, a controversial anti-subversion bill, which is shelved.
2005	Tung Chee-hwa resigns and is succeeded by Donald Tsang, a career civil servant under the British. His reform proposals are rejected by democracy campaigners, who say they do not go far enough. Disneyland opens on Lantau.
2006	Hong Kong's Bishop Zen, an outspoken advocate of democracy, becomes a cardinal. In July thousands of Hong Kong people demonstrate for full democracy. In December the Star Ferry pier in Central is demolished, despite local opposition.
2007	Donald Tsang is re-elected to a new 5-year term as Hong Kong's leader, by a committee loyal to Beijing. Hong Kong's 7,000,000 people have no direct say. Nevertheless, the 10th anniversary of the Handover in July is celebrated with verve, as the economy booms once again, and none of the worst fears of mainland rule have been born out.

1982: Margaret Thatcher takes tea in a resettlement estate during one of her visits to negotiate the handover of Hong Kong.

1997: lowering the Union Jack on handover day.

2003: the Sars outbreak caused global panic.

2007: celebrations to mark the 10th anniversary of the handover of Hong Kong to China.

Hotels

Hong Kong has some of the most luxurious hotels in the world catering for some of the wealthiest business travellers on the globe. Unsurprisingly, nearly all the big international hotel groups are represented here. In contrast to the UK and the rest of Europe, hotels in Hong Kong are used as much by the local population as they are by visitors; Hong Kongers frequent hotels for dining, meeting and socialising. The big hotels' afternoon teas and Sunday brunches are renowned, and some of the city's top restaurants and bars are located within the five-star and boutique properties.

Central and the Peak

Bishop Lei International House
4 Robinson Road, Mid-Levels; tel: 2868 0828; www.bishopleihtl.com.hk; $;
MTR: Central, then bus to Robinson Road or walk to Mid-Levels Escalator; map p.136 B2
A good low-cost option – owned by the Catholic Diocese of Hong Kong – located 15 minutes' walk away from the nightlife hub of Lan Kwai Fong, and with SoHo on its doorstep (via the Mid-Levels Escalator). There is nothing remarkable about the decor, but with

many of the services and facilities of an upper-scale European hotel – including a gym, business centre, pool, free in-room Broadband, 24-hour room service and babysitter and concierge services – and low-season rates from HK$650 this hotel offers exceptional value for money. Some suites even have impressive harbour views.

Four Seasons
8 Finance Street, Central; tel: 3196 8888; www.fourseasons.com/hongkong; $$$;
MTR: Central, Hong Kong Airport Express; map p.136 C4
With its dazzling facilities (including a large spa and two rooftop pools), hip bars, place-to-be restaurants and jaw-dropping views, the Four Seasons is Hong Kong at its most decadent, glamorous, flaunt-it best. If you do not stay, at least try a cocktail in the bar. The hotel has covered access to the Airport Express station and the adjacent chic IFC mall.

Left: the indulgent Four Seasons.

The Hong Kong Hotel Association operates meet-and-greet services at exits A and B at the North and South ends of the Airport. Reservations are strongly recommended, particularly in summer and at Christmas, but the association also offers reservation services at its counters located beyond the customs hall. If you arrive without a hotel booking, the HKHA should be able to help find you a room.

Hotel LKF
33 Wyndham Street, Lan Kwai Fong; tel: 3518 9333; www.hotel-lkf.com.hk; $$–$$$;
MTR: Central; map p.137 C3
Not to be confused with the Lan Kwai Fong Hotel (see p.54), the 95-room LKF is one of the city's hippest addresses, smack in the middle of Lan Kwai Fong. Rooms have espresso machines and DVD players, and guests can avail themselves of butler services and complimentary shoeshine. The sexy 29th-floor cocktail bar and supper lounge, AZURE, was at time of going to press strictly

Left: a taipan-style room at the Mandarin Oriental.

Price ranges, which are given as a guide only, are for a standard double room with bathroom per night, including service and tax but without breakfast. Note, though, that hotels frequently offer lower promotional rates online, and outside peak seasons.

$ under HK$1,000
$$ HK$1,000–2,000
$$$ over HK$2,000

'residents only' but this policy may become more relaxed. If it has, book ahead.

Island Shangri-La
Pacific Place, Supreme Court Road, Central; tel: 2877 3838; www.shangri-la.com; $$$; MTR: Admiralty; map p.137 E2

The jaw-dropping 17-storey atrium at 'the Shang' says it all: this is the Shangri-La group's flagship property, and comes with all the bells, whistles and first-class service one would expect from this revered local chain. Large rooms with oversize bathrooms have broadband, DVDs, in-room copier/printers and other gadgets, and views of the harbour or Victoria Peak. The restaurants are heavily patronised by local gourmets – always a good sign.

The Landmark Mandarin Oriental
15 Queen's Road, Central; tel: 2132 0188; www.mandarinoriental.com; $$$; MTR: Central; map p.137 D2

The Mandarin Oriental group opened this 113-room boutique hotel a stone's throw from its famous sister hotel in 2005, to give a slightly more intimate style of luxury. Claiming the city's largest rooms, it has warm, contemporary decor throughout. Facilities include a bar on the ground floor, a stunning restaurant and vast spa that spreads over two floors.

Mandarin Oriental Hong Kong
5 Connaught Road, Central; tel: 2522 0111; www.mandarinoriental.com; $$$; MTR: Central; map p.137 D3

Mandarin Oriental's first and flagship property reopened at the end of 2006 after a major refit, with larger rooms, multilingual butlers on every floor and iPod docking stations as standard. Service remains

Below: Island Shangri-La.

Above: greeting guests at the Mandarin Oriental.

exemplary, and the hotel has lost none of its charm to modernity. The Mandarin also houses a clutch of popular restaurants and bars, including the Conran-revamped **Mandarin Grill** and a bar that has a special license to permit smoking, in spite of Hong Kong's recent smoking ban.
SEE ALSO RESTAURANTS, P.88

Western

Lan Kwai Fong Hotel
3 Kau U Fong, Sheung Wan; tel: 2311 6280; www.lankwaifong hotel.com.hk; $$; MTR: Sheung Wan; map p.136 C3
There is a boutique Asian charm to this 162-room hotel, and its location – west of the real Lan Kwai Fong district, not far from Hollywood Road, the Man Mo temple and SoHo – is excellent. There is in-house dining and Internet access, and five suites have balconies (almost unheard of in Hong Kong) with spectacular views across Central to the harbour. The balconies are not for vertigo sufferers, however.

Wan Chai and Causeway Bay

Cosmo Hotel
375–7 Queen's Road East, Wan Chai; tel: 3552 8388; www.cosmohotel.com.hk; $;

MTR: Causeway Bay; map p.138 C2
The Cosmo, with its colour-coded orange, mod-green or pastel yellow rooms and retro wallpaper, is funky and an exceptionally well-priced option. Its location, in a historic building a stone's throw from Happy Valley Racecourse and the Causeway Bay shopping district, makes it perfect for keen shoppers, and Wan Chai's nightlife is also on the doorstep. There's free WiFi access throughout, and the many nice touches for a hotel in this price range include flat-panel PCs with Broadband access in the executive rooms.

Empire Hotel
33 Hennessy Road, Wan Chai; tel: 2866 9111, www.empire hotel.com.hk; $$; MTR: Wan Chai; map p.139 C3
A good-value hotel in the heart of Wan Chai, the 360-room Empire has many of the services and facilities of its higher-priced neighbours, including a pool, gym and business centre. Rooms are pleasantly comfortable, and there is no scrimping on in-room amenities.

Fleming Hong Kong
41 Fleming Road, Wan Chai; tel: 3607 2288; www.the

fleming.com.hk; $$; MTR: Wan Chai; map p.138 B3
Dubbing itself Hong Kong's 'Urban Lifestyle Hotel', the Fleming is a new 66-room boutique property in the thick of Wan Chai. WiFi, cordless phones and plasma TVs are standard, and there is free access to a DVD library. Deluxe and executive rooms have kitchenettes. Asia's first female-only floor caters for women guests with in-room beauty kits, jewellery boxes, facial steamers and toiletries.

Grand Hyatt Hong Kong
1 Harbour Road, Wan Chai; tel: 2588 1234; www.hong kong.grand.hyatt.com; $$$; MTR: Wan Chai; map p.138 A3
The Hyatt has magnificent views of the Convention Centre and harbour, and its grand Art Deco-style lobby with black marble pillars, mosaic floor and sweeping staircase is a sight to behold. Hints of Art Deco continue through the public areas and luxuriously minimalist guest rooms. The hotel is also known for its **Plateau Spa** – a state-of-the-art fitness, spa and pool complex that extends over 7,000sq m. Other facilities include tennis courts, a golf driving range, jogging track and a fabulous **Champagne Bar**.
SEE ALSO BARS, P.26; PAMPERING, P.81

Price ranges, which are given as a guide only, are for a standard double room with bathroom per night, including service and tax but without breakfast. Note, though, that hotels frequently offer lower promotional rates online, and outside peak seasons.
$ under HK$1,000
$$ HK$1,000–2,000
$$$ over HK$2,000

You will want for nothing at one of Hong Kong's upmarket hotels: excellent city and/or harbour views are pretty much guaranteed, and in low season you should not have to pay any more for a view. Interconnecting rooms are often available for families. Always request a view when booking, and ask about free room upgrades and seasonal packages: many of these include benefits such as food and drinks credits, and free laundry service.

Also, remember that almost all hotels offer free local phone calls, and many of the newer establishments and smaller boutique hotels now offer free WiFi access and other gadgets as an added incentive to stay.

What these smaller independent hotels lack in views they more than make up for in individuality and money-saving incentives. Most of the boutiques offer free breakfast and DVD libraries, and some feature kitchenettes and grocery delivery services.

Jia

1–5 Irving Street, Causeway Bay; tel: 3196 9000; www.jia-hongkong.com; $$–$$$; MTR: Causeway Bay; map p.139 D3

Stylish, urbane and stuffed with *objets d'art*, the Jia was Hong Kong's first true boutique hotel. Bearing plenty of the quirky hallmarks associated with designer Philippe Starck, it has lost none of its appeal in spite of recent competition. The 54 studio-rooms are far from large, but they are certainly stunning, and you will want for nothing in this service-oriented hotel. Complimentary breakfast, afternoon cakes, cocktail-hour wine and gym access make the rates very good value, and an added bonus is the hip and award-winning **Opia** restaurant.

SEE ALSO RESTAURANTS, P.91

Lanson Place

133 Leighton Road, Causeway Bay; tel: 3477 6999; www.lansonplace.com; $$$; MTR: Causeway Bay; map p.139 C2

Opened in mid-2006, the Lanson differentiates itself from Hong Kong's other boutique hotels with its distinctly European accent. Smart, airy and sophisticated, it offers free WiFi and use of the DVD and book library, a complimentary 'wellness' breakfast and gym access. Some rooms have kitchenettes. Sip a martini in their lounge or ask the sommelier to recommend a vintage wine.

Southside

Le Méridien Cyberport

100 Cyberport Road, Pok Fu Lam, near Aberdeen; tel: 2980 7788; www.hongkong.lemeridien.com; $$–$$$; bus: 40 to Pok Fu Lam, or free hotel shuttle bus

Perched on the edge of Telegraph Bay west of Aberdeen, the 173-room Le Méridien Cyberport is one of Hong Kong's most spectacular, 'world of its own' hotels (although Central is only a 15-minute bus or taxi ride away), and one of the city's funkiest to boot. The panoramas from the ocean-view rooms are memorable, and cocktails in its trendy bar are a must at sunset. It is a stone's throw away from Cyberport, a revolutionary digital city that also features a cinema and a plethora of high-end shops, and the hotel's electronic facilities are accordingly state of the art. Nearby attractions include Repulse Bay, South Bay beach, Stanley Market, and Big Wave Bay. Ocean Park is only minutes away too.

Kowloon

Harbour Plaza Hong Kong

20 Tak Fung Street, Whampoa Gardens, Hung Hom; tel: 2621 3188; www.harbour-plaza.com; $$; KCR: East line to Hung Hom Station, ferry: Hung Hom pier

With its rooftop resort-style pool and impressive waterfront views, the Harbour Plaza, in the recently-developed Whampoa Gardens area on the east side of Kowloon, is a popular choice among visiting Europeans. Though it is slightly out on a limb, there are still scores of shops and restaurants on the doorstep, plus convenient ferry access to three island destinations and a free shuttle bus to Tsim Sha Tsui MTR and Hung Hom KCR stations.

Below: Harbour Plaza hotel.

It is only a short ferry ride or MTR journey between the two, but make sure you know which side of the harbour you want to be on before booking your accommodation: Kowloon (Tsim Sha Tsui) or Hong Kong island (where Central, Lan Kwai Fong, Wan Chai and Causeway Bay are the key areas). Kowloon is where most of the night markets and tourist shopping is located, but if nightlife is a key criteria then you should opt to stay on Hong Kong Island.

Holiday Inn Golden Mile
50 Nathan Road, Tsim Sha Tsui; tel: 2369 3111; www.golden mile.com; $–$$; MTR: Tsim Sha Tsui; map p.134 C1

This hotel is conveniently located in the midst of Nathan Road's 'Golden Mile' shopping strip; the modern rooms, in the usual Holiday Inn style, are a good size and feature floor-to-ceiling windows, although any hope of a view is blocked by nearby buildings. It has a varied mix of good restaurants, such as the **Avenue**, and there is a rooftop swimming pool and spa. Low online rates make it good value.

SEE ALSO RESTAURANTS, P.94–5

Intercontinental Grand Stanford
70 Mody Road, Tsim Sha Tsui East; tel: 2721 5161; www.hong kong.intercontinental.com; $$$; MTR: Tsim Sha Tsui; map p.135 D2

Near the waterfront on the east side of Tsim Sha Tsui, with views over the harbour, this 579-room hotel is also near Hong Kong's Coliseum stadium, and has hosted the likes of David Bowie and Elton John. Around half the rooms have harbour views. The hotel has French, Italian and Cantonese restaurants, and there is a heated outdoor pool.

Intercontinental Hong Kong
18 Salisbury Road, Tsim Sha Tsui; tel: 2721 1211; www.hong kong-ic.intercontinental.com; $$$; MTR: Tsim Sha Tsui; map p.134 C1

Below: the pool at the Harbour Plaza Hotel

Opposite: the Intercontinental Hong Kong has some of the city's finest views.

One of Hong Kong's top hotels, with possibly the best harbourfront views in town, right on the Tsim Sha Tsui waterfront. The Lobby Bar and rooftop infinity spa pools are not to be missed, and the hotel also boasts Asia's most decadent presidential suite, cantilevered over the harbour (with its own infinity pool and gym). Dining options include the region's first **Nobu** outside Tokyo, as well as **SPOON by Alain Ducasse**. There is also the luxurious **I-Spa**. Rooms are generously sized and well appointed, and most have harbour views.

SEE ALSO PAMPERING, P.80;
RESTAURANTS, P.95

Langham Hotel
555 Shanghai Street, Mong Kok; tel: 3552 3388; www.langham hotels.com; $$; MTR: Mong Kok; map p.132 B3

This hotel is part of a multi-purpose office, leisure and hotel complex that rises like a shiny new incisor from a formerly rundown patch of Mong Kok. The hi-tech rooms have floor-to-ceiling windows over a fascinatingly vibrant district of Hong Kong, and facilities include guest phones that can be taken anywhere in the hotel (and let you check the world weather, news headlines and your stocks and shares), WiFi throughout, huge in-room plasma screens and DVD. The impressively large **Chuan Spa** is among the city's best hotel spas. A 15-storey entertainment complex, which includes a **UA Cinema**, is next door.

SEE ALSO FILM, P.43;
PAMPERING, P.80

Luxe Manor
39 Kimberley Road, Tsim Sha Tsui; tel: 3763 8888; www. theluxemanor.com; $$$; MTR: Tsim Sha Tsui; map p.134 C2

The first boutique designer hotel in Kowloon, Luxe Manor offers a modern, or perhaps post-modern, interpretation of a European mansion. Some of its design features recall the works of 20th-century surrealists, and the whimsically-themed rooms are sure to appeal to anyone with a sense of humour, and maybe adventure. Each room has a great rain shower, but no bath; free breakfast is served at the hotel's Aspasia restaurant. The Luxe also offers a good location, at the heart of the Tsim Sha Tsui shopping district and just a short walk away from the Knutsford Terrace dining and bar area.

Nathan Hotel
378 Nathan Road, Yau Ma Tei, tel: 2388 5141, www.nathan hotel.com; $–$$; MTR: Yau Ma Tei; map p.134 C4

This renovated, quiet and pleasant hotel is close to the Temple Street Night Market, and has 180 spacious and well-decorated no-frills rooms. The Penthouse restaurant serves Cantonese and Western food, and there is a Starbucks on site.

Right: Langham Hotel.

Above: Salisbury YMCA.

Park Hotel

61–5 Chatham Road South, Tsim Sha Tsui; tel: 2731 2100; www.parkhotel.com.hk; $; MTR: Tsim Sha Tsui; map p.135 C2
Among the best of the larger hotels in the moderate price range, the Park is located across from the Science Museum, a few streets back from the harbourside in Kowloon. The lobby is attractive and the large rooms well-furnished; there are Western and Cantonese restaurants, plus a coffee and cake shop.

Peninsula

Salisbury Road, Tsim Sha Tsui; tel: 2920 2888; http://hongkong.peninsula.com; $$$; MTR: Tsim Sha Tsui; map p.134 C1

The much-loved 'Pen' opened in 1928, making it Hong Kong's most historic hotel; Nöel Coward was only one of the globetrotting celebs who stayed here in its first golden era. Today, one only has to step into the magnificent lobby, where the famous afternoon tea is served, to imbibe the ambience of yesteryear. But the Peninsula also has both feet planted firmly in the present. Rooms are the pinacle of luxury, matching the hotel's helipad and fleet of Rollers, and the views from the famous corner-suite baths are legendary. In-house establishments include the Philippe

Starck-designed **Felix** top-floor bar, with its celebrated men's loo with a view and the **Peninsula Spa by ESPA**.
SEE ALSO PAMPERING, P.81; RESTAURANTS, P.95

Royal Garden Hong Kong

69 Mody Road, Tsim Sha Tsui East; tel: 2721 5215; www.rghk.com.hk; $$$; MTR: Tsim Sha Tsui; map p.135 D2
At one of Kowloon's most attractive upmarket hotels all rooms open onto terraces overlooking a plant-filled 15-storey atrium with pools and waterfalls. Rooms are cosy and inviting; some have harbour views. Leisure facilities include the spectacular Mediterranean-style Sky Club – featuring a 25-m year-round pool with great harbour views – a well-equipped gym, a spa and a tennis court.

Salisbury YMCA

41 Salisbury Road, Tsim Sha Tsui; tel: 2268 7000; www.ymcahk.org.hk; $; MTR: Tsim Sha Tsui; map p.134 B1
Its room rates do not follow those found in your typical YMCA, but the Hong Kong Y is nonetheless one of the best bargains in the city, offering the facilities and service of much more

Below: the Peninsula, Tsim Sha Tsui, Kowloon.

Hong Kong's hotel rates can seem steep, especially when 10 per cent service charge and 3 per cent government tax are added to the bill. But standards are among the best in the world, and you can be assured of modern and tasteful rooms, first-rate facilities, spotless public areas, 24-hr room service, a staggering choice of bars and dining options and exceptional service. Many hotels also have shopping malls on site. And there are ways of cutting down on the cost of staying in Hong Kong, above all by booking online: hotels are continually offering special rates on their websites, which are often far lower than their theoretical standard rates.

expensive hotels at a fraction of the cost. Rooms are utilitarian but comfortable and well equipped, and there is a pool, gym, squash courts, climbing wall and on-site dining.

New Territories

Hong Kong Gold Coast Hotel

1 Castle Peak Road, Castle Peak Bay; tel: 2452 8888; www.gold coasthotel.com.hk; $$$; bus: 962B from Admiralty bus station, or hotel shuttle bus approximately every hour from Tsim Sha Tsui via Tsing Yi and Tsuen Wan

Set in 4 hectares of landscaped gardens overlooking the South China Sea, this is as close as Hong Kong gets to a resort-style hotel. Lie by the huge pool and you could almost be in Thailand. Each of the 450 rooms and suites features a panoramic sea view, and many have private balconies. Children are well catered-for, and leisure facilities are extensive.

Royal Park

8 Pak Hok Ting Street, Sha Tin; tel: 2601 2111, www.royal park.com.hk; $$; KCR: East line to Sha Tin

This newly refurbished and surprisingly stylish hotel near Sha Tin's New Town Plaza shopping complex and overlooking the Shin Mun River is easily accessed from the city by KCR, or on the hotel's own shuttle buses to and from Tsim Sha Tsui. There are three Asian restaurants, a coffee shop, squash and tennis courts, jogging facilities and a swimming pool and health centre. Special facilities are also provided for guests with disabilities.

The Outer Islands

Hong Kong Disneyland Hotel and Disney's Hollywood Hotel

Hong Kong Disneyland Resort, Lantau; tel: 3510 6000, 3510 5000; www.hongkongdisney land.com; $$$; MTR: Sunny Bay, then change onto Disneyland Resort Line

If visiting Hong Kong with younger children, you might find it hard to miss out on spending at least one night here. Both hotels are 10 min from the airport and 25 min from downtown, and there are complimentary shuttle buses between the hotels and Disneyland itself. The former hotel is Victorian style, the latter all-American. A

Price ranges, which are given as a guide only, are for a standard double room with bathroom per night, including service and tax but without breakfast. Note, though, that hotels frequently offer lower promotional rates online, and outside peak seasons.

$	under HK$1,000
$$	HK$1,000–2,000
$$$	over HK$2,000

Above: Royal Garden Hong Kong.

variety of packages is available, combining hotel accommodation with park entrance.

Silvermine Beach Hotel

Silvermine Bay, Mui Wo, Lantau; tel: 2984 8295; www.resort. com.hk; $–$$; ferry: Central to Mui Wo (Silvermine Bay), bus: Hong Kong International Airport

A basic but pleasant 128-room hotel overlooking Silvermine Bay on Lantau Island, a half-hour ferry ride from Central, and convenient for country walks and visiting some fine beaches and the bronze Buddha at the Po Lin Monastery. There is a coffee shop and Chinese restaurant, and though the beach is nothing to write home about, the hotel has an outdoor swimming pool, gym, sauna and tennis courts.

Warwick Hotel

East Bay, Cheung Chau; tel: 2981 0081; www.warwick hotel.com.hk; $; Ferry: Cheung Chau

Hong Kong's best international-style island-resort beach hotel houses 70 rooms, albeit in an ugly grey concrete building. All rooms have balconies with views straight onto a fine beach, and facilities include a children's playground, babysitting services, a pool and watersports facilities.

59

Language

Hong Kong's official languages are Chinese and English. The main Chinese dialect is Cantonese, spoken by more than 90 per cent of the population and an inseparable part of the sound and rhythm of the city. Mandarin Chinese (Putonghua), the official language of the People's Republic of China, is gaining in popularity. This reflects the importance of doing business with the mainland and inbound tourism rather than government directives. Cantonese can seem rather daunting to speakers of European languages, but an attempt at a simple phrase or two will generally be well-received.

A Language Minefield

Hong Kong people use a standard form of Cantonese when they write, or in a business situation, but speak colloquial Cantonese in everyday conversation. Colloquial Chinese is rich in slang, and some spoken words do not have characters.

To confuse you further, Hong Kong (like Taiwan) uses a slightly different style of characters to the rest of China. During reforms initiated by Mao in the 1950s to increase literacy, the People's Republic of China simplified its characters. Hence the characters used on the mainland are referred to as Simplified Chinese, while Hong Kong's more complex characters are called Traditional Chinese.

> The written form of Chinese was originally derived from pictures or symbols that represented objects or concepts, so there is no correlation between the appearance of Chinese characters and the sound that they represent.

TONES

If all this was not enough to master, many an enthusiastic linguist has been defeated by Cantonese tones. Each word has a distinct pitch that goes higher, lower or stays flat within each word. Among the Cantonese there is no real agreement as to how many tones there are – some say as many as nine – but most people use six in daily life.

The Jyutping transliteration system devised by the Linguistic Society of Hong Kong classifies the six main tones as: **1**, high falling/high flat; **2**, high rising; **3**, middle; **4**, low falling; **5**, low rising; **6**, low.

Each word has one syllable, and is represented by one distinct character. A word is made up of three sound elements: an initial, e.g., 'f', plus a final sound, e.g. 'an', plus a tone.

A few rare words just have a final sound and a tone, e.g. 'm' in *'m goi'* (thank you).

Therefore, when combined with a tone, 'fan' has seven distinct and contradictory meanings: to divide (high rising 1); flour (high falling 2); to

teach (middle flat 3); fragrant (high flat 1); a grave (low falling 4); energetic (low rising 5); and a share (low flat 5).

The wealth of sound-alike words (homonyms) that can be easily mispronounced play a part in many Cantonese traditions and the development of slang. However, for the visitor or new learner tones mean that utter bafflement is a common reaction to your attempt simply to say the name of the road you wish to visit. Persevere, and try to mimic the way a Cantonese speaker says each part of the phrase.

Pronunciation

j as in the 'y' of yap
z similar to the sound in bei**ge** or the zh in Guang**zh**ou
c as in chip
au as in how
ai as in buy
ou as in no
i as in he

Useful Words & Phrases

NUMBERS

0	*ling*
1	*jat*
2	*ji*
3	*saam*

Left: the written word can be a dlicate art.

PEOPLE
mother *maa maa*
father *baa baa*
son *zai*
daughter *neoi*
baby *be be*
friend *pang jau*
boyfriend *naam pang jau*
girlfriend *neoi pang jau*
husband *lou gung*
wife *lou po*

ADJECTIVES
small *sui*
big *dai*
good *ho*
bad *mm ho*
expensive *gwai*
cheap *peng*
slow *maan*
fast *faai*
pretty/beautiful *leng*
hot *jit*
cold *dung*
very... *hou ...*
delicious *ho sick*

4	*sei*
5	*ng*
6	*luk*
7	*cat*
8	*baat*
9	*gau*
10	*sap*
11	*sap jat*
12	*sap ji*
20	*ji sap*
21	*ji sap jat*
100	*baak*
140	*jat sei ling*

COMMON EXPRESSIONS
Good morning *zou san (joe san)*
Good afternoon *ng on*
Good night *zou tau*
Goodbye *bai bai*
Hello (on phone) *wai!*
Thank you (service) *m goi*
Thank you (gift) *do ze*
You're welcome *M sai m goi*
No problem *mou man tai*
How are you? *Nei hou maa? (neigh ho marr)*
Fine, thank you *gay ho, yau sum*
yes *hai*
no *m hai*
OK *hou aa*
Please take me to *m goy chey ngor hur-ee*

My name is... *ngor geeu*
yesterday *kum yut*
today *gum yut*
tomorrow *ting yut*
hotel *zau dim*
key *so si*
manager *ging lei*
room *haak fong*
telephone *din wa*
toilet *ci so*
bank *ngan hong*
post office *yau jing guk*
passport *wu ziu*
restaurant *zaan teng*
bar *zau ba*
bus *ba si*
taxi *dik si*
train *fo ze*

QUESTIONS
Who? *bin go a?*
Where? *bin do a?*
When? *gei si a?*
Why? *dim gaai a?*
How many? *gei do a?*
How much does that cost? *gei dor chin a?*
Do you have...? *yau mo ... a?*
What time is the train to Guangzhou...? *Guangzhou ge for che, gay dim hoy a?*

HEALTH AND EMERGENCIES
I have (a) ... *ngo...*
headache *tau tung*
stomach ache *tou tung*
toothache *nga tung*
fever *faat sui*
I am sick *ngo jau beng*
doctor *ji sang*
nurse *wu si*
ambulance *gau surng che*
police *ging chaat*

Right: a calligrapher's shop.

Museums and Galleries

Hong Kong's museums and galleries have an enviable task: to document the thriving, modern culture of Hong Kong set against rich Chinese traditions, and all the while preserve a unique colonial past. This puts the city's heritage at the visitor's fingertips, whether in the delicacy of tea ware at Flagstaff House or the sweeping political changes recorded at the Hong Kong Heritage Museum. There is also a vibrant art scene, revealed at the Hong Kong Museum of Art and Arts Centre.

Art Museum of the Chinese University of Hong Kong

Ma Liu Shui, near Sha Tin, New Territories; tel: 2609 7416; www.cuhk.edu.hk/ics/amm; daily 10am–5pm; free; KCR: East line to University station, then shuttle bus

The Chinese University campus enjoys a panoramic view over the scenic inland waters of Tolo Harbour. The purpose-built Art Museum showcases Chinese art to brilliant effect and, in association with mainland Chinese museums, has brought many Chinese treasures to Hong Kong in exciting temporary exhibitions. The permanent collection includes paintings, calligraphy, bronze seals and jade carvings.

Flagstaff House Museum of Tea Ware

10 Cotton Tree Drive, Hong Kong Park, Central; tel: 2869 0690, www.lcsd.gov.hk; daily 10am–5pm; free; MTR: Admiralty, bus/tram: Queensway and Hennessy Road; map p.137 D2

The building housing this museum, the oldest surviving colonial building in Hong Kong, is every bit as interesting (or more so) as the exhibit itself. Flagstaff House was completed in 1846, and for over a century was the residence of the Commander-in-Chief of the British army in Hong Kong, as the centre of the area known as Victoria Barracks. Today, the large expanse is the lush, green Hong Kong Park, which is also the site of a popular aviary. The museum hosts a very extensive display of historic pots, cups and the many different artefacts associated with tea in China, as well as temporary exhibits on various aspects of Chinese tea and tea-drinking, and occasionally of modern potters' teaware.

Hong Kong Correctional Services Museum

45 Tung Tau Wan Road, Stanley, Southside; tel: 2147 3199; www.csd.gov.hk/english/hkcsm; Tue–Sun 10am–5pm; free; bus: 6, 6X, 40, 66, 260

A Hong Kong oddity: in the peaceful setting of Stanley, this museum charts the history of the Hong Kong penal system from the early days of the colony, with creepy exhibits like a mock gallows and cells.

Below: Museum of Tea Ware.

Left: Hong Kong Arts Centre.

Bank of China), but in 1982 was dismantled stone by stone and put into storage. It was re-assembled in Stanley in 2001 (with some problems, as some components had been mis-labelled). Above the museum Murray House also contains a handful of Western-style restaurants, overlooking Stanley Bay.

Hong Kong Museum of Art

Hong Kong Cultural Centre, 10 Salisbury Road, Tsim Sha Tsui, Kowloon; tel: 2721 0116; www.lcsd.gov.hk/hkma; Fri and Sun–Wed 10am–6pm, Sat 10am–8pm; entrance charge, but free Wed; MTR: Tsim Sha Tsui; map p.134 C1

The distinctive 'skateboard-ramp'-roofed Museum of Art on the Kowloon waterfront is a great place to while away a few hours. The museum houses some of the world's finest examples of ancient Chinese art, from the Han to the Ming and Qing dynasties, along with hundreds of traditional and contemporary oil paintings, drawings, etchings and calligraphy. It also displays historic photographs,

Hong Kong Heritage Museum

1 Man Lam Road, Sha Tin, New Territories; tel: 2180 8188; www.heritagemuseum.gov.hk; Mon and Wed–Sat 10am–6pm, Sun 10am–7pm; entrance charge; KCR: East line to Sha Tin

Designed to preserve and interpret the cultural identity of Hong Kong, and opened in 2000 in the new town of Sha Tin, this is also the territory's largest museum, with 12 exhibition halls in an all-new building designed to evoke traditional Chinese architecture through a series of attractive courtyards.

In addition to hosting changing thematic exhibitions, the permanent galleries include an exquisite gallery of Chinese art and exhibits devoted to the development of the New Territories and their varied ethnic groups, the history of

Some of Hong Kong's attractions are especially suited to little travelers. For more information on child-friendly places to visit, see p.28–29.

Cantonese opera and even the evolution of local toys. Displays are comprehensive and imaginative.

Hong Kong Maritime Museum

Murray House, Stanley Plaza, Stanley; tel: 2813 2322; www.hkmaritimemuseum.org; Tue–Sun 10am–6pm; entrance charge; bus: 6, 6X, 40, 66, 260

With its 18th-century Chinese archery bows, pirate tales and hands-on exhibits that include the bridge of a container ship and a navigation simulator and radio room complete with dials, gadgets and sound effects, the waterfront Maritime Museum in the little Southside town of Stanley is one of Hong Kong's most child-friendly museums.

It traces centuries of Hong Kong's seafaring history, in Ancient and Modern galleries. It also has another striking location: the colonial arcades of **Murray House**, built as a British Army officers' mess in 1848. It originally stood in Central (on the site now occupied by the

Below: Hong Kong Maritime Museum, Murray House.

Above: Hong Kong Museum of Art.

prints and artefacts from Hong Kong, Macau and Guangzhou. Four of the seven exhibition galleries are taken up with Chinese antiquities, Chinese fine arts, historical pictures and contemporary local art. Worldwide collections are also showcased, in two special exhibition galleries.

Hong Kong Museum of Coastal Defence

175 Tung Hei Road, Shau Kei Wan, east of Causeway Bay; tel: 2569 1500; www.lcsd.gov.hk; Fri–Wed 10am–5pm; entrance charge, but free Wed; MTR: Shau Kei Wan or Heng Fa Chuen
Located in the restored 19th-century Lei Yue Mun Fort, this museum documents Hong Kong's military past, from the Ming and Qing dynasties to colonial times, World War II and the present day. The permanent exhibition is located in the 1887 Redoubt, which is the starting point for a historical trail where visitors can view restored military installations, including a World War II tank.

Hong Kong Museum of History

100 Chatham Road South, Tsim Sha Tsui East, Kowloon; tel: 2724 9042; www.hk.history. museum; Mon and Wed–Sat 10am–6pm, Sun 10am–7pm;

entrance charge, but free Wed; bus: Chatham Road South; map p.135 D3
Conveniently opposite the Science Museum *(see opposite)* this large and lavish modern showcase museum, opened in 2001, documents 6,000 years of Hong Kong history, from its earliest settlement to the Chinese dynasties, the colonial era and the 1997 Handover through its permanent exhibition *The Hong Kong Story*. Imaginative, lively and sometimes perhaps surprisingly controversial displays include lifelike mock-ups of old-style teahouses, cinemas and a Cantonese opera stage, and a fascinating array of old photographs.

Hong Kong Museum of Medical Sciences

2 Caine Lane, Western; tel: 2549 5123; www.hkmms.org.hk; Tue–Sat 10am–5pm, Sun 1–5pm; entrance charge; MTR: Central, then Mid-Levels Escalator, bus: Caine Road; map p.136 B3
Housed in a historic monument – a distinguished Edwardian building from 1906 that was Hong Kong's first purpose-built medical laboratory – this museum is one of the first in the world to compare the traditional Chinese and Western

approaches to medicine. The old Bacteriological Institute laboratory is still intact.

Hong Kong Racing Museum

2/F Happy Valley Stand, Happy Valley; tel: 2966 8065; www. hkjc.com; Tue–Sun 10am–5pm; free; bus/tram: Happy Valley; map p.138 C1
Horse racing began in Hong Kong at the justifiably famous Happy Valley Racecourse in 1845, but if you can not make it to the actual races, visit this colourful museum, opened in 1996. The museum's glass wall looks over the high-tech racecourse and stands, and it tells the history of racing in the former colony via eight galleries, a cinema and interactive videos.
SEE ALSO SPORT, P.113–4

Hong Kong Railway Museum

13 Shung Tak Street, Tai Po Market, Tai Po, New Territories; tel: 2653 3455; www.heritage museum.gov.hk; Wed–Mon 9am–5pm; free; KCR: East line

Hong Kong is a famously safe city for visitors, with street and petty crime a rare occurrence. But for a glimpse into Hong Kong's underworld, and the infamous triads, be sure to pop into the **Police Museum**, in the former Wan Chai Gap police station.
It traces the history of the former Royal Hong Kong Police Force, which today has dropped the 'Royal', through four sections: an orientation gallery, a gallery for temporary exhibitions, and, most gripping, the Triad Societies and Narcotics Galleries.
27 Coombe Road, The Peak; tel: 2849 7019; Tue 2–5pm, Wed–Sun 9am–5pm; free; bus: 15, 15B from Central.

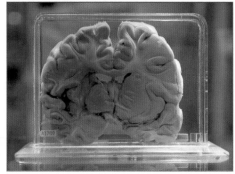

Above: Hong Kong Museum of Medical Sciences.

to Tai Po Market, bus: 271 from Canton Road, Kowloon

This small, picturesque museum is a must-see for railway enthusiasts, but its historical charm and quaintness will also appeal across the board. It is located in the Chinese-temple-style former Tai Po Market railway station on the Guangzhou line, which first opened in 1913, and is now a historic monument. The museum charts the development both of the Kowloon-Canton Railway (KCR) and of the town of Tai Po – one of the oldest in the New Territories – and exhibits include atmospheric photographs and a full-size model of an electric train compartment, as well as real steam locomotives and vintage coaches.

Hong Kong Science Museum

2 Science Museum Road, Tsim Sha Tsui East, Kowloon; tel: 2732 3232; http://hk.science. museum; Mon–Wed and Fri 1–9pm, Sat–Sun 10am–9pm; entrance charge, but free Wed; bus: Chatham Road South; map p.135 D3

Unreservedly directed at the young, whether in families or school groups, the Science Museum displays more than 500 scientific and technological interactive exhibits, including robotics, computers, phones, a miniature submarine, a DC–3 aeroplane and a 22-m high Energy Machine which, when activated, triggers a series of spectacular audiovisual displays. With 80 per cent of its exhibits hands-on, this is a great place for kids to explore the basic concepts of science and technology. It is enormously popular, but adults without kids in tow might find it less interesting.

Hong Kong Space Museum

Salisbury Road, Tsim Sha Tsui, Kowloon; tel: 2721 0226; www.lcsd.gov.hk; Mon and Wed–Fri 1–9pm, Sat–Sun 10am–9pm; entrance charge, but main exhibition free Wed; MTR: Tsim Sha Tsui; map p.134 C1

The igloo-like Space Museum with its trademark domed roof abuts the Hong Kong Museum of Art on the Kowloon waterfront. There are two exhibition halls – the Hall of Space Science and Hall of Astronomy – with the emphasis, as in the Science Museum, on interactive exhibits, with plenty to keep kids fascinated. There is also the giant Space Theatre planetarium (extra charge), which presents two types of show: the Sky Show, on a 23-m dome screen, and documentaries on a 360-degree Omnimax screen.

Below: Hong Kong Science Museum.

Above: Chinese painting, past and present.

Hong Kong Visual Arts Centre

Hong Kong Park, 7A Kennedy Road, Central; tel: 2521 3008; www.lcsd.gov.hk; Wed–Mon 10am–9pm; free; MTR: Admiralty, bus/tram Queensway and Hennessy roads; map p.137 D2
Housed in the officers' quarters of the former Victoria Barracks, this centre is a strong supporter of local art and artists, specialising in the fields of sculpture, printmaking and pottery. It comprises nine working studios, an exhibition space and a lecture theatre, and hosts a varied mix of events, workshops and exhibitions.

Pao Galleries, Hong Kong Arts Centre

4–5/F, Hong Kong Arts Centre, 2 Harbour Road, Wan Chai; tel: 2824 5330; www.hkac.org.hk; daily 10am–8pm; free; MTR: Wan Chai (exit C); map p.138 A3
The Pao Galleries inside the multi–purpose Hong Kong Arts Centre regularly exhibit works by acclaimed international artists, and are a fine showcase for contemporary art. The exhibition programme changes frequently and is very mixed, but international and local exhibitions of paintings, photography, crafts and design are staged.

Pottery Workshop

Old Dairy Farm, 2 Lower Albert Road, Central; tel: 2525 7949; www.ceramics.com.hk; exhibitions Mon–Sat 11am–7pm; free; MTR: Central; map p.137 C2
This workshop was established in the basement of the Old Dairy Farm Building in 1985 as part of the **Fringe Club**, Hong Kong's leading alternative arts complex. Its aim was to revive interest in hand-made ceramics in Hong Kong, covering both traditional skills and new designs: beginning with a humble 15 students and a small gallery in a garage, it has expanded into four galleries, and has workshops in Jingdezhen and Shanghai on the mainland as well as in Hong Kong. The Workshop has won international recognition for its role in revitalising the Chinese tradition in ceramics and developing pottery-making in Hong Kong, and it commands a tremendous local reputation. Its frequent exhibitions showcase new work with a fascinating mix of traditional techniques and originality.
SEE ALSO MUSIC, DANCE AND THEATRE, P.71–2, NIGHTLIFE, P.79; RESTAURANTS, P.87–8

Sun Yat-sen Museum and Historical Trail

7 Castle Road, Western; tel: 2367 6373, http://hk.drsun yatsen.museum; Mon–Wed and Fri–Sat 10am–6pm, Sun 10am–7pm; entrance charge; MTR: Central, then Mid–Levels Escalator, bus: Caine Road; map p.136 B2

One of Hong Kong's newest museums, dedicated to the life and teachings of Chinese revolutionary Dr Sun Yat-sen. In 1911 Dr Sun, who had studied and worked as a doctor in both Hong Kong and Macau, succeeded in overthrowing the Qing Dynasty, and with it some 2,000 years of Chinese autocracy.

Located in the historic Kom Tong Hall, an impressive Edwardian-style residence built for a wealthy local merchant in 1914, the museum's galleries bring the revolutionary activities of the era to life through artefacts, manuscripts, letters, photographs and a well-narrated audio guide, and demonstrate how a tolerant colonial government in Hong Kong indirectly acted as a catalyst for the development of revolutionary activities in China.

The museum is also the starting point for exploring the cluster of sites in the Central and Western districts

One–stop Museum Pass

The museum pass, valid for a week (HK$30) or a month (HK$50) allows unlimited admission to seven of Hong Kong's most popular museums: the Hong Kong Museum of Art, the Hong Kong Science Museum, the Hong Kong Space Museum (excluding the Space Theatre), the Hong Kong Museum of History, the Hong Kong Museum of Coastal Defence, the Hong Kong Heritage Museum and the Sun Yat-sen Museum. It is available from participating museums and Hong Kong Tourist Board visitor Information centres (see p.37).

that form the **Sun Yat-sen Historical Trail**. These include the shop that was the first meeting place for the 'four desperados' (Sun and his first three co-revolutionaries), and the old site of the College of Medicine for Chinese, where Sun received his medical training in the 1880s. Pick up a map of the trail at the museum; free guided tours are also available on Saturdays (booking advisable, through Hong Kong Tourist Board offices or website). They are usually in Cantonese, so check when any are available in English.

University Museum and Art Gallery

University of Hong Kong, 94 Bonham Road, Pok Fu Lam, Western; tel: 2241 5500; www.hku.hk/hkumag; Mon–Sat 9.30am–6pm, Sun 1.30–5.30pm; free; bus: 3B, 23, 40, 40M, 103 from Central; map p.136 A3

Easily located by the main entrance of the University of Hong Kong, the highly respected Fung Ping Shan Museum became the University Museum in 1996, with the addition of a new wing. The museum now occupies the whole of the attractive Edwardian Fung Ping Shan building, while the art gallery is in the lower storeys of the TT Tsui Building; a bridge links the two. UMAG's collections have grown to include over 1,000 Chinese antiquities, notably bronzes, ceramics and paintings dating back to the 7th century. Most prized is the world's largest collection of bronze crosses produced during the Yuan dynasty by the Nestorians, a Christian sect that arrived in China around AD 600. Also on display are over 300 items of Chinese ceramics and carvings from the world-renowned Tsui collection, lodged in the museum on long-term loan.

Below: Sun Yat-Sen Museum.

Music, Dance and Theatre

B e it Chinese or Western, the arts are a significant and growing part of the Hong Kong landscape. Whether your interests run from classical music to pop or contemporary dance, the city offers a wealth of sophisticated performances. Spend a magical evening with the Hong Kong Chinese Orchestra, a night being dazzled by the pyrotechnic shows of global pop superstars or an afternoon at a glitzy Western musical; it is all there for the taking in this East-meets-West artistic hub.

Chinese Arts

Hong Kong Chinese Orchestra

tel: 3185 1600; www.hkco.org
One of the largest of its kind in the world, the Hong Kong Chinese Orchestra remains Hong Kong's only full-scale professional orchestra dedicated to playing traditional Chinese music. The 85-strong orchestra has performed at many famous venues and festivals around the world, but also appears regularly at the **Hong Kong Cultural Centre** (see p.72) and other venues around the Territory. Under the baton of artistic director and principal conductor Yan Huichang, it has taken on the mission of promoting Chinese music worldwide, and its repertoire includes both traditional folk music and contemporary full-scale works, many commissioned for the orchestra. Among its most famous recordings are *The Butterfly Lovers* and *Journey to Lhasa*.

Hong Kong Dance Company

tel: 3103 1888;
www.hkdance.com

Above: the Hong Kong Dance Company.

A uniquely Hong Kong mixture: the city's special culture and history is a rich artistic source for Hong Kong Dance, whose style vividly coalesces East and West. Committed to maintaining Chinese dance, the company performs both traditional folk dances and dance dramas and entirely original works that freely incorporate western techniques, and since its foundation in 1981 the HKDC has staged over a hundred productions choreographed by local, mainland and overseas choreographers, to critical acclaim. It adheres to a belief that dance derives from tradition but is not restricted by boundaries; the results are vibrant and spectacular.

Western Dance and Music

BALLET AND CONTEMPORARY DANCE
City Contemporary Dance Company

tel: 2329 7803;
www.ccdc.com.hk
The flagship of modern dance in Hong Kong, the CCDC is renowned for its distinctive and diverse style of programmes. Founded by choreographer (and still the company's director) Willy Tsao in 1979, it endeavours to rally the best of Chinese talents to create dance in a contemporary Chinese context, and as well as presenting Tsao's own work has

Check www.discoverhongkong.com or the websites of *bc* and *HK* magazines for forthcoming programmes, and www.hk.artsfestival.org for information on the Hong Kong Arts Festival.

Left: Chinese opera still has mass appeal in Hong Kong.

tion with Cantopop artists. The orchestra also attracts world-class soloists to perform on the same stage.

Hong Kong Sinfonietta
tel: 2836 3336;
www.hksinfonietta.org

Hailed as 'one of the world's great small orchestras', the Hong Kong Sinfonietta was founded by music graduates in 1990 with the aim of bringing music closer to the community. Today, under the leadership of Music Director Yip Wing-sie, the orchestra performs over 70 times a year – mainly at **Hong Kong City Hall** *(see p.72)* – and is renowned for its impassioned performances, innovative audience development concerts, crossover productions and new commissions. Over the years, the orchestra has collaborated with an illustrious array of international musicians, including Pavarotti and Zukerman, and has been a regular guest at festivals at home and abroad.

Contemporary Music

CANTOPOP

The first generation of Cantonese pop stars – launching the style quickly dubbed *Cantopop* –

nurtured some of the best choreographers in town, including Helen Lai and Mui Cheuk-yin. The company also tours widely, enlightening audiences worldwide with innovative works and reaching around 100,000 people each year.

Hong Kong Ballet
tel: 2573 7398;
www.hk.ballet.com

Hong Kong is home to one of the foremost classical ballet companies in Asia. For the past few years the Hong Kong Ballet has served as a cultural ambassador for the Territory, performing in Europe, North America, Singapore and major cities in mainland China. The Company presents a broad-based repertoire ranging from classical and neoclassical to contemporary works, and commissions new works. A new chapter opened for the Hong Kong Ballet when John Meehan joined the Company as Artistic Director in July 2006. His first season highlight, *Balanchine and Beyond*, received the Hong Kong Dance Award 2007.

ORCHESTRAL MUSIC
Hong Kong
Philharmonic Orchestra
tel: 2721 2030; www.hkpo.com

Now under artistic director Edo de Waart, this acclaimed orchestra is in residence at the **Hong Kong Cultural Centre** *(see p.72)* from September to July. After enriching Hong Kong's cultural life for over a century the HKPO is one of Asia's leading orchestras, a formidable ensemble of Chinese and international talents. It presents over 150 performances each year, from core symphonic classics to collabora-

Below: Cantopop stars Orchids Eighteen.

M

Chinese Opera remains an integral part of Chinese culture and, however alien it may seem at first to most westerners, it is certainly worth going to see a performance while you are here. In Hong Kong opera performances (Cantonese operas are naturally the most popular) are customary during important festivals on the Chinese calendar. Traditionally, they were put on in temporary bamboo-and-mat theatres in public squares, but they have now moved into Hong Kong's modern venues. To foreign ears, the high-pitched wails of a Chinese opera, interrupted by deafening gongs and drums, seem bizarre and discordant, but Chinese singers undergo long training to achieve a properly pitched falsetto. Every part of the performance has a special meaning: make-up, movements, props and costume colours identify an actor's age, sex and personality the moment he or she appears on stage. Most traditional opera performances in Hong Kong form what are known as *sumkung* (eulogy of the gods), as they are performed to celebrate special festivals or the birthdays of different gods. Many are related to Taoism and Buddhism; during the Hungry Ghost Festival, operas are staged intermixed with other ceremonies to expiate the sins of the dead. It is perfectly acceptable for audiences to arrive late, leave early, walk around, chat or even eat during a Chinese opera, which may run from 3hrs to a whole day. When an actor sings especially well, the audience is expected to respond by shouting out praise and applauding.

Above: extravagant characters from a Chinese opera.

appeared in the mid-1970s. There have been a handful of genuine stars, but the genre is generally dominated by teen idols whose popularity

tends to depend more on their looks than their voices.

Foremost in fan-appeal since the early 1990s were the 'Four Heavenly Kings' – Leon Lai, Jackie Cheung, Andy Lau and Aaron Kwok – and pop-rock band Beyond, who broke up in 2005. Female singers are equally ubiquitous, such as Sally Yeh, Kelly Chen, Sammi Cheng and Hong Kong's greatest superstar, Beijing-born 'Heavenly Queen' Faye Wong, who is phenomenally popular across East Asia.

More recent arrivals include Leon Ku, Hacken Lee and bad-boy star Nicholas Tse, who enjoyed a tortured relationship with Faye Wong that captivated local gossip columns. Cantopop stars fre-

quently cross over into Hong Kong movies, and have massive followings. When heart-throb singer/actor Leslie Cheung died – in a suicide jump from the top floor of the Mandarin Oriental hotel in 2003 – the city was practically paralysed by grief.

MUSICALS
Broadway and West End musicals have a big audience in Hong Kong, and touring productions frequently visit the city for runs of a month or so, usually at the **Hong Kong Cultural Centre** or the **Academy for Performing Arts** *(see p.72)*. Major crowd-pullers have included Andrew Lloyd Webber's *The Phantom of the Opera, The Sound of Music, Saturday Night Fever,*

Abba-based *Mamma Mia!*, and *Singin' In The Rain*. There are also local productions, such as one of Tony Award-winning rock musical *Rent*, starring Hong Kong celebrity Karen Mok.

POP AND ROCK

Hong Kong has finally made it onto the international concert circuit. Programming possibilities were long limited by the lack of suitable venues, but the situation has changed since the opening of the **AsiaWorld-Expo Arena** *(see right)* at the end of 2005. This has now hosted Oasis, Coldplay, Avril Lavigne and the Black-eyed Peas, and has been a stop on the world tours of pop divas Cristina Aguilera and Gwen Stefani. Less stadium-sized acts still tend to play at the Convention Centre or smaller venues in town.

JAZZ

The Hong Kong Jazz Association is a non-profit organisation of jazz lovers and professional musicians dedicated to promoting jazz among Chinese communities. Sadly, a couple of the city's best jazz venues have closed in recent years, but a jazz contingent is included as part of the annual Arts Festival (2007's line-up included the Chucho Valdés Quartet and Julia Migenes) and a handful of venues, including the **Blue Door** and **Fringe Club** (both in Central) that all have regular jazz slots.
SEE ALSO NIGHTLIFE, P.79

Theatre

Hong Kong Repertory Theatre

tel: 3105 5930; www.hkrep.com
Established in 1977, the HKRep is the Territory's leading professional theatre company, with a repertoire covering Chinese and international drama and original local plays. Under its director, US-trained Fredric Mao, the company also pursues an energetic policy of cultural exchanges with mainland China, other Chinese communities and the rest of the world. Productions, presented at the **Hong Kong Cultural Centre** *(see p.72)* and other venues, are usually in Cantonese or Mandarin, with English subtitles.

Venues

For the latest programme information visit www.discover hongkong.com, or *bc* and *HK* magazines or their websites.

AsiaWorld-Expo Arena

AsiaWorld-Expo, Hong Kong International Airport, Lantau; tel: 3608 8828; www.asiaworld-expo.com; Airport Express from Central
This giant 13,500-seat hall has opened up Hong Kong to a flow of suitably giant-scale pop acts. It is part of the huge AsiaWord-Expo site, right next to the airport.

Fringe Club

2 Lower Albert Road, Central; tel: 2521 7251; www.hkfringe club.com; MTR: Central; map p.137 C2
Housed in the various buildings of an old colonial-era dairy, the Fringe is Hong Kong's foremost centre for

Below: the Blue Door Jazz Club.

has space for 12,500 people. It is the favourite venue for Cantopop stars, but international acts sometimes appear too. It will close for renovation from July to December 2008.

Hong Kong Convention and Exhibition Centre
1 Expo Road, Wan Chai; tel: 2582 8888; www.hkcec.com; MTR: Wan Chai (exit C); map p.134 A4
AsiaWorld Arena has displaced the Convention Centre from its role as Hong Kong's largest venue, but it still hosts many visiting acts and musicals: Cliff Richard, Elaine Paige and Roger Waters have all played here recently.

Hong Kong Cultural Centre
10 Salisbury Road, Tsim Sha Tsui, Kowloon; tel: 2734 9009; www.hkculturalcentre.gov.hk; MTR: Tsim Sha Tsui; map p.134 B1
Opened in 1989, this giant slab-like structure on the Kowloon waterfront is Hong Kong's premier arts venue, with three fine auditoria and many other facilities. It hosts most performances by the Hong Kong Philharmonic and the Hong Kong Chinese Orchestra and many visiting

alternative arts, with a small theatre and studio, the **Pottery Workshop**, galleries and a roof garden-bar. The programme is a rich mix, and includes jazz, avant-garde new music and rock.
SEE ALSO MUSEUMS AND GALLERIES, P.66; NIGHTLIFE, P.79; RESTAURANTS, P.87–8

Hong Kong Academy for Performing Arts
1 Gloucester Road, Wan Chai; tel: 2584 8500; www.hkapa.edu; MTR: Wan Chai (exit C); map p.138 A3
One of the foundation-stones of Hong Kong's cultural effervescence, with courses in every field from TV to Chinese opera, the Academy also contains the Lyric Theatre – used by the Hong Kong repertory and visiting companies – and presents fine concerts by its own students and international musicians.

Hong Kong Arts Centre
2 Harbour Road, Wan Chai; tel: 2582 0200; www.hkac.org.hk; MTR: Wan Chai (exit C); map p.138 A3
As well as containing art galleries and a cinema this multi-purpose venue hosts theatre groups (some in English) and occasional concerts.

Hong Kong City Hall
5 Edinburgh Place, Central; tel: 2921 2840; www.cityhall. gov.hk; MTR: Central; map p.137 D3
City Hall contains a 1,424-seat concert hall and a theatre, which hosts Chinese opera and Western music, and many Festival events.

Hong Kong Coliseum
9 Cheong Wan Road, Hung Hom, Kowloon; tel: 2355 7234; www.lcsd.gov.hk; bus: 101, 104, 110; map p.135 E3
This inverted-pyramid arena

Right: Hong Kong Arts Centre.

Above: City Hall hosts many live events.

artists, including musicals. There are also frequent and varied free concerts, especially during the day.

Ko Shan Theatre
77 Ko Shan Road, Hung Hom, Kowloon; tel: 2740 9222; www.lcds.gov.hk; bus: 101, 106, 107, 108, 111
A modern venue popular for Chinese opera, which sometimes hosts pop shows too.

Sha Tin Town Hall
1 Yuen Wo Road, Sha Tin, New Territories; tel: 2694 2509; www.lcsd.gov.hk/stth; KCR: East line to Sha Tin
A product of the Hong Kong government's plan to decentralize culture in the Territory, this modern multispace venue hosts a range of traditional Chinese and other performances.

Queen Elizabeth Stadium
18 Oi Kwan Road, Wan Chai; tel: 2591 1346; www.lcsd.gov.hk; bus: 5A, 10; map p.138 C2
An indoor sports hall (hence, awful acoustics) that has hosted many gigs by medium-sized international acts. It is due to undergo major renovation, and reopen in July 2008.

Festivals
Festivals play a big part in Hong Kong's cultural calendar. The **Hong Kong Arts Festival** (tel: 2824 3555, www.hk.artsfestival.org), running through February and early March, is the main event, which every year features the best Hong Kong and Chinese artists and first-class international performers such as the Moscow Philharmonic, Youssou N'Dour, the Royal Shakespeare Company and Welsh National Opera. Performances are mainly held in City Hall, the Hong Kong Cultural Centre and the Academy for Performing Arts.

On a much smaller scale, the **Fringe Festival** is organized from the **Fringe Club** each January, with three weeks of new and alternative concerts, performances, art exhibits, street events and more at the Club and other venues around the city.

Below: Hong Kong Convention and Exhibition Centre.

73

Nightlife

Big expense accounts, a status as an international trading capital and a large expat community translate into neon-dusted nights of delight in this town of edgy excess. Hong Kong knows how to party well into the wee hours. So, whether its international DJs in a monolithic warehouse space, or sweaty moments in a postage-stamp sized back alley room, there is bound to be something to suit every taste. Just remember, the better you dress, the more you will impress. When it comes to status, the more flamboyant you are with the luxury labels, the more velvet ropes will be brushed aside.

Central and Western: Lan Kwai Fong and SoHo

The younger set mostly heads for the bars and clubs in Lan Kwai Fong and SoHo (South of Hollywood Road) above Central. The Fong used to be the only real hang-out for Westerners, until the Mid-Levels Escalator opened and breathed new life into what was essentially a quiet local residential neighbourhood. Scores of former disused shop houses, workshops and general produce stores have re-opened as restaurants, hip boutiques, cafés and bars, creating a whole new shop-

Opening hours and admission charges for nightclubs vary dramatically, and we have only listed information for clubs with a consistent policy. Weeknights are often free, while on weekend nights cover charges are the norm, and special events could make getting in pretty expensive. As far as closing times go, there is little worry in ever getting sent home before dawn.

Above: having a drink in SoHo.

ping, dining and clubbing hub. While lively Lan Kwai Fong still retains a whiff of its old hedonistic backpacker days, SoHo is slightly more chi-chi and has bags more character. It is easy enough to dip in and out of them both in one evening, however, and you should certainly try both during your visit.

Wan Chai

Forever associated with *The World of Suzie Wong* tag from the 1960s, Wan Chai has always played second fiddle

to its brassier neighbour Lan Kwai Fong. But if you are prepared to look there are some real finds here too. Most notable recently is the new nightlife hub that has mushroomed around **Star Street**, where a handful of sophisticated bars and restaurants has transformed this little-known patch of Wan Chai.

Many revellers from Lan Kwai Fong and SoHo cab it to Wan Chai around midnight to finish off the night in more spit-and-sawdust style at venues like **Joe Bananas** *(see p.76)*. While it does still have a sleazy side, the number of 'hostess bars' (many of them dressed-up brothels, catering for a predominantly business clientele) and other seedier bars in Wan Chai is dwindling. But, *caveat emptor*, and do not go without a fat wallet, even for a drink.

Kowloon

Until a few years ago nightlife in Tsim Sha Tsui was fairly restricted to a couple of bars along Knutsford Terrace, the glam and expensive Felix at The Peninsula and a slew of

Left: Lan Kwai Fong at night.

Club '97
9 Lan Kwai Fong, Central; tel: 2810 9333; MTR: Central; map p.137 C2
One of the longest-running but still one of the hippest clubs in town; Friday night is gay night, but the crowd is always pretty mixed. Above it is the similarly sleek and fashionable Post '97 bar.
SEE ALSO BARS, P.25

Devil's Advocate
48–50 Lockhart Road. Wan Chai; tel: 2865 7271; www.devils advocate.com.hk; MTR: Wan Chai; map p.138 A2
Late-night dancing, big sports screens and a 'sinfully delicious' menu set the scene at this relaxed bar and dance spot, with a slightly cheesey 'devilish' theme.

other hotel bars with their nightly in-house entertainment, usually a Filipino four-piece. Although it does not have the volume of bars that Central does, there is no need for anyone staying on Kowloon to go rushing over to Central for their nightlife fix. Today TST offers far more in the way of choice, not to mention some truly stylish bar-restaurants like **Aqua Spirit** (see p.95) – one of the places to be in Hong Kong – and an ever-wider selection along the alfresco **Knutsford**

Terrace. A good selection of bars and pubs can also be found on **Ashley Road**, or the side streets around **Carnarvon Road**. The advantage to drinking here is that you will be among locals as well as expats and tourists. New boutique hotels opening up in the area look set to raise the bar even more in TST.

Clubs

Big Apple Pub and Disco
20 Luard Road, Wan Chai; tel: 2529 3461; MTR: Wan Chai; map p.138 A3
An after-hours dance venue-cum-raunchy singles' hook-up and nightspot.

C Club
B/F, 30–32 D'Aguilar Street, Lan Kwai Fong; tel: 2526 1139; MTR: Central; map p.137 C3
European DJs are a fixture at this ever-popular establishment, where you will most certainly have to dress to impress. One of the few designer drinking spots where you do not have to pay a members' fee to get in.

Right: the city above sleeps while Lan Kwai Fong beats.

Nightclubs and bars in Hong Kong open and close faster than cheetah out for the kill. What is hot one day could be packed with tumbleweed the next. Stay in the know by checking the listings at **www.hkclubbing.com**. This valuable website posts listings, details on theme nights, reviews and even comments from local residents. Women should especially look out for postings that detail 'Ladies Nights' and other free entry and drink specials.

Above: out and about in SoHo.

Drop
Basement, On Lok Mansion, 39–43 Hollywood Road, Central; tel: 2543 8856; www.drophk.com; MTR: Central; map p.136 B6

Low tables, high ceilings, cool sounds and always a queue at the door; Drop also serves the best fresh-fruit martinis in town. A smooth cocktail bar in the early evening, ramping up to a jam-packed party venue at night. After 11pm only members are admitted, so get in early.

Dragon-i
UG/F, The Centrium, 60 Wyndham Street, Central; tel: 3110 1222; www.dragon-i.com.hk; Mon–Thur noon–2am, Fri–Sat noon–4am; free; MTR: Central; map p.137 C3

The current celebrity haunt of choice is this bar-restaurant-nightclub that has seen everyone from David Beckham to Naomi Campbell grace its hallowed halls. Very expensive, but worth it if you like to party with international jet-setters.

Home
2/F, 23 Hollywood Road, Central; tel: 2545 0023; MTR: Central; map p.136 C3

The place to go in the wee hours of the morning: keep the party going through the night by joining the throngs on the soul-fuelled dance floor, or crash out in the chill-out space, featuring massive leather beds. Open until 9am every weekend.

Joe Bananas
23 Luard Road, Wan Chai; tel: 2529 1811; www.maddogs pubs.com; Mon–Tue and Thur 11am–5am, Wed and Fri–Sat 11am–6am, Sun 3pm–5am; free; MTR: Wan Chai; map p.138 A2

Pretty much non-existent before the Handover, Hong Kong's members' club scene is burgeoning. There are now a handful of exceptional members' clubs, and not all of them are as off limits to visitors as you may think. The new M1NT club, for example, has a sister club in London, and members of London-owned Quintessentially will enjoy club privileges in Hong Kong. The trick is to butter-up your highly regarded hotel concierge. Concierges at a clutch of five-star hotels in the city have the connections – and the power – to oil the doors. This is a prime example of the way Hong Kong's village mentality really comes to the fore and you might as well work it.

The 'one and only' Joe Bananas has been around as long as most local partygoers can remember: far from sophisticated, but it sure is fun. Ladies should check out Rhythm and Booze on Wednesdays, when drinks are free from 10pm–3am.

Kee Club
6/F, 32 Wellington Street, Central; tel: 2810 9000; MTR: Central; map p.137 C3

Is that a Picasso I see on the wall before me? Why, yes it is! And that is not the only work of elite art at Hong Kong's most exclusive bar. Dancing does occur – sort of – but most patrons are too busy checking out each other's clothes, wallet and beauty (in that order), and would never risk working up a sweat. Go if you can, if only to see how the other half lives just this once.

Kiss
4/F California Tower, 30–32 D'Aguilar Street, Lan Kwai Fong; tel: 2522 6580; MTR: Central; map p.136 C3

A DJ-fuelled drinking spot in the California Tower. Nothing much to write home about, but convenient for a night of club and bar hopping in Lan Kwai Fong.

Lux

UG/F, California Tower, 30–32 D'Aguilar Street, Lan Kwai Fong; tel: 2868 9538; MTR: Central; map p.136 C3

Smart and sophisticated, with DJs nightly. A bit more of the same vibe as in the many other crammed venues along D'Aguilar Street.

M1NT

108 Hollywood Road, Central; tel: 2261 1111; www.m1nt.com. hk; MTR: Central; map p.136 B3

As well as offering its members all the trappings of a luxury lifestyle, this new venue has one of the hottest nightclubs in town. Marvel at the Swarovski crystal chandelier that dangles like a waterfall between floors, and watch Hong Kong high society doing business by the baby shark tank.

Mes Amis

83 Lockhart Road, Wan Chai; tel: 2527 6680; Sun–Thur noon–1am, Fri–Sat noon–2am; MTR: Wan Chai (exit A1, C), bus: Gloucester and Hennessy roads; map p.138 A2

More of a sports/wine bar than a nightclub, it becomes a true dance spot late in the evening after the wine has been drunk and the rugby and football matches fade from the TVs. Do not expect anything too sleek or chic.

SEE ALSO BARS, P.26–7

Mink

19 Hollywood Road, Central; tel: 3171 1989; MTR: Central; map p.136 C3

Creamy leather couches and hip resident DJs bring the elite to this hot nightspot on a nightly basis. Wednesdays are especially recommended,

Above: fancy-dress party goer.

when Obsession on Ice transforms the space into a salute to all things glamorous and glitzy, featuring a UK and US house soundscape.

The Sin Bar

G/F, Tonnochy Towers, 250–74 Jaffe Road, Wan Chai; MTR: Wan Chai; map p.139 C3

The biggest sin to occur at this club is the overplaying of Top 40 hits by the likes of Britney Spears and Canto-pop divas. Thursday to Saturday is when you can get your fix.

Tribeca

4/F, Renaissance Harbour View Hotel, Convention Plaza, 1 Harbour Road, Wan Chai; tel: 2824 0523; MTR: Wan Chai; map p.138 B3

Formerly the Club ING, this hotel-based club used to cater for visiting executives and conservative local girls looking to snag a white-collar boyfriend. After renovation, it is now on the radar of Hong Kong's picky 20-something crowd, drawn by international DJ's and hot hip-hop. On Thursdays ladies get in free.

Typhoon

37–9 Lockhart Road, Wan Chai; tel: 2527 2077; MTR: Wan Chai; map p.138 B3

Left: there is no place like Home.

Above: a narrow alleyway in Lan Kwai Fong.

More pub than club, this typical Wan Chai establishment serves up the usual shooters and happy-hour mix to a standard top dance hits soundtrack.

Volar

38 D'Aguilar Street, Lan Kwai Fong; tel: 2810 1510; Mon–Thur 6pm–2am, Fri 6pm–4am, Sat 9.30pm–4.30am; MTR: Central; map p.136 C3

When it opened in 2004, Volar made a huge impression on locals by hiring huge international DJs and spending a fortune on mood-enhancing lighting. You will need to look good to get in, as the velvet ropes are notoriously hard to get behind thanks to some of the city's most picky doormen.

Yumla

Lower Basement, Hariela House, 79 Wyndham Street, Central; tel: 2147 2382; www.yumla.com;

Mon–Thur 5pm–2am, Fri–Sat 6pm–4am; no cover charge; MTR: Central; map p.137 C3

'Yumla' means drinking in Chinese, and boy will you do a lot of it at this combo bar/club in the heart of the Central–Fong bar-hopping zone. Minuscule in size, it more than makes up for it with a powerful sound system that belts out great music spun by local DJs.

Live Music

All Night Long

9 Knutsford Terrace, Tsim Sha Tsui, Kowloon; tel: 2367 9487; MTR: Tsim Sha Tsui; map p.135 C2

Meat market or great place to just get down and boogie? You decide. The bands are mostly Filipino and vary wildly in quality, but you are always guaranteed a good time. And where else can you indulge your passion for getting down to the best of Wang Chung?

Blue Door

5/F, 37 Cochrane Street, Central; tel: 2858 6555; www.bluedoor.com.hk; Fri–Sat 10.30pm–2am; no cover charge; MTR: Central; map p.136 C3

A jazz club and bar with live music every Friday and Saturday; no cover charge.

SEE ALSO MUSIC, DANCE AND THEATRE, P.71

Karaoke is extremely popular with locals and should be tried at least once, especially if you are travelling as part of a group. Private rooms are the way to go, so book ahead and get a room together with your crooning friends.
(See also Bars, p.26.)

Right: the Fringe's rooftop terrace.

The Edge
Shop 2, G/F, The Centrium, 60 Wyndham Street, Central; tel: 2523 6690; www.clubedge. com.hk; MTR: Central; map p.136 C3

A premier live music venue (shows from 10pm) with a specially designed sound system. Regular house band, guest bands and a Latin night once a week. Closed Sundays and Mondays.

Fringe Club
2 Lower Albert Road, Central; tel: 2521 7251; www.hkfringe. com.hk; MTR: Central; map p.137 C2

More than just a live music venue, this alternative arts space also hosts live performance, art openings, music and more.

SEE ALSO MUSIC, DANCE AND THEATRE, P.71–2

Gecko
Ezra Lane, Lower Hollywood Road, Central; tel: 2537 4680; MTR: Central; map p.136 C3

Break out the expense account, because this elite and exclusive bar caters for those who appreciate the best in life, including great live Jazz, on several evenings each week. At

weekends, they tend to make way for DJs.

Music Room Live
2/F, 34–6 D'Aguilar Street, Lan Kwai Fong; tel: 2845 8477; MTR: Central; map p.136 C3

Formerly just the Jazz Club; now a venue for a whole range of international and local live acts.

Ned Kelly's Last Stand
11A Ashley Road, Tsim Sha Tsui, Kowloon; tel: 2376 0562; MTR: Tsim Sha Tsui; map p.134 B1

There is live music nightly (except Sunday) from 9.30pm at this rip-roaring, good-time Australian pub. Dixieland sounds are the speciality of this long-standing institution, with hearty,

Left: live music can be anything from rock cover bands to Cantopop.

no-frills Aussie food to go with them.

27 Restaurant and Bar
27/F, Park Lane Hotel, 310 Gloucester Road, Causeway Bay; tel: 2839 3327; MTR: Causeway Bay; map p.139 C3

Live lounge music every Tuesday to Saturday from 9.30pm. The hotel lounge atmosphere can sometimes give it a staid feel.

Dine and Dance

Red Rock
57–9 Wyndham Street, Central; tel: 2868 3884; MTR: Central; map p.136 C3

A trendy Italian restaurant and bar that combines an excellent international beer selection, enjoyable food, an outside terrace and late-night dancing to R&B and mainstream pop.

Pampering

The Chinese are firm believers in the benefits offered by traditional medicine, and both Western and Eastern health treatments abound in Hong Kong. From acupuncture and cupping, to t'ai chi and feng shui; Hong Kong has all the traditional Eastern techniques covered. Additionally the main hotels offer extensive treatments tailored to the tastes (and stresses) of Western business travellers. Whether it is a foot massage in a Chinese-style spa or a full-on splurge at one of the numerous hotel spas, you will certainly not go short of indulgent, invigorating options in this city.

Hotel Spas

Virtually all Hong Kong's bigger hotels offer some kind of relaxation and beauty facility, but those listed here are the cream of the crop, and are open to non-residents.

Chuan Spa

Level 41, Langham Hotel, 555 Shanghai Street, Mong Kok, Kowloon; tel: 3552 3510; www.chuanspa.com; daily 8am–10pm; MTR: Mong Kok; map p.132 B3

One of the most impressive and respected luxury spas in Hong Kong, the 41st-floor Chuan Spa has stunning views over Kowloon and offers every conceivable form of holistic pampering. Chuan takes the pillars of traditional Chinese medicine to its heart, and a visit here is a must if Chinese therapies are top of your list. The treatments draw on the five pillars of Chinese medicine – wood, earth, metal, fire and water – and the consultants are trained in Chinese medicine, massage and naturopathy. An opulent range of international treatments is also available.

I-Spa at the Intercontinental Hong Kong

Intercontinental Hong Kong Hotel, 18 Salisbury Road, Tsim Sha Tsui, Kowloon; tel: 2721 1211; www.hongkong-ic.intercontinental.com; daily 8am–10pm; MTR: Tsim Sha Tsui; map p.134 C1

I-Spa was Hong Kong's first feng-shui inspired spa, and the pool complex boasts a famous and much-photographed trio of infinity-edge Jacuzzi pools of different temperatures, each one 'bleeding' into the harbour. Half or full-day programmes are available, as well as a huge choice of Chinese and western treatments. The Jet Lag Relief is a speciality, and you have not lived until Henry 'Magic Toes' (or one of the other expert masseuses) has 'walked' on your back while he hangs from bars on the ceiling. There are dedicated treatments for men, and should you really want to push the boat out, try King or Queen for a Day. Nearby, the hotel also has an equally lavish fitness suite.

If you start to notice people walking around the streets of Hong Kong with huge yellow bruises up and down their arms and necks, relax: it is likely to be a result of cupping. This ancient form of therapeutic massage involves glass light-bulb-shaped jars being fixed on various points on the body. The ugly residual bruises are a result of the jars being 'pumped' to create a vacuum that is used to draw out impurities. Cupping is quite popular in Hong Kong, and is said to be particularly effective for arthritis sufferers.

OM Spa

3/F Regal Airport Hotel, 9 Cheong Tat Road, Hong Kong International Airport, Lantau; tel: 2286 6266, www.regalhotel.com; daily 8am–10pm; Airport Express from Central

Regal International has spent HK$10 million constructing the sumptuous OM Spa, the first spa to open at Hong Kong International Airport – offering the prospect of complete recuperation after a long flight. With a Thai-influenced

SEE ALSO HOTELS, P.57

Left: a quiet, Chinese retreat.

Plateau Spa

Grand Hyatt Hong Kong, 1 Harbour Road, Wan Chai; tel: 2584 7688; www.hongkong.grand. hyatt.com; daily 8am–midnight; MTR: Wan Chai; map p.138 A3

Open to day spa visitors as well as the hotel's guests, this vast 7,500 sq-m spa features 23 treatment rooms, residential Plateau guest rooms, a 50-m outdoor pool with a poolside grill, a tree-lined courtyard and a gym. It will take you an hour just to absorb the treatment menu. Five-hour relaxation, fitness, aesthetics, and culinary programmes are all included.

Day Spas

The Foot and Hand Cave

LG/F, 11 Lyndhurst Terrace, Central; tel: 2815 1666; daily 8am–10pm; MTR: Central, then Mid-Levels Escalator; map p.136 C3

This shop is conveniently located between SoHo and Lan Kwai Fong, and so is perfectly placed for an afternoon of lunching, boutique shopping and pampering. There is an extensive menu of reasonably-priced hand and foot treatments and nail

design, it features one of the city's most extensive massage treatment menus, with more than 30 different options. The spa also contains two Spa Suites, five cabana-style treatment rooms, 11 superior treatment rooms and a foot-massage salon. In the Karma residential suite, right beside the main spa, guests can enjoy alfresco massages and use the outdoor whirlpool bath.

Peninsula Spa by ESPA

Peninsula Hotel, Salisbury Road, Tsim Sha Tsui, Kowloon; tel: 2315 3322; http://hongkong. peninsula.com; daily 8am–11pm; MTR: Tsim Sha Tsui; map p.134 C1

The product of collaboration between the august Peninsula Hotel and the worldwide ESPA spa group, this lavish facility opened in 2006. Located on the 7th and 9th floors of the hotel, it has its aesthetic roots in classical Chinese design. Heritage aside, everything else about the spa is as cutting edge as is possible. The single and double treatment suites all

have en suite showers and other facilities, as well as ESPA's customised foot-ritual seating.

Treatments are a combination of East and West: there is also an Asian Tea Lounge surrounded by a crystal water wall, men's and women's relaxation lounges and male and female thermal suites, each featuring a sauna with hypnotic harbour views. The Roman-style pool is pretty spectacular, and it too offers views across the harbour.

Below: Yue spa.

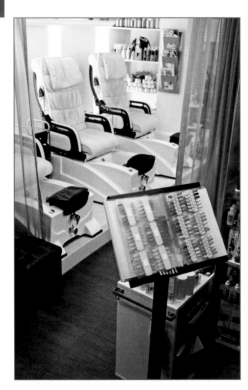

Left: the Foot and Hand Cave.

massages incorporating flower and plant extracts certainly will. Definitely one for the girls, though there are men's treatments too.

Spa MTM
Shop A, G/F, 3 Yun Ping Road, Causeway Bay; tel: 2923 7888; www.mtmskincare.com; Mon–Fri 10.30am–10pm, Sat–Sun 10.30am–8pm; MTR: Causeway Bay; map p.139 D3

MTM is an oasis of calm in the middle of one of Hong Kong's busiest shopping districts. While undergoing a 'skin assessment' and courtesy foot bath you will be asked to select a treatment; try the divine Sakura Revival Therapy. Perfect for wilting shopaholics, the experience begins with a full body mask and a thermal blanket 'wrap' that lets you sweat out your toxins. After cooling down with a cold towel the wrap is washed off in the bath, in preparation for your 90-minute massage. Each treatment ends with tea and a small dessert.

Sampar Beauty Pod
Lane Crawford, Pacific Place, Central; tel: 2526 2963; www.lanecrawford.com; daily 10am–9pm; MTR: Admiralty; map p.137 D2

Trust the swanky department store Lane Crawford to up the pampering stakes with its über-slick in-store 'beauty pod'. The Sampar is tucked behind the cosmetics counters at Lane Crawford's Pacific Place store, and is yet another convenient pit stop for weary shoppers. A selection of tailor-made pampering beauty rituals is available. There is also a

care services, and the more traditional Chinese treatments include ear candling (not as uncomfortable as it sounds) and reflexology.

Frederique Spa
4/F Wilson House, 19–27 Wyndham Street, Central; tel: 2522 3054; www.paua.com.hk; daily 8am–10pm; MTR: Central; map p.137 C3

With three decades of pampering Hong Kong under its belt, Frederique must be doing something right. The European-style salon offers everything from tooth whitening and 'Time for Men' to 'Pregnancy Beautiful' packages and eye therapies. Prices match the opulent facilities. The Paua group also has five other spas around Hong Kong, including

the recently-opened and very luxurious **Paua Spa at Centre Stage**, 108 Hollywood Road, Central, tel: 2522 3054. Check the website for a list of locations and current promotions.

ManiPedi
9/F Soho Square, 21 Lyndhurst Terrace, Central; tel: 2815 3319; www.manipedi.com.hk; daily 8am–10pm; MTR: Central, then Mid-Levels Escalator; map p.136 C3

Perfect for *Sex and the City* types, ManiPedi does what it says – nails, hands and feet – in a contemporary, minimalist white space in trendy SoHo. Oh, and did we mention the 9th-floor views of Central? If the dreamy oversized leather armchairs do not have you swooning, the vast choice of nail polishes and leg-reviving

Opposite: varnish for colourful fingers and toes.

Pod in the IFC Mall branch, tel: 2118 3388.

SEE ALSO SHOPPING, P.101

Sunny Paradise Sauna
341 Lockhart Road, Wan Chai; tel: 2831 0123; daily noon–7pm; MTR: Wan Chai; map p.138 B3

Ask any expat-about-town where he or she goes for their sauna, facials or massage and a good number will say Sunny's. This cheap and cheerful option offers no-frills but perfectly good massage services in the heart of Wan Chai: the most popular is the Chinese body massage. The price includes towels, tea and fruit. Separate floors for men and woman make this a great budget option for groups of guys or girls who just want to hang out.

Tai Pan Reflexology, Beauty and Foot Spa
G/F and Basement, 83 Nathan Road, Tsim Sha Tsui, Kowloon; tel: 2301 1990; daily 8am–1am; MTR: Tsim Sha Tsui; map p.134 C2

After walking down the stairs and across a glass-covered fish pond, you will find a surprisingly large space here, peppered with screens, lanterns and Buddhist paintings, yet somehow the traditional decor is charming and intimate. Ambience aside, the Tai Pan is also reasonably priced: a one-hour session in the massage chair enjoying a foot jet bath followed by reflexology costs around HK$200; a combination head-and-neck massage followed by one-hour foot reflexology is HK$259. Last appointments are around midnight. There is also a branch in Wan Chai, at 441 Lockhart Road.

Yue Spa
3/F Pearl City Plaza, 22–36 Paterson Street, Causeway Bay; tel: 2688 0919; daily 8am–10pm; MTR: Causeway Bay; map p.139 D3

The ambiance at Yue is relaxingly Oriental, with plenty of dark wood, water and Chinese decoration. Organic tea served on arrival, soft music, the calming waft of essential oils and the friendly staff all help set the tone, too. The hefty treatment menu is photo-album thick, and draws on the elements of Destiny (nourishment), Soil (wraps), Metal (circulation), Wood (body balance), Water (removal of toxins), Fire (soothing) and Earth. It can be tricky to find, so ask your concierge to write down the full address in Chinese.

Western health treatments abound in Hong Kong, but while here, it is worth trying things the Chinese way.
Chinese medicine dates back almost 5,000 years; traditionally, it sees the body as a delicate balance of two opposing forces: *yin* and *yang*. When the balance is upset, it leads to a blockage in the flow of Qi (pronounced chi) or vital energy. Take baby steps and start with a relaxing toe rub: a reflexologist will massage your feet to boost circulation and free the flow of *qi*, and can also provide an all-over diagnosis of your body health. If you enjoy this, another must is an acupuncture session.
Acupuncture originated in China almost 2,000 years ago. It works on the principle that there are primary and secondary meridians running through the body, connected by thousands of acupressure points, which can be stimulated by the insertion of fine needles. Acupuncture is one of the most widely-used medical procedures in the world, and increasingly accepted in the West, but you will be hard pushed to find such a wide variety of expert acupuncturists as there is in Hong Kong.

Parks and Gardens

A lthough you will not find parks here on the scale of London's green swathes, or akin to New York's Central Park, Hong Kong has a handful of good, much-appreciated urban parks that are well stocked with facilities including swimming pools and tennis courts. Outside the city there are even more places to spend time with nature, where you can take five, pause from sightseeing, join the locals in a t'ai chi session or even indulge in a bit of bird-watching. For more on the outdoors, *see* Walks and Views, p.128.

Hong Kong Park

19 Cotton Tree Drive, Central; daily 6am–11pm; free; MTR: Central, bus, tram: Queensway and Hennessy Road; map p.137 D2

Hong Kong Park is an oasis of green amid the surrounding urban landscape. Occupying most of the one-time British army garrison area known as Victoria Barracks, the park encompasses the **Edward Youde Aviary**, greenhouses, the **Flagstaff House Museum**, the **Hong Kong Visual Arts**

If you have ever fancied your hand (and feet) at kung fu, head to Kowloon Park on a Sunday afternoon (Sculpture Walk; 2.30–4.30pm) where you will find a variety of traditional kung fu demonstrations taking place, along with performances including ceremonial drumming and lion dances. Onlookers are invited to have a bash, and instructors are happy to guide visitors through the typical movements. It is a great introduction to Chinese Martial Arts.

Centre, playgrounds, a restaurant and a marriage registry, plus water features that include fountains and lily ponds. Amid the vegetation are fine specimens of large trees, which were originally planted by the military. The aviary allows you to walk through a spectacular mix of habitats, with over 150 bird species in a convincing tropical 'rainforest' environment. Twitchers should head to the

Left: morning exercises at Victoria Park.

Above: Hong Kong Park.

Conservatory on Wednesdays at 8am for a free two-hour morning bird watch.
SEE ALSO MUSEUMS AND GALLERIES, P.62, 66

Hong Kong Zoological and Botanical Gardens

Albany Road, Central; tel: 2530 0154, www.lcsd.gov.hk; daily 6am–10pm; free; MTR: Central, bus: 3B, 12, 23, 40; map p.137 C2

Located near the former British governors' residence, these gardens were laid out in 1864 on the northern slope of Victoria Peak to the design of a nature-loving governor. This is a popular spot for morning t'ai chi exercises. The zoo collection occupies a large part of

Left: Hong Kong Park.

Victoria Park

Between Victoria Park Road and Causeway Road, Causeway Bay; daily 24hrs; free; MTR: Causeway Bay, Tin Hau; map p.139 D/E 3/4

Opened in 1957, Hong Kong's largest park boasts a raft of facilities, including swimming pools, jogging tracks and tennis courts. You can even massage your feet on a special pebble path, and it is naturally another popular early-morning t'ai chi venue. Thousands gather here at festival-times, and at weekends the park is full of people exercising, relaxing and simply enjoying the sunshine. Victoria Park also offers the shade of over 5,500 trees.

the gardens – particularly on the western side – with about 500 birds, 70 mammals, notably apes, monkeys and lemurs, and 70 reptiles. Many of them are from endangered species, which are being bred successfully in the park.

Kowloon Park

Kowloon Park Drive, Tsim Sha Tsui, Kowloon; daily 5am–midnight; free; MTR: Tsim Sha Tsui, Jordan; map p.134 B2–3

With a sports complex offering Olympic-sized indoor and outdoor swimming pools and an open-air Sculpture Walk (2.30–4.30pm), Kowloon Park is a tranquil oasis at the heart of Tsim Sha Tsui that is especially popular with locals. Others among its many attractions include an aviary and bird lake, where birds range from local sparrows to exotic imported flamingos, wading in landscaped pools, a maze garden, banyan court, and a Chinese garden. The park was opened in 1970 by the then Governor Sir David Trench, and was redeveloped at a cost of HK$300 million in 1989 by the Hong Kong Jockey Club.

Kadoorie Park and Botanic Garden

If you are interested in Hong Kong's take on conservation, head up to the Kadoorie Park and Botanic Garden, to the west of Tai Po in the New Territories. Set up in 1951 by the Jewish Kadoorie brothers, with the twin aims of assisting conservation and local village agriculture, the park concentrates on protecting native orchids and birds of prey, and showcases Hong Kong's wealth of natural flora and fauna in a wild park and lovely gardens. The orchards and vegetable fields here are almost fully organic. Local farmers receive training in crop and livestock management, and the park has helped thousands of farmers to become self-sufficient. Lam Kam Road, Tai Po; tel: 2488 1317; www.kfbg.org.hk; daily 9.30am–5pm; entrance charge; train: KCR East line to Tai Po Market or Tai Wo, then bus 64K towards Yuen Long (west).

Below: some use the parks for jogging, others are more sensible.

Restaurants

It has been said that when the Chinese are confronted with something they have never seen before or do not understand, their first impulse is to try eating it. This folk philosophy has helped inspire one of the greatest cuisines the world has known, as well as some of the most bizarre dishes Western visitors have ever seen: from chicken feet to fish eyes, everything is available if you know where to look. It would be a shame not to indulge in the indigenous food on offer, but there are endless restaurants catering for the city's business tourists, putting world cuisine from Thai curries to American burgers on your doorstep.

Central and the Peak

CHINESE
Luk Yu Tea House
24–6 Stanley Street; tel: 2523 1970; daily 7am–10pm; $–$$; MTR: Central; map p.136 C3
This famous and popular tea house opened in the early 1930s, and is a living piece of colonial history. With its carved wood panelling and doors, ceiling fans, spittoons, marble tabletops, couples booths and stained-glass windows it is also fabulously atmospheric. This is a great place to try the full range of Chinese teas, and is famed for its excellent *dim sum* (served until 5.30pm). But ask for the English menu, as dealing with the staff can be daunting for non-locals.

Lumière/Cuisine Cuisine
3101–07, Level 3, IFC Mall, Finance Street; tel: 2393 3933; www.lumiere.hk; Lumière daily noon–2.30pm, 7–11pm, Cuisine Cuisine Mon–Fri noon–2.30pm, 6–10.30pm, Sat–Sun 11am–3pm, 6–10.30pm; both $$$; MTR: Central; map p.137 D4
Huge, high-ceilinged and highly designed space with indoor and outdoor dining –

Above: *dim sum* made to order.

each restaurant has magnificent views – this two-sided restaurant showcases two classic Chinese cuisines, each with refined modern touches: spicy Sichuan in Lumière, and Cantonese in Cuisine Cuisine.

Ning Po Residents Association
4/F Yip Fung Building, 10 D'Aguilar Street, Lan Kwai Fong; tel: 2523 0648; daily noon–2.45pm, 6–10.45pm; $$; MTR: Central; map p.136 C3
A typical, clattering canteen-style local restaurant hidden inside a commercial building. It is a Hong Kong institution, and the enormous range of dishes from Shanghai and Ningpo in northeast China come well recommended. Suck it and see: it will be atmospheric, if nothing else.

Peking Garden
Shop 003, Pacific Place, 88 Queensway; tel: 2845 8452; Mon–Sat 11.30am–3pm, 5.30–11pm, Sun 11am–3pm, 5.30–11pm; $$; MTR: Admiralty; map p.137 E2
This lively restaurant specialises in northern Chinese dishes. Watch fresh noodles being made each evening, and enjoy the Peking Duck-carving exhibitions and Beggar's Chicken clay-breaking ceremonies. There are several other branches, among them those at the **Empire Centre**, 68 Mody Road, Tsim Sha Tsui East, tel: 2721

Prices are for an average three-course meal, with one beer or glass of wine:

$	under HK$150
$$	HK$150–300
$$$	HK$300–500
$$$$	over $500

Left: Chinese restaurant, Central.

and, unusually for the Chinese palate, cured hams and dairy products.

EUROPEAN
Finds
2/F Lan Kwai Fong Tower, 33 Wyndham Street; tel: 2522 9318; www.finds.com.hk; Mon–Fri noon–midnight, Sat 7pm–3am, Sun 10.30am–5.30pm; $$$; MTR: Central, then Mid-Levels Escalator; map p.136 C2

An acronym of Finland, Iceland, Norway, Denmark and Sweden, Finds has a menu that offers a melange of specialities from the Nordic region. It is also a very cool place to dine, with a fabulous wooden deck for pre-dinner cocktails and a great location at the heart of vibrant Lan Kwai Fong. Service is attentive, and the quality .

M at the Fringe
2 Lower Albert Road, Central; tel: 2877 4000; www.m-restaurants.com; Mon–Fri noon–2.30pm, 7–10.30pm, Sat–Sun 7–10.30pm; $$$$; MTR: Central; map p.137 C2

If you are travelling alone or just fancy a quick box-style lunch, try the Central offshoot of Lamma Island's popular Deli Lamma restaurant. **Deli Lamma Lan Kwai Fong** has a choice of set lunches for a flat HK$70, and five options for main courses. Dishes are internationally inspired, and the menus change daily. A better-value lunch in Hong Kong will be hard to find. 1/F unit F, Winner Building, 37 D'Aguilar Street, Lan Kwai Fong; tel: 2522 1292; MTR: Central; map p.137 C3.

8868, and at 500 Hennessy Road, Causeway Bay, tel: 2577 7231.
Shui Hu Ju
G/F 68 Peel Street; tel: 2869 6927; www.aqua.com.hk; daily 6pm–midnight; $$$$; MTR: Central; map p.136 B3

Another of the Aqua group's elegant restaurants around Hong Kong, this has a traditional, wood-embellished exterior and heavy antique door that gives way to a delightful, atmospheric and intimate setting conjuring up images of old China, smack

in the heart of hip SoHo. Named after a mystical mountain in an old Chinese fable, Shui Hu Ju's menu encompasses rustic recipes from around Northern China, including deep fried lamb shank, deep fried chicken with Szechuan chilli, and dried beancurd paper roll.
Yun Fu
Basement, 43–55 Wyndham Street; tel: 2116 8855, www.aqua.com.hk; Mon–Fri noon–3pm, 6–11.30pm, Sat–Sun 6–11.30pm; $$$; MTR: Central, then Mid-Levels Escalator; map p.136 C3

Tucked away on Wyndham Street, Yun Fu offers cutting-edge Cantonese and other South Chinese cuisines. As in all the Aqua group's restaurants, the design plays cleverly and very elegantly with traditional Chinese motifs, with minimalist decor that is remarkable in its simplicity. The food draws many influences from Yunnan province, offering the rare flavours of local mushrooms, flowers

Right: small local restaurants offer a unique experience.

Vegetarian Options

In Hong Kong you will find restaurants offering cuisines from all over Asia, and the gamut of Western cuisines, not just French or Italian but also Scandinavian, Dutch and Mexican, as well as steakhouses, pizza parlours and kosher food. Vegetarians do not have an easy time here, though. Things are improving, but compared with other Asian countries, such as Thailand and India, there is a noticeable lack of vegetarian choices, and Chinese chefs routinely add chicken or other meat stocks to otherwise 'vegetarian' dishes, to add flavour, so even these may not be what you are looking for. However, there is a handful of restaurants devoted to purely vegetarian cooking.

The majority are, naturally, Chinese in their cooking style, often with Buddhist connections, and are thus also frequented by monks. Most of their food should be vegan, and dishes containing eggs are usually labelled on the menu. Indian restaurants are also a good bet, and some hotels also cater for vegetarians, if notified in advance (**Avenue**, at the Kowloon Holiday Inn, has a good vegetarian range at all times, *see p.94–5*). There are few four-star-and-above chefs in Hong Kong who will not rise to the veggie challenge. For more vegetarian possibilities, in addition to those listed in this chapter, try MSG-free **Kung Tak Lam** in Causeway Bay, 31 Yee Wo Street; tel: 2890 3127 or **Veggie XP**, 140 Wan Chai Road, tel: 2115 8880 in Wan Chai. Finally, do not forget the **Po Lin Monastery** on Lantau (*see Temples and Monasteries, p.119*). The **Hong Kong Vegan Society** has a list of vegan-related shops and restaurants at: www.ivu.org/hkvegan.

Extravagant prices for wonderfully elaborate pan-European cuisine (and decor) that some insist is the best in town. M, curiously, occupies a charming space on an upper floor of the same former dairy farm that is home to the **Fringe Club** alternative arts centre. The intricate menu changes every three months.

SEE ALSO MUSEUMS AND GALLERIES, P.66; MUSIC, DANCE AND THEATRE, P.71–2; NIGHTLIFE, P.78

FRENCH
Le Tire Bouchon
Basement, 45 Graham Street; tel: 2523 5459; www.hkdining. com/ltb; Mon–Sat noon– 2.30pm, 7–10.30pm; $$$; MTR: Central, then Mid-Levels Escalator; map p.136 C3
After two decades in the city, this intimate French favourite is still going strong. The traditional daily menu includes classics such as garlic snails (in the shell) and French onion soup. As one would expect in an old favourite like this, service is impeccable.

FUSION
Mandarin Grill
Mandarin Oriental Hotel, 5 Connaught Road, Central; tel: 2825 4004, www.mandarin oriental.com; $$$$;

MTR: Central; map p.137 D3
One of Hong Kong's best-loved grills, the Mandarin has recently benefited from a Terence Conran makeover. Although the menu is pricey, the Grill experience is sublime and worth every penny. You might never taste steak this good (fish, pasta and sushi are also on the menu) or be treated to such finely tuned service anywhere in the world. Book, book, book.
The Peak Lookout
121 Peak Road, The Peak; tel: 2849 1000; www.peaklookout. com.hk; Mon–Thur 10.30am– 11.30pm, Fri 10.30am–1am, Sat–Sun 8.30am–1am; $$; MTR: Central, then Peak Tram
Formerly the famous Peak Café, the Lookout serves sumptuous food on a delightful terrace on one of the highest points of the city, alongside the Peak Tower, with, of course, a fabulous view. The menu pleases every imaginable taste with a mix of Chinese, Indian, European and more, and it is a good, lower-cost alternative to the restaurants in the Peak Tower. It is also great for afternoon tea, or even for a breakfast treat at weekends, after you have worked up an appetite with a Peak stroll.

Below: Le Tire Bouchon.

Above: Jashan.

Pearl on the Peak

L1, The Peak Tower, 128 Peak Road; tel: 2849 5123; www.the peak.com.hk; Mon–Fri noon–2.30pm, 6–10.30pm, Sat–Sun noon–2.30pm, 6–11.30pm; $$$; MTR: Central, then Peak Tram

More than 10 new food outlets have opened at the refurbished Peak Tower, but Pearl on the Peak is one of the most spectacular. It is the Hong Kong sibling of chef Geoff Lindsay's Pearl Restaurant in Melbourne, and offers refined Pacific Rim cooking along with sweeping city views through floor-to-ceiling windows. The same 270-degree views can also be enjoyed from a lovely terrace.

INDIAN
Jashan

1/F Amber Lodge, 23 Hollywood Road; tel: 3105 5300, www. jashan.com.hk; Mon–Sat noon–3pm, 6–11pm; $–$$; MTR: Central, then Mid-Levels Escalator; map p.136 C3

Richly decorated, Jashan offers an extensive menu of Indian cuisine, with dishes from both north and south. A speciality is the exceptional-value lunchtime buffet, but it also offers fine dining in the evening.

Veda

8 Arbuthnot Road; tel: 2868 5885; www.veda.com.hk; daily noon–2.30pm, 6–11.30pm; $$–$$$; MTR: Central, then Mid-Levels Escalator; map p.136 C3

One of a new breed of Indian restaurants in Hong Kong, Veda has a spacious and restrained interior, and a menu highlighting lesser-known dishes from all over India. This makes for a dining experience that bucks the norm if you can bear to prize yourself away from the old

favourites. Starters include quail samosa; mains include tandoori Tasmanian salmon, and there is an intriguing Sunday brunch. Set-price buffets make it much cheaper at midday than in the evenings.

ITALIAN
Goccia Restaurant and Champagne Bar

G/F, 73 Wyndham Street; tel: 2167 8181; Mon–Fri noon–2.30pm, 6–11pm, Sat 6–11.30pm; $$$; MTR: Central, then Mid-Levels Escalator; map p.136 C3

Not only has Goccia made lunch in Central fast and healthy, but it also has a Michelin-starred chef. A lunch salad bar with over 15 selections of greens and toppings allows for as many different flavour combinations as you can put together, and a selection of side orders such as seared tuna gives you the option of a well-balanced meal that can still be enjoyed in 30 min.

Isola Bar and Grill

Levels 3–4, IFC Mall, Finance Street; tel: 2383 8765, www. isolabarandgrill.com; Sun–Thur noon–2.30pm, 6.30–11pm, Fri–Sat noon–2.30pm, 6.30–11.30pm; $$$$; MTR: Central; map p.137 D4

It is a tough choice: outside on the stunning terrace, or inside in the two-storey, all-white interior. The whiter-than-white and 'understated glam' decor befits the modern Italian menu, all of which is served up accompanied by a

89

R

Classified is something of a departure for Hong Kong, and is the city's hottest current grazing spot. Charcuterie, cheeses, wines, fine teas, coffees and preserves fill the shelves of this very European-style deli-café, and there are wooden tables surrounded by chalkboards that engender a try-before-you-buy philosophy. Grab a seat, order a cheese platter and pair it with one of a vast selection of quality wines and champagnes.
The airy **Press Room** *(right)* next door (part of the same stable) is a relaxed French brasserie-style restaurant in the one-time print shop of the *South China Morning Post*. Weekend brunch is naturally a strong point. Both are at 108 Hollywood Road, Central; tel: 2525 3444/3454; www.thepressroom.com.hk.

unique harbour view. The outdoor terrace is one of the best in town, which may mean you have to come here more than once...

Pasta e Pizza
B/F 11 Lyndhurst Terrace; tel: 2545 1675; Mon–Fri noon–3pm, 6–10.30pm, Sat noon–3pm, 6pm–late; $$; MTR: Central, then Mid-Levels Escalator; map p.136 C3
A cheerful, homely Italian restaurant complete with red-checked tablecloths. Pizzas are served straight from its stone-based oven, just the way they should be. An ample range of pastas and salads is also on offer, and there are good-value set lunches and live jazz on Saturday nights.

Va Bene
17–22 Lan Kwai Fong; tel: 2845 5577; www.vabeneristorante. com; Mon–Thur noon–2.30pm, 6.30–11.30pm, Fri noon–2.30pm, 6.30pm–midnight, Sat 6.30pm–midnight, Sun 6.30–11pm; $$$$; MTR: Central; map p.137 C2
The newly relocated, rustically upmarket Va Bene remains one of the city's most enduringly popular dining spots. It also has about the most genuinely European atmosphere of any Hong Kong restaurant.

JAPANESE
Kiku Japanese Restaurant
Basement, Gloucester Tower, The Landmark, Des Voeux Road East; tel: 2521 3344; daily 11.30am–3pm, 6–10.30pm; $$$; MTR: Central; map p.137 D2
A properly traditional, pine–panelled restaurant serving *teppanyaki* and *sushi* delicacies, *kaiseki*, or *sukiyaki* or *shabu-shabu* set meals. The à la carte menu features Kyoto-style cuisine; grilled cod and eel are especially recommended.

MIDDLE EASTERN
Beirut
27 D'Aguilar Street, Lan Kwai Fong; tel: 2804 6611; daily noon–3pm, 6pm–midnight, bar open noon–midnight; $$–$$$; MTR: Central; map p.137 C3
Subdued lighting, mosaic mirrors and Lebanese music add to the ambience at Beirut. The restaurant offers an extensive menu of Lebanese specialities, and the homemade hummus is the best in Hong Kong. A fine spot for lunch.

Habibi
G/F 112–14 Wellington Street; tel: 2544 9298; Mon–Sat 11.30am–11.30pm; $$–$$$; MTR: Central; map p.136 C3
Welcome to a Cairo-esque bazaar from the 1930s, with high ceilings, dazzling mirrors, hubble-bubble pipes and even belly dancers. Serving authentic, delicious

Opposite: the vegetarians' choice: Life Organic.

Right: the highly themed
Water Margin.

Egyptian food, Habibi does a
great value two-course set
lunch. Specialities include
mashwiaat, Egyptian mixed
grill and cold *mezze*, all
prepared by an Egyptian chef
(and all halal). Similar dishes
are available deli-style, and
for lower prices, at the same
owners' **Koshary Café**,
alongside.

SOUTHEAST ASIAN
Good Luck Thai Food
G/F 13 Wing Wah Lane; tel: 2877
2971; Mon–Sat 11am–2am;
$–$$; MTR: Central, then Mid-
Levels Escalator; map p.137 C3
Cheap and cheerful dining
the way the expats love it:
off plastic tables, and in a
smelly but very authentic
Hong Kong alleyway just off
the bar and nightlife hub of
Lan Kwai Fong. Famously
cheap, and also famous for
its *tom yam* soup.
Qing
3 Mee Lun Street; tel: 2815
6739; Mon–Sat 11.30am–
11.30pm; $$; MTR: Central, then
Mid-Levels Escalator; map
p.136 B3
Contemporary Vietnamese
tapas, in the recently-labelled
NoHo (North of Hollywood
Road) area. Qing has a com-
fortable bar and an outdoor
terrace, and good set lunch
menus for around HK$80.

VEGETARIAN
Life Organic Health Café
10 Shelley Street; tel: 2810
9777; www.lifecafe.com.hk;
Mon–Fri 8am–midnight (meals
served noon–10.30pm), Sat–
Sun 10am–midnight (meals
served 10am–10.30pm); $–$$;
MTR: Central, then Mid-Levels
Escalator; map p.136 C3
A very popular vegetarian
café and restaurant where
dreadlocked backpacking
travellers and gym-toned
executives alike munch on
freshly-made flapjacks and
alfalfa, between sips of
freshly-squeezed passion
fruit and carrot juice.

Wan Chai and Causeway Bay

CHINESE
Water Margin
Shop 1205, Food Forum, Times
Square, 1 Matheson Street,
Causeway Bay; tel: 3102 0088;
www.aqua.com.hk; daily noon–
3pm, 6–11pm; $$$$; MTR:
Causeway Bay; map p.139 C3
Festooned with handmade
Chinese lanterns that evoke
all the atmosphere of recent
Chinese movies like *Hero*,
this very smart Chinese
restaurant serves the contemporary Northern cuisine
of chef Calvin Yeung, in a
setting that is completed by
antique sofas, tables made
from Chinese paintings and
individual dining areas
partitioned by silk curtains.

FUSION
Opia
Jia Hotel, 1–5 Irving Street,
Causeway Bay; tel: 3196 9100,
www.jiahongkong.com; Mon–
Sat 7–11pm; $$$$; MTR: Causeway Bay; map p.139 D3
Young Australian chef Dane
Clouston cooks up a storm
of contemporary taste experiences at this trendy and
award-winning eatery
tucked inside one of Hong

Prices are for an average three-course meal, with one beer or glass of wine:	
$	under HK$150
$$	HK$150–300
$$$	HK$300–500
$$$$	over $500

91

Kong's sleekest designer hotels.

INDIAN
Viceroy
2/F Sun Hung Kai Centre, 30 Harbour Road, Wan Chai; tel: 2827 7777; www.chiram.com. hk; daily noon–3pm, 6–11pm; $$–$$$; MTR: Wan Chai; map p.138 B3

This long-standing popular Indian restaurant with panoramic harbour views also has an outdoor terrace with good views of the Wan Chai waterfront. It serves subtly flavoured tandoori, curry and vegetarian speciali-ties, and an all-you-can-eat weekday buffet feast.

JAPANESE
Kokage
9 Star Street, Wan Chai; tel: 2529 6138; Mon–Fri noon–3pm, 6pm–midnight, Sat–Sun 6pm–midnight; $$$; MTR: Wan

Chai; map p.138 A2
Its location in trendy, up-and-coming Star Street says a lot about the award-winning Kok-age, and one of the city's most popular and stylish new bars is located conveniently above the restaurant. All minimalist dark wood and candles, Kok-age offers nnovative Japanese cuisine in the Nobu style, in a very hip part of town.

Wasabisabi
Shop 130, Times Square, 1 Matheson Street, Causeway Bay; tel: 2506 0009; www.aqua. com.hk; daily noon–3pm, 6–11pm; $$$; MTR: Causeway Bay; map p.139 C3

A backlit catwalk-style colonnade splits the plush **Lipstick Lounge+Bar** from the restaurant's main dining area at this hip Japanese restaurant, part of the chic Aqua group. The menu is modern and creative, and the *sashimi* is jet-fresh from

Prices are for an average three-course meal, with one beer or glass of wine:

$	under HK$150
$$	HK$150–300
$$$	HK$300–500
$$$$	over $500

Tokyo's Tsukiji market. Swiv-elling sofas move through 360 degrees to cater for parties and so that diners can face the bar at night. Be sure to try the signature Lychee Mojito.

MIDDLE EASTERN
Zahra
409A Jaffe Road, Wan Chai; tel: 2838 4597; daily 7–11pm; $$; MTR: Wan Chai, Causeway Bay; map p.139 C3

A fabulous, tiny Lebanese restaurant with a failsafe menu, Zahara almost transports you to the Beirut of the 1950s. Favourites include Lebanese *mezze*, shrimp Phoenician, lamb and okra stew, and baked fish in tahini sauce. If in doubt, ask the friendly staff for sugges-tions. Do not miss out on the black Lebanese coffee.

SOUTHEAST ASIAN
Indonesian
Restaurant 1968
28 Leighton Road, Causeway Bay; tel: 2577 9981; daily 11.30am–11.30pm; $$; MTR: Causeway Bay; map p.139 C2

The original restaurant did open here back in 1968, hence the name. It has had a major facelift, and is now a funky joint decorated in deep reds and browns, creating a romantic ambience more effectively than many Hong Kong restaurant redesigns. The food is great here too: all the Indonesian favourites from *nasi goreng* to cuttlefish curry. A branch has recently opened in Observatory Court, in Tsim Sha Tsui, tel: 2619 1926.

Below: Indonesian Restaurant 1968.

Above: Jumbo Kingdom.

Saigon

2/F Sun Hung Kai Centre, 30 Harbour Road, Wan Chai; tel: 2598 7222; daily noon–3pm, 6–11pm; $$–$$$; MTR: Wan Chai; map p.138 B3

This restaurant captures well an air of bygone Saigon in its decor, while offering contemporary Vietnamese cuisine. The menu changes with each season, and offers daily set menus and specials and a separate vegetarian list. Must-try dishes include the seasoned fried soft–shell crab and Hanoi beef and noodle soup. There is a branch in Stanley, at 1/F, 90 Stanley Main Street, tel: 2899 0999.

Southside

CHINESE
Jumbo Kingdom

Shum Wam Pier Drive, Wong Chuk Hang, Aberdeen; tel: 2553 9111; www.jumbo.com.hk; main restaurant Mon–Sat 11am–11.30pm, 7am–11.30pm; $$–$$$; bus: 70, 98 to Aberdeen

These 30-year-old floating restaurants in the middle of Aberdeen harbour are a fun Hong Kong institution: very touristy, but the fantastic over-the-top decor is an attraction in itself. The restaurant offers free sampan rides to the two boats from the Aberdeen quayside, and once on board the food is seafood and other Cantonese favourites: signature dishes include Flamed Drunken Shrimp and shark's fin soup with lobster and cognac. The Kingdom has recently been expensively refurbished, and now also has the more international **Top Deck** space to give it more chic–appeal *(see above)*.

EUROPEAN
Verandah

109 Repulse Bay Road, Repulse Bay; tel: 2292 2822; www.the repulsebay.com; Tue–Sat noon–11pm, Sun 11am–11pm; $$$; bus: Repulse Bay from Central bus station

With its whirring ceiling fans, metres of wood and rarified atmosphere, this is an atmospheric survivor from the colonial era, with a stunning sea view. It is also one of Hong Kong's best and most popular weekend brunch venues, although lunch, afternoon tea and dinner are just as enjoyable. It makes a good stop off en route to Stanley, but book as far ahead as possible for weekends.

FUSION
Top Deck

Shum Wam Pier Drive, Wong Chuk Hang, Aberdeen; tel: 2552 3331; www.cafedecogroup.com; Tue–Thur 6–11.30pm, Fri 6pm–1am, Sat 11.30am–1am, Sun 9am–11.30pm; $$–$$$; bus: 70, 98 to Aberdeen

Top Deck bills itself as Hong Kong's first 'lifestyle' restaurant, and seeks to be the hipper, younger alternative to the boisterous **Jumbo Kingdom** on the lower decks *(see left)*. A bar and lounge is housed under a dramatic three-storey Chinese pagoda roof, and this opens onto the main dining area, and a broad outdoor sun deck. Soak up the southside views and atmosphere while relaxing in a couch or deck

93

You are spoilt for choice when it comes to dining with a view in Hong Kong. On the south side of Hong Kong Island, try the **Verandah** at Repulse Bay *(see p.93)* for a spectacular harbour view, or the eateries along Stanley Main Street. Alternatively, take a ferry to Lamma or Cheung Chau for their harbourside seafood restaurants.

On clear nights, the **Peak Lookout** *(see p.88)* and other restaurants on Victoria Peak offer breathtaking views. **Felix** at the Peninsula *(see opposite)* and **Aqua** at One Peking Road *(see opposite)* are the big hitters in Kowloon. Book in advance.

chair. The menu is an eclectic Chinese, European and pan-Asian mix: Sunday brunch is a speciality, and comes with unlimited bubbles for adults.

Kowloon

AMERICAN

Ruth's Chris Steakhouse
Empire Centre, 68 Mody Road, Tsim Sha Tsui East; tel: 2366 6000; www.ruthschris.com; daily noon–3pm, 6.30–11pm; $$$; MTR: Tsim Sha Tsui, bus: Salisbury Road; map p.135 D2
If you are a carnivore craving a juicy steak this American chain, serving cuts of fillet, strip, rib-eye, porterhouse and T-bone, should hit the spot. Other mains include tuna, chicken, lamb chops, and lobster, and salads and sandwiches are also available. Another branch is in the Lippo Centre, 89 Queensway, Central, tel: 2522 9090.

CHINESE

Hutong
28/F, One Peking, 1 Peking Road, Tsim Sha Tsui; tel: 3428 8342; www.aqua.com.hk; daily noon–3pm, 6pm–midnight; $$$$; MTR: Tsim Sha Tsui;

map p.134 B1
One floor down from the same owners' sleekly international **Aqua** *(see opposite)*, Hutong is just as exquisitely designed, but this time reminiscent of an ancient family courtyard in one of Beijing's fast-disappearing *hutongs* (courtyard houses). The restaurant has atmosphere in spades, as well as fabulous views. The food – refined modern variations on North Chinese cuisine – is superb; dishes include crispy boned lamb ribs Hutong Style, bamboo clams steeped in Chinese rose wine and chilli *padi*, crispy soft shell crab with Szechuan red pepper and scallops with fresh pomelo.

Jade Garden
4/F Star House, 3 Salisbury Road, Tsim Sha Tsui; tel: 2730 6888; Mon–Sat 11am–5pm, 5.30pm–midnight, Sun 10am–midnight; $–$$; MTR: Tsim Sha Tsui; map p.134 B1
Jade Garden offers excellent *dim sum* till 5pm – order from the English menu, rather than deal with the trolley staff – and beautiful harbour views.

Spring Deer
42 Mody Road, Tsim Sha Tsui East; tel: 2366 4012; daily

noon–3pm, 6–11pm; $$; MTR: Tsim Sha Tsui, bus: Salisbury Road; map p.135 C2
There is nothing fancy about Spring Deer, but this Beijing-style restaurant is a local institution for Peking Duck and other northern specialities, and a favourite among in-the-know Westerners and visitors as well as locals. It is handily located too, around the corner from Nathan Road. Book ahead because it is always packed.

EUROPEAN

Avenue
Holiday Inn Golden Mile, 50 Nathan Road, Tsim Sha Tsui; tel: 2315 1118; www.goldenmile.com; Mon–Sat noon–2.30pm, 6–10.30pm, Sun 11.30am–2.30pm; $$$$; MTR: Tsim Sha Tsui; map p.134 C1
Glass-curtain windows looking over the Golden Mile

Prices are for an average three-course meal, with one beer or glass of wine:

$	under HK$150
$$	HK$150–300
$$$	HK$300–500
$$$$	over $500

Left: the view from Peak-top restaurants.

Felix
28/F, Peninsula Hotel, Salisbury Road, Tsim Sha Tsui; tel: 2315 3188, http://hongkong.peninsula. com; restaurant daily 6–11pm, bar 6pm–2am; $$$$; MTR: Tsim Sha Tsui; map p.134 C1
This restaurant-cocktail bar is not to be missed: the marvellous view and the striking Philippe Starck design are as memorable as the delectable Pacific Rim fusion cuisine. Visit for a cocktail at the bar if nothing else, but dress up.

MOS Burger
Shop 1, L4A Langham Place, 8 Argyle Street, Mong Kok; tel: 3514 4301; daily noon–midnight; $, MTR: Mong Kok; map p.132 B3
The second Hong Kong branch of trendy Japanese rice-burger chain MOS (sticky organic rice replaces the bread bun). It is a handy place to know if you are exploring Mong Kok and do not fancy Chinese, but expect to wait up to 30 min for your burger at lunch times. It is worth waiting for a healthy seafood rice burger 'cake' of scallops, veg and prawns. The plain old beef version is also available.

shopping hub and a modern European menu make this hotel restaurant a popular Kowloon dining spot. The menu is particularly generous in vegetarian dishes.

Jimmy's Kitchen
1/F Kowloon Centre, 29 Ashley Road, Tsim Sha Tsui; tel: 2376 0327; www.jimmys.com; daily 11.30am–3pm, 6–11.30pm; $$; MTR: Tsim Sha Tsui; map p.134 B2
One of Hong Kong's oldest restaurants, open since the 1930s, wood-panelled Jimmy's specialises in British and European food, but also has curries and a variety of other Asian dishes. There is also a Jimmy's in the South China Building, 1–3 Wyndham Street in Central, tel: 2526 5293.

FRENCH
SPOON by Alain Ducasse
Intercontinental Hong Kong, 18 Salisbury Road, Tsim Sha Tsui; tel: 2313 2323; www.hongkong-ic.intercontinental.com; Mon–Sat 6pm–midnight, Sun noon–2.30, 6pm–midnight; $$$$; MTR: Tsim Sha Tsui; map p.134 C1
Floor-to-ceiling windows

and spectacular views are the icing on multi-Michelin-starred Ducasse's cake in this, his first Asian venture. A ceiling installation of hand-blown Venetian glass spoons barely detracts from the pick-n-mix menu, based on the idea that diners can combine different culinary traditions and flavours: perfect for those who like to graze.

FUSION
Aqua
29–30/F, One Peking, 1 Peking Road, Tsim Sha Tsui; tel: 3427 2288; www.aqua.com.hk; Mon–Sat noon–3pm, 6–11pm, Sun noon–4pm, 6–11pm, bar Thur–Sun 5pm–1 or 2am; $$$$; MTR: Tsim Sha Tsui; map p.134 B1
A jaw-dropping must-see, Aqua is, quite simply, where Hong Kong is at. It is made up of **Aqua Roma** (Italian) and **Aqua Tokyo** (Japanese) on the 29th floor and the mezzanine **Aqua Spirit** bar on the 30th, accessed by a sultry mirrored catwalk; whichever you come for, Aqua is all about high chic, glamorous decor and staggering views through double-story windows.

The first humanoid waiters in the world are now taking orders at the **Robot Kitchen** in the Park Central mall in Tseung Kwan O, on the easternmost side of Kowloon. Our futuristic friends greet customers and take orders, and their bright flashing lights are a big hit with children. A dancing robot also performs daily to diners enjoying the selection of pizzas, pasta, steak and other Western favourites.

95

With both the Chinese and their British colonizers batty about tea, it is hardly surprising that afternoon tea is a much-loved tradition shared by locals, expats and tourists alike. When in Hong Kong, you should experience High Tea at least once in your stay. Popular hotel venues include the **Peninsula**, **Mandarin Oriental**, **Intercontinental** and **Grand Hyatt**. Be sure to push the boat out, since you will only be saving a small amount to downgrade, and some things really are worth doing properly. Britannia may no longer rule the roost, but you could be forgiven for thinking otherwise when you step into the venerable Peninsula hotel *(see p.58)*. The classical grandeur of the lobby and the string quartet set the scene, while the generously-laden cake stand and coffees and loose-leaf teas, served in bone china crockery, put many of Britain's own set afternoon teas to shame. You will also pay about half the price London's top hotels charge for the privilege. Afternoon tea at 'The Pen' is an Asian institution, and well worth crossing the harbour for (served daily, 2–7pm).

INDIAN
Gaylord
1/F Ashley Centre, 23–5 Ashley Road, Tsim Sha Tsui; tel: 2376 1001; www.chiram.com.hk; daily noon–2.30pm, 6.30–11pm; $$$; MTR: Tsim Sha Tsui; map p.134 B4

This Kowloon Indian has been around since 1972 and serves North and South Indian cuisine, with plenty of seafood and vegetarian dishes. The decor is bland, but live music is a nightly feature and the lunch and dinner buffet menus are good value.

New Sangeet
Shop 1–3, G/F Wah Fung Building, 17–23 Minden Avenue, Tsim Sha Tsui; 2367 5619; daily noon–3pm, 6–11pm; $$$; MTR: Tsim Sha Tsui; map p.134 C1

Sangeet means music in Hindi, and that is exactly what you will find each evening after 8pm, when a Bhangra band plays Indian classics. Indian classics also grace the menu, but the decor is modern, with moody blues and purples, couches bedecked with cushions and a certain Bollywood-glamour vibe pervading the restaurant.

ITALIAN
Fat Angelo's
Shop B, Basement, The Pinnacle, 8 Minden Avenue, Tsim Sha Tsui; tel: 2730 4788; www.fatangelos.com; daily noon–midnight; $$; MTR: Tsim Sha Tsui; map p.134 C1

A friendly, uncomplicated, very American-style Italian restaurant dishing up huge portions of pasta favourites that can feed up to eight people. Children get an activity menu, but it can also be a romantic setting, with its checked tablecloths and wine served in tumblers. There are five more branches around Hong Kong and the New Territories.

Pizzeria
2/F Kowloon Hotel, 19–21 Nathan Road, Tsim Sha Tsui; tel: 2734 3722; www.harbour-plaza.com; daily noon–3pm, 6–11pm; $$$; MTR: Tsim Sha Tsui; map p.134 C1

Located on the second floor of this Kowloon hotel, Pizzeria actually specialises in sophisticated pasta dishes more than pizza, although it is naturally on the menu. The atmosphere is relaxed, and there is a wide range of northern Italian dishes on the frequently-changing menu.

JAPANESE
Nobu
Intercontinental Hong Kong, 18 Salisbury Road, Tsim Sha Tsui; tel: 2313 2323, www.hongkong-ic.intercontinental.com; daily noon–2.30pm, 6–11pm; $$$$; MTR: Tsim Sha Tsui; map p.135 C1

Yawning views of the harbour and city skyline are on a par with the bluefin at the famed sushi-meister's first Asian venture outside Japan. The waiting list is long, but if you fail to bag a table try the small sushi bar with its nine non-bookable stools, or retreat with sake martinis to the sexy lounge bar clad in 7,700 river rocks, which shares the same vistas.

Prices are for an average three-course meal, with one beer or glass of wine:

$	under HK$150
$$	HK$150–300
$$$	HK$300–500
$$$$	over $500

SOUTHEAST ASIAN

La Cuisine de Mekong

2/F, 15 Knutsford Terrace, Tsim Sha Tsui; tel: 2316 2288; www.mhihk.com; daily 6pm–3am; $$; MTR: Tsim Sha Tsui; map p.135 C2

One of 13 varied restaurants in this Knutsford Terrace mall, offering a menu of spicy sauces, soups, grilled-meat salads, stir fries and exotic desserts that represent the cuisines of the whole Mekong region: southwest China, Burma, Laos, Cambodia, Thailand and Vietnam. Decor reflects French colonial times, and there is an outdoor 'garden' surrounded by tropical palms.

Her Thai

Shop 1, Promenade Level Tower 1, China Hong Kong City, 33 Canton Road, Tsim Sha Tsui; tel: 2735 8898; daily noon–midnight; $$; MTR: Tsim Sha Tsui; map p.134 B2

Offering reasonably priced, enjoyable Thai food, this modest restaurant also has fabulous views of the harbour, taking in the Central skyline. The interior, with its gentle lighting and red hanging lanterns, is one of Hong Kong's most romantic settings.

Spice Market

3/F Marco Polo Prince Hotel, Harbour City, 23 Canton Road, Tsim Sha Tsui; tel: 2113 6046; www.marcopolohotels.com; daily 6am–10.30pm; $$$; MTR: Tsim Sha Tsui; map p.134 B1

Do not be put off by the hotel location: this is a pleasant, relaxed restaurant presenting a wide variety of Asian foods, including Japanese, Chinese, Thai and Indian specialities, hotpots, satays and more. Buffets are the order of the day, so this is a great option if you are not sure what you feel like, want to pick and mix or if you have fussy children in tow. It is also accessible from the Gateway mall.

VEGETARIAN

Joyful Vegetarian

530 Nathan Road, Yau Ma Tei; tel: 2780 2230; daily 11am–11pm; $$; MTR: Yau Ma Tei; map p.132 B1

It is hard to find strictly vegetarian food in Hong Kong, as most chefs add at least a little meat broth to vegetable-based dishes, but this restaurant is one of a handful that specialises in truly vegetarian food. Try the delicious country-style hotpot, from the impressive variety on the menu.

Light Vegetarian Restaurant

G/F New Lucky House, 13 Jordan Road, Yau Ma Tei; tel: 2384 2833; daily 11am–11pm; $; MTR: Jordan; map p.134 C4

The menu here offers lots of dishes based on Cantonese favourites, but in vegetarian form: rice noodles, ho–fun, udon, noodles in soup, Chinese congee and imitation meat dishes. Vegetarian dim sum is available to eat in or take-away. There is a branch at North Point on Hong Kong Island (Kiu Fai Mansion, 413–21 King's Road, tel: 2561 8123), which does a great-value evening buffet from 6pm.

New Kowloon

SOUTHEAST ASIAN

Ayuthaiya

Shop G23, Festival Walk, Kowloon Tong; tel 3105 5055, www.aqua.com.hk; daily noon–3pm, afternoon tea 3–6pm, 6.30–11pm; $$; MTR, KCR: Kowloon Tong

Inspired by the new wave of Thai cafés and restaurants springing up in Bangkok, Ayuthaiya is the Aqua group's take on contemporary Thai cuisine, in an off-the-beaten-track location in a new mall in Kowloon Tong. Signature platters include baby lobster sashimi with raw garlic, green chilli and Nahm Jim, served in sharing–style portions. Long tables add to the relaxed, informal feel. Afternoon tea is a speciality. In summer, ask for a table on the non-smoking outdoor dining platform.

Below: everything you can wish for is true.

97

Shopping

Shopping in Hong Kong is a rich, varied, seven-days-a-week pursuit. Atmospheric street markets contrast with flagship designer stores, local 'lanes' and cheap-and-cheerful factory outlets selling everything from cut-price trainers to affordable chinoiserie. There are great sales with big discounts, and the summer sales are now marked by an annual 'Shopping Festival', which offers visitors fantastic deals on Hong Kong 'must-buys'. Whether it is international styles, home-grown design, Chinese antiques or high-tech electronics, there is something here to satisfy every whim.

Shopping in Hong Kong

As well as to make money, it is fair to say that Hong Kong Chinese live to shop. Their appetite for designer fashion labels, gadgets and the latest… well, anything, is pretty insatiable. There are shops just about everywhere you go in the urban centres, and more acreage of glittering multi–levelled mall than you can visit in a month. The shopping experience is not restricted to malls, however. There is a range of atmospheric markets to discover, off the beaten track 'lanes' to explore and characterful antiques shops and boutiques.

Although not quite the bargain haven it once was, Hong Kong offers much in the way of variety and keen pricing, if you know where to look. And, for local colour, Hong Kong, home to many a 'Hansom Tailor' but perhaps only one 'Always Sweetly Smell florist', reigns supreme. Where else in the world would you find grade-A shark's fin on the same street as Marks & Spencer's scones for afternoon tea?

Shopping Areas

CENTRAL AND THE PEAK

Central and the neighbouring Admiralty are known for big department stores, brand-name luxury goods, designer labels, malls (including **Pacific Place** and **IFC Mall**) and smaller but still glittering shopping centres, such as **Chater House**, **Prince's Building** and **The Galleria**.

But there is plenty in the way of character shopping here too. If you want a zip repaired, a watch battery replaced or a leather bag stitched, head for **The Lanes** (officially **Li Yuen** streets, **East** and **West**), two parallel streets between Queen's Road Central and Des Voeux Road Central that are lined with small shops selling and repairing watches, luggage, clothes and costume jewellery. And further up the steep slopes inland (easily reached via the Mid-Levels Escalator) Central is the starting point of Hong Kong's **SoHo** (South of Hollywood Road, shared with Western), currently the most chic shopping zone in town.

Left: Stanley Market antiques.

attracting local fashion designers, independent jewellers and design boutiques, particularly along **Staunton** and **Elgin** streets.

WAN CHAI AND CAUSEWAY BAY

Although not a major shopping district **Wan Chai** is gaining a name for its trendy furniture stores, and for a number of excellent rattan and Chinese furniture stores along Queen's Road East. **Spring Garden Lane Market** *(see p.103)* is a good place to shop for clothes. It also connects to the area's fascinating wet and dry markets, which offer a great insight into locals' daily shopping. At the other end of the continuum, up-and-coming **Star Street** houses lifestyle boutiques, home-ware shops, galleries, flower shops and cafés.

Causeway Bay, on the other hand, is far more hectic. Try to stand still outside **Sogo** on Hennessy Road on a Saturday afternoon and you may well be carried along by a sea of shoppers riding on a gargantuan wave of designer

Below: hand carved *chops*.

Opening Hours

Shopping hours vary, but in the main mall shopping starts at around 10am–11am and goes on to 9pm. Shops in the major shopping districts of Causeway Bay and Tsim Sha Tsui stay open later, till 9.30/10pm, and the major markets keep going until at least 10pm, often later. As a rule of thumb, shops in Central and Western open 10am–6.30pm; Causeway Bay and Wan Chai 10am–9.30pm (or later); Tsim Sha Tsui, Yau Ma Tei and Mong Kok 10am–9pm and in Tsim Sha Tsui East 10am–7.30pm. Avoid weekday lunchtimes and weekends if you do not like crowds, and do not expect Sunday to offer any respite from credit card temptation. Shopping in Hong Kong is every bit a seven-days-a-week affair.

WESTERN

The old district of **Sheung Wan**, around and south of the MTR station, is one of the most atmospheric parts of Hong Kong and still a centre of traditional Chinese street life. **Western Market** *(see*

p.103–4) is one of its most accessible hubs. Head south and west of here, across streets like **Wing Lok Street**, packed with scores of shops selling bizarre traditional medicines and unrecognisable dried seafood. You will come to **Hollywood Road** and its web of side streets stuffed with antiques, carpet and furniture shops, including **Cat Street Bazaar**, the popular name for **Upper Lascar Row**, a great spot for local ambiance with a string of shops and stalls selling antique watches, coins and stone carvings.

Man Wa Lane, east of the MTR station between Queen's Road and Des Voeux Road, is the place to find a Chinese *chop* – a traditional hand-carved personal seal, in stone or other materials – or some fine quality calligraphy brushes.

Further south and up the hillsides, the Western district is also home to **SoHo** (South of Hollywood Road, running across into Central), which has blossomed into an über-chic neighbourhood shopping bags; the 'Sogo junction' around Causeway Bay MTR station is home to some of the world's most expensive retail space. As well as Japanese department stores and glitzy multi-storey malls (**Times Square**, **Island Beverley**, **Lee Gardens**), Causeway Bay also has open-air markets selling clothes and costume jewellery, an abundance of cosmetics outlets and shops specialising in shoes, computer equipment and cutting-edge young fashion (especially **Fashion Walk** and Island Beverly malls). This really is 'shopping central' in every sense of the word.

KOWLOON

The days of Kowloon being regarded as the Island's slightly unsophisticated and downmarket sister in shopping terms are long gone. Kowloon's major shopping artery **Nathan Road**, ambitiously dubbed the **Golden Mile**, is of most appeal these days to those doing some serious electrical shopping, and not very attractive for anything else. Kowloon, though, is also home to the 500-shop **Harbour City**, Hong Kong's largest mall, and **One**

Peking Road, with its high-end fashion labels and chic restaurants. Further north in **Mong Kok**, the glass and metal **Langham Place** rises from a warren of backstreets like a vision of the future, with over 300 shops spread over 15 floors.

There are plenty of bargains to be had in the grid of side streets that fan out to the east of Nathan Road. Explore the world of washable silk along **Mody Road**, where you will find wall-to-wall inexpensive local boutiques, or head to **Granville Road** for factory outlets loaded with export overruns, plus great buys in leatherware and luggage. Kowloon is also famous for its specialist street markets, selling everything from clothes and flowers to goldfish and jade.

Malls

Hong Kong is one of the great centres of the shopping mall, with some of the largest, most all-out-dazzling retail temples on the planet. The giant mega-malls are natural attention grabbers, but hip, more individual and often quirky fashions and a less predictable experience can often be found in tiny shops in the many smaller

malls around town, beloved of trendy young locals.
Fashion Walk
Kingston and Cleveland streets, Causeway Bay; MTR: Causeway Bay; map p.139 D3
Pedestrianised streets rather than a true mall, but lined by restaurants and stylish small boutiques.
The Galleria
9 Queen's Road Central, Central; MTR: Central; map p.137 D3
Smart little mall, dwarfed by the Landmark alongside, but with branches of **Joyce Boutique**, the very trendy streetwear line i.t. and more.
Harbour City
Canton Road, Tsim Sha Tsui, Kowloon; MTR: Tsim Sha Tsui; map p.134 B2
The biggest of all Hong Kong's malls: actually five interconnecting malls, including the Ocean Centre and Ocean Terminal, with just about every brand and store represented.
IFC Mall
Harbour View Street, Central; www.ifc.com.hk; MTR: Central, Hong Kong Airport Express; map p.137 D4

Below: The Landmark.

Above: Times Square shopping mall.

The gleaming new mall at the heart of Hong Kong's showpiece IFC development has drawn towards it all the big fashion names, and a giant new Lane Crawford store.

Island Beverley
1 Great George Street, Causeway Bay; MTR: Causeway Bay; map p.139 D3
The favourite mini-mall of Hong Kong's young and hip, packed with 70 micro-outlets for local, Japanese or European fashion. Many shops only open after midday.

The Landmark
Queen's Road Central, Central; MTR: Central; map p.137 D3
Vast mall, built in the 1980s but recently opulently updated, and packed with grand luxury brand names.

Lee Gardens
Hysan Avenue, Causeway Bay; MTR: Causeway Bay; map p.139 D3
Relatively low-key mall that nevertheless hosts Chanel, Dior and other upmarket labels. The recently-opened Lee Gardens 2 has several good shops for children.

One Peking Road
21 Peking Road, Tsim Sha Tsui; MTR: Tsim Sha Tsui; map p.134 B1
The spectacular One Peking Road skyscraper, home of restaurants like **Aqua**, has a luxury fashion mall at its foot.
SEE ALSO RESTAURANTS, P.95

Pacific Place
88 Queensway, Admiralty; www.pacificplace.com.hk; MTR: Admiralty; map p.137 E2
Huge, four-level mall, with branches of many major stores.

Prince's Building
Chater Road, Central; MTR: Central; map p.137 D3
Medium-sized mall, known for top-range fashion and jewellery labels.

Times Square
Russell Street, Causeway Bay; www.timessquare.com.hk; MTR: Causeway Bay; map p.139 C2
Another blockbuster-size mall, with plenty of major fashion names, but also a big food court, electronics stores and more.

Department Stores

Western-style and Japanese department stores – often installed in the main malls – are big hitters in Hong Kong's retail game. Chic and sleek **Lane Crawford** is Hong Kong's equivalent to Bloomingdale's or Harrods, i.e. classy and expensive. It is comfortable for browsing, but you will not find much that is too different from home. The several branches of **Marks & Spencer**, too, are little pieces of Britain in the sub-tropics, with small food halls (for a fairly high price) if you are pining for familiarity.

The Japanese stores in Causeway Bay – **Seibu** and **Sogo** – have a huge following among locals and the Japanese expatriate community.

Lane Crawford
Pacific Place, 88 Queensway, Admiralty; tel: 2118 3668; www.lanecrawford.com; MTR: Admiralty; map p.137 E4
Founded in 1850, this colonial-era store has adapted very well to modern times. Other large branches are at the IFC mall, Times Square and Harbour City.

Marks & Spencer
Pacific Place, 88 Queensway, Admiralty; tel: 2921 8891; www.marksandspencer.com; MTR: Admiralty; map p.137 E4
Other M&S branches are at Central Tower, Queen's Road, Central; Times Square; and Harbour City.

Seibu
Pacific Place, 88 Queensway, Admiralty; tel: 2868 0111; MTR: Admiralty; map p.137 E4
Lavish, very stylish Japanese

101

store with fashion and other luxuries from around the world, and a food hall to match. A smaller branch is at Windsor House, Gloucester Road, Causeway Bay.

Sincere

173 Des Voeux Road Central, Sheung Wan, Western; tel: 2544 2688; www.sincere.com.hk; daily 10am–7.30pm; MTR: Sheung Wan; map p.136 C4

Long-established store with international fashion and other products and Chinese specialities, at down-to-earth prices. Also branches in Kowloon.

Sogo

555 Hennessy Road, Causeway Bay; tel: 2833 8338; www.sogo. com.hk; daily 10am–10pm; MTR: Causeway Bay; map p.139 D3

Slightly more modest Japanese store, still with huge, mostly Japanese, stocks, including superior household goods. Also at 12 Salisbury Road, Tsim Sha Tsui.

Wing On

211 Des Voeux Road Central, Sheung Wan, Western; tel: 2852 1888; www.wingonet.com; daily 10am–7.30pm; MTR: Sheung Wan; map p.136 C4

Another long-running, great-value Hong Kong store, with

> ### Shipping it Home
> Many larger stores will help with the packaging and shipment of purchases and can offer advice about insurance policies to cover fragile items. These can be bought at most of the bigger stores as a simple add-on to purchases. Many of the larger hotels can also organise a mailing service, and Hong Kong's Post Offices cater well for shoppers, with a range of on-site packaging materials available. Staff can offer advice and relevant documents for land and sea shipments. Postage rates are reasonable, and the service is very reliable.

a huge range of stock, from electronics to traditional *cheongsam* dresses. There are four more Wing On stores around Hong Kong.

Markets

Flower Market

Flower Market Road, Mong Kok, Kowloon; daily 7am–7.30pm; MTR: Prince Edward (exit B1); map p.132 B4

Exquisitely colourful, Kowloon's flower market sells everything from Dutch tulips to exotic orchids. As usual, fortune plays a part: particular blooms and plants are associated with different festivals, especially Chinese New Year.

Goldfish Market

Tung Choi Street, Mong Kok, Kowloon; daily 9am–11pm; MTR: Prince Edward (exit B1); map p.132 B4

Aquariums are popular in Hong Kong because of their perceived luck-bringing qualities, so long as they are

Opposite: flowers and fish have their own markets.

properly positioned in the home. Mong Kok's Goldfish Market stocks fish, corals, exotic amphibians and tanks.

Jade Market
Junction of Kansu and Battery streets, Yau Ma Tei, Kowloon; daily 10am–4pm; MTR: Jordan; map p.132 B1

A mecca for collectors from all over the world, Hong Kong's Jade Market is a wonderful place to spend a morning browsing and soaking up the atmosphere. According to Chinese belief, jade wards off evil spirits and protects travellers, and you will find everything from rare and valuable jade carvings to small, inexpensive trinkets. Do not invest in expensive jade, though, unless you have an expert on hand.

Ladies' Market
Tung Choi Street, Mong Kok, Kowloon; daily 12.30–10.30pm; MTR: Mong Kok (exit E2); map p.132 B3

While it sells many other things as well as those specifically for women, the Ladies' Market is especially good for bags, accessories and inexpensive women's clothing. It is more manage-able than Temple Street, so it is worth popping in here late afternoon before tackling the nearby Night Market.

Spring Garden Lane Market
Spring Garden Lane, between Queen's Road East and Johnston Road, Wan Chai; daily 10.30am–8pm; MTR: Wan Chai; map p.139 A2

With stalls and factory outlets selling at big discounts designer fashions, sports-wear and other goods

originally meant for export, this is the place to come for real rock-bottom bargains. Around it is the rest of Wan Chai's pungent main market, with plenty of fresh fish stalls, so be ready to negotiate some slippery pavements.

Stanley Market
Stanley Village Road, Stanley, Southside; daily 9am–6pm; bus: 6, 6A, 6X or 260 from Central

The historic fishing lanes of Stanley are jam-packed with vendors selling Chinese artwork, silk collectibles and curios. Locals and visitors flock here for its relaxed seaside atmosphere and restaurants.

Temple Street Night Market
Temple Street, Yau Ma Tei, Kowloon; daily 4–11pm; MTR: Jordan (exit A); map p.132 B1

Awash with rows of brightly lit stalls hawking an astonish-ing variety of clothing, pens, watches, CDs, cassettes, electronic gadgets, hardware and luggage, the Night Market is ordered chaos in action. Busy food stalls do a roaring trade in fresh seafood and hotpot dishes, and fortune-tellers and Chinese opera enthusiasts cluster at the Yau Ma Tei end of the street. It does not really get going until after sunset.

Western Market
Junction of Morrison Street and Connaught Road, Sheung Wan, Western; daily 10am–7pm; MTR: Sheung Wan; map p.136 B4

Sheung Wan's main market is a handsomely renovated Edwardian building filled with Chinese handicraft stores and fabric shops.

Right: colourful goods and characters at the Jade Market.

Above: Temple Street Night Market.

Yuen Po Street Bird Garden

Yuen Po Street, Mong Kok, Kowloon; daily 7am–8pm; MTR: Prince Edward (exit B1); map p.132 C4

You will hear the warble of the Bird Garden, on one side of the Flower Market (see p.102), before you see it. This charming Chinese-style garden is the favourite gathering place for Hong Kong's songbird owners, and the street and garden contains some 70 songbird stalls as well as courtyards and 'moon' gates. The market sells everything from intricately crafted cages (which make good souvenirs) to nutritious grasshoppers. Birds are priced according to their singing ability.

WEEKEND MARKETS

Hong Kong also has a new, more international-style street market, the open-air **Borrett**

Road Market in Mid-Levels (reached via Cotton Tree Road from Admiralty, or Minibus 9; www.borrettroadmarket.com). Its stalls sell original and traditional crafts, organic produce, clothing, jewellery, sculpture, art, aromatherapy oils and gifts. It offers children's entertainment, and is open on the 2nd Sunday of each month. The same organisers have recently added a second site, **Pok Fu Lam Market** (Level 4 CyberPlaza, Cyberport 2; 3rd Sun of each month), on a grassy spot in Hong Kong's quiet, upmarket and residential south side, not far from Repulse Bay.

Factory Outlets, Seconds and Wholesale

As well as markets, other Hong Kong trademarks are the scores of places that, for a fraction of the prices you would probably pay back home, sell samples, over-runs and slightly damaged seconds of locally-made clothes originally intended for export.

As a rule of thumb, bargain-priced womenswear, menswear, T-shirts and jeans, trainers and and other footwear and children's clothes can be found in the **factory outlets** along **Spring Garden Lane Market** and **Johnston Road** in Wan Chai; **Jardine's Crescent** and **Lee Garden Road** in Causeway Bay; at **Stanley Market;** and in Kowloon, along **Haiphong** and **Granville** roads in Tsim Sha Tsui; and around the **Ladies' Market** and Fa Yuen **Street** in Mong Kok. **Temple Street Night Market** in Yau Ma Tei, Kowloon, has cheap menswear. The shops in the **Pedder Building**, Pedder Street, Central, are a good choice for European fashions at competitive prices, and the nearby **Lanes** (**Li Yuen Streets East** and **West**) are renowned for bargain shopping. But caveat emptor: not all of the so-called designer merchandise is genuine.

Although it is slightly off the beaten track, **Horizon Plaza** in Aberdeen (2 Wing Lee Street, Ap Lei Chau, Aberdeen; bus:

Below: Bird Garden Market.

Above: antiques and abaci.

70, 98, 590) is a must if you are looking for bargain furniture to ship home. It houses both furniture and fashion outlets: **Tequila Kola** (1/F) is a must for contemporary Asian furniture; **Shambala** (2/F) is another wooden furniture specialist. And locals flock to Horizon Plaza for **Joyce Warehouse** (2/F), where the chic Joyce Boutique fashion stores sell 'old season' lines at hugely discounted prices.

Milan Station
26 Wellington Street, Central; tel: 2736 3388; MTR: Central; map p.136 C3
An enterprising local chain that stocks all kinds of (authentic) second-hand designer bags in mint condition. Branches in Percival Street, Causeway Bay, and around the city.

Sasa
G/F World Trade Centre, 280 Gloucester Road, Causeway Bay; tel: 2805 6838; www.sasa.com; daily 11am–11pm; MTR: Causeway Bay; map p.139 D3
One of the cheapest cosmetics shops around, with vast ranges of local and international brands, many imported direct from the manufacturer, but the most exciting thing is the super-low prices for just-

launched luxury brand perfumes. Branches all around Hong Kong.

Shopping For…

ART, ANTIQUES, FURNITURE AND ASIAN HANDICRAFTS

> **Buyer Beware**
> Though there is nothing you can not buy in Hong Kong, it has ceased to be the guaranteed 'amazing bargain' it once was for electronics products. Be wary of tricksters who sell fake peripherals, CDs and so on in apparently-original, branded packaging, and try to avoid buying anything that does not have an international guarantee. Do not be fooled by signs advertising that a shop has 'Tax Free' prices either: Hong Kong is a free port, so all of the city's shops enjoy tax-free status.
> Look out for the Hong Kong Tourism Board's black and gold 'QTS' (Quality Tourism Services) scheme logo on shop doors or windows, or visit the website (www.discoverhongkong.com/qts) for a list of accredited shops and restaurants. Especially useful when buying jewellery, watches and electronics, it indicates retailers accredited by the tourism board for quality in goods and service.

Hong Kong is a thriving centre for arts and crafts from the whole of Asia as well as China, with museum-quality antique furniture, ceramics, sculptures, textiles and traditional paintings from Tibet, Japan and Southeast Asia. More affordable are modern Chinese or Vietnamese paintings, rugs, reproduction Korean chests and antique Chinese furniture or ceramics, Thai Buddha figurines, Balinese woodwork and Chinese folk paintings. For shops that deal specifically in Chinese art, craftwork, clothing and so on, *see under* **Chinese Fashion, Arts and Crafts**, *p.106*.

The greatest concentrations of antiques and carpet dealers are around **Upper Wyndham Street** in Central and **Hollywood Road** in Sheung Wan, where **Upper Lascar Row**, also known as **Cat Street Bazaar**, is always good for browsing. **Queen's Road East** in Wan Chai is the best place to look for customised rattan and reproduction rosewood furniture.

There are also a number of top-quality antiques dealers in malls, such as **Pacific Place** in Admiralty and at

105

Above: Mao memorabilia for sale at Cat Street.

Harbour City and **New World Centre** on Kowloon-side. For more competitive prices on Chinese and Asian antiques and contemporary clothes, furnishings and design items, check out too the wholesale import/export outlets in **Aberdeen** (bus 70, 98, 590). They are conveniently concentrated in two big warehouse-style buildings: the **Hing Wai Centre,** 7 Tin Wan Praya Road; and **Horizon Plaza**, (see p.105).

Fine art galleries are also concentrated in Central, mostly around **Wyndham Street** and **SoHo**, and many host regular exhibitions. Check under exhibition listings in the local newspapers, or in the free *HKTB Hong Kong Diary* and *bc* or *HK* magazines.

Alan Chan Creations
Peak Galleria, Peak Road; MTR: Central, then Peak Tram Stylishly nostalgic graphic design items by one of Hong Kong's leading design gurus.

Amazing Grace Elephant Company
Star House, Salisbury Road, Tsim Sha Tsui, Kowloon; tel: 2730 5455; www.amazing gracehk.com; daily 9am–9.30pm; MTR: Tsim Sha Tsui; map p.134 B1
Lively store with sarongs, batiks, jewellery, carvings and so on from across Asia as well as China. Also has a shop at the airport.

Banyan Tree
214–18 Prince's Building, Chater Road, Central; MTR: Central; map p.137 D3
All-Asian crafts, and reproduction and antique furniture. Branches in Harbour City and Horizon Plaza, Aberdeen.

Hong Kong Museum of Art
10 Salisbury Road, Tsim Sha Tsui, Kowloon; tel: 2721 0116; Fri and Sun–Wed 10am–6pm, Sat 10am–8pm; MTR: Tsim Sha Tsui; map p.134 C1
The museum's gift shop is a fine place to pick up smaller gift items and cards.

Mountain Folkcraft
12 Wo On Lane, off D'Aguilar Street, Central; tel: 2525 3199; MTR: Central, then Mid-Levels Escalator; map p.137 C3
Little shop with unusual items mostly from China and Tibet.

OVO
16 Queen's Road East, Wan Chai; tel: 2526 7226; MTR: Wan Chai; map p.138 A2
Modern shop filled with sleek, high-quality custom-made furniture.

Vincent Sum Collection
15 Lyndhurst Terrace, Central; tel: 2542 2610; MTR: Central, then Mid-Levels Escalator; map p.136 C3
Fine pan-Asian furniture, ornaments and gorgeous silks.

CHINESE FASHION, ARTS AND CRAFTS
For the Rolls-Royce of things Chinese, do not miss the designer-chic **Shanghai Tang**. You can also pick up cheaper *cheongsams* and other Chinese garments in the **Lanes** (**Li Yuen Streets East** and **West**) and **Des Voeux Road** in Central, at Chinese department stores

Hong Kong Shopping Festival
The annual summer-long shopping festival organised by the Hong Kong Tourism Board usually runs from the end of July to the end of August, and offers bargain-hunters great deals on fashion, beauty products, jewellery and watches, electronics and traditional Chinese products. Nightly entertainment is part of the programme, and visitors can use their Festival Passport to claim special offers and discount coupons in participating stores and restaurants across the city's major food and shopping districts. Check www.discoverhongkong.com for each year's dates *(see p.38).*

and in the scores of local boutiques on the roads that lead off **Nathan Road** in Tsim Sha Tsui, towards TST East.

Markets are also a good bet for Chinese clothes and accessories. The **Ladies Market** *(see p.103)* stocks a wide selection of dresses and handbags, and **Stanley Market** *(see p.103)* sells everything from a complete mandarin suit for a three-month old baby to exquisite *cheongsams* for five-year-olds, and far, far cheaper (but good quality) versions of the silk scarves sold in Shanghai Tang.

G.O.D

Leighton Centre, Sharp Street, Causeway Bay; tel: 2890 5555; www.god.com.hk; daily noon–10pm; MTR: Causeway Bay; map p.139 C2

A hip and humorous take on Chinese crafts and other local products. Home-grown G.O.D (pronounced 'gee-oh-dee', a phonetic play on the Cantonese for 'live better') is a browser's playground stuffed with funky home-wares, unusual clothing and quirky Asian knick-knacks. There is plenty of local humour in its range of unique bags, which feature among other things images of housing estates and a play on the blue, red and white *amah* bags, carried by the city's thousands of Filipina maids. Other branches are in Central and Tsim Sha Tsui.

Hong Kong Design Gallery

Level 1, Hong Kong Convention and Exhibition Centre, 1 Harbour Road, Wan Chai; tel: 2584 4146; www.hkdesigngallery.tdctrade. com; Mon–Fri 10am–7.30pm, Sat 10–7pm, Sun noon–7.30pm; MTR: Wan Chai; map p.138 A3

Inspiring new jewellery, accessories, household design, gadgets and more by up-and-coming Hong Kong designers, in an official showcase gallery.

Shanghai Tang

Pedder Building, 12 Pedder Street, Central; tel: 2525 7333; www.shanghaitang.com; Mon–Sat 10am–8pm, Sun 11am–7pm; MTR: Central; map p.137 C3

These ultra-stylish, artfully 1930s-style stores have their own imaginative lines of retro-nostalgic Chinese fashions in lush velvets, silk jacquards and acid pinks and greens. An expert made-to-measure service is offered. Gift items include novelty watches with tiny *dim sum* servings instead of numbers, and Chairman Mao cufflinks. Branches in Pacific Place, the Peninsula and Interconti-nental hotels and the airport.

ELECTRONICS, COMPUTERS AND PHOTOGRAPHIC

If you are prepared to shop around, you can still find very competitive prices on electronic goods here. Shops selling digital cameras, DVD players, music systems, MP3 players, computers and all kinds of other gadgets cluster mainly in **Causeway Bay** and, above all, **Tsim Sha Tsui**, Kowloon, especially along **Nathan**, **Peking**, **Mody** and **Carnarvon** roads. As in tourist hot spots around the world, you need to keep an eye out for unscrupulous shopkeepers. Compare prices, resist pressure-sales tactics and always check the goods and receipt before leaving the shop. If in doubt, stick to traders listed in the HKTB's official Dining, Entertainment and Shopping Directory *(see box. p.108)*. If you are not comfortable with the haggling process, the fixed-price chains **Broadway** or **Fortress** are good alternatives.

Computers can be found in the same areas as other elec-tronics, running up in Kowloon to the upper stretches of **Nathan Road** in Mong Kok. A wide range of hard- and soft-ware is available, and you will shave a little, if not a great deal, off home prices for actual computers and basic programmes. What you will find is a vastly extended variety of peripherals, from games, specialist pro-grammes, novelty add-ons and mice of all colours and sizes to laptop bags, with plenty to tempt you.

In the small shops that make up the 'computer malls', be prepared for sometimes very pushy (but sometimes also helpful) service. Comput-

Below: Stanley Market.

Though Hong Kong's economy is generally very strong, the pegging of the Hong Kong dollar to the weak US dollar means that it is possible to pick up some excellent deals, especially on iPods, cameras and other gadgets. Before you start browsing, pick up a copy of the HKTB's official *Dining, Entertainment and Shopping Guide* and *Essential: The Official Hong Kong Guide*. These free booklets contain useful tips. Visit from July to September or December to February, for example, and you can take advantage of some fantastic sales. Some of the top stores discount by up to 70 per cent, and great bargains can be had on designer good and labels during these periods.

ers and peripherals sold here have overwhelmingly been made, naturally, for the Asian market. Always check the keyboard before you leave the shop – some come with Chinese characters only, others a mix of English and Chinese and some just English. Check too that all modem or other ports are compatible with those in your home country.

298 Computer Zone
298 Hennessy Road, Wan Chai; daily, shop times vary; MTR: Wan Chai; map p.139 C3

A famous/notorious mall, a labyrinth of tiny stores over three floors. Prices are rock-bottom, but this can be because some of the goods are pirated or poor-quality non-branded copies. A place to know what you are doing.

Broadway
Shop 714–15, Times Square, 1 Matheson Street, Causeway Bay; tel: 2506 1330; Sun–Thur 11am–9.30pm, Fri–Sat 11am–11pm; MTR: Causeway Bay; map p.139 C3
Broadway has every kind of electronic and camera product displayed in user-friendly fashion, and are also official Apple resellers. Several branches around Hong Kong.

Computer Mall, Windsor House
Gloucester Road, corner of Great George Street, Causeway Bay; daily, shop times vary; MTR: Causeway Bay; map p.139 D3
Three floors of shops with every kind of computer and peripherals.

Fortress
Shops 718–19, Times Square, 1 Matheson Street, Causeway Bay; tel: 2506 0031; www.fortress.com.hk; Mon–Fri 11am–11pm, Sat–Sun 10.30am–10pm; MTR: Causeway Bay; map p.139 C3
Cameras, audio, computers and more. Over 30 branches.

Golden Shopping Centre
Yen Chow and Fuk Wa streets, Sham Shui Po, New Kowloon; daily, shop times vary; MTR: Sham Shui Po
HK's original electronics mall, with ultra-low prices; has had a reputation for selling non-branded or pirated goods, but things are said to have improved.

Mongkok Computer Centre
8 Nelson Street, Mong Kok, Kowloon; daily, shop times vary; MTR: Mong Kok; map p.132 C3
Three floors of every computer product you can think of.

Photo Scientific Appliances
6 Stanley Street, Central; tel: 2522 9979; Mon–Sat 9am–7pm; MTR: Central; map p.136 C3
Many local professional photographers buy their equipment at this superior store.

Star Computer City
Star House, Salisbury Road, Tsim Sha Tsui, Kowloon; daily, shop times vary; MTR: Tsim Sha Tsui; map p.134 B1
Another computer mall, with lots of tiny shops.

FASHION AND DESIGNER SHOPPING
All the fashion heavyweights have been in Hong Kong for years, but this has not stopped a spate of hi-profile launches and re-launches, often coinciding with the revamping or opening of major

Below: Temple Street Night Market.

Above: designer shops are easily found.

malls. This is particularly so in the Central district, where the stylish triumvirate of the **Landmark** *(see p.101)*, neighbouring **Prince's Building** *(see p.101)* and the stylish new **Chater House** (Chater Road) fly the flag for the world's designer fashion fraternity.

Superbrands **Louis Vuitton** and **Gucci** have both opened architecturally striking flagship stores in the renovated **Landmark** *(see p.101)*. Vuitton, with its fourth 'global concept' store, occupies three floors and is fronted by an enormous trunk-shaped hoarding featuring the famous cherry monogram. This has set the scene for the arrival of a slew of upmarket brands, which attract the fashion cognoscenti like bees to honey. First came a mini version of the UK's **Harvey Nichols**, to be joined by another Brit, **Paul Smith**, and the über-trendy Japanese label **A Bathing Ape**. These stop-the-traffic flagships are upstaged only by the veritable fiefdom being created by **Armani**, a few hundred metres away in the Chater Building.

Further on towards the harbour, labels from **Agnès b** (who has opened her first and only travel concept store in Hong Kong) to local designer **Vivienne Tam** can be found in the **IFC mall** *(see p.101)*, where it is worth calling into the city's largest **Lane Crawford** *(see p.100)* store for a seat at the trendy CD Bar. At the in-store Martini Bar flagging shoppers can relax with a cocktail while engulfed in Bose surround-sound and check their stock and shares on the Hang Seng index.

More labels abound at **Pacific Place** and **Times Square** *(see p.101)* in Causeway Bay, in the arcades in many top-flight hotels, and in the **New World Centre** and **Harbour City** *(see p.100)* complexes and on **Canton Road** in Tsim Sha Tsui, Kowloon. Low- to mid-range fashion chains have outlets in virtually every shopping district in Hong Kong, with top international brand names competing with locally produced labels such as Jessica, Bossini, U2, Giordano and Episode.

Aside from Vivienne Tam, other home-grown designer talent to look out for includes Lu Lu Cheung, Allan Chiu, Anna Sui, Barney Cheng and Walter Ma. And do not miss **Island Beverey** mall in Causeway Bay *(see p.101)*,

for an innovative crop of young designers.

Not to be ignored is another aspect of Hong Kong shopping: its many factory outlets and discount houses. For these, *see p.104*.

A Bathing Ape
G/F, 10 Queen's Road Central, Central; tel: 2868 9448; www.bape.com; daily 11am–8pm; MTR: Central; map p.137 C3
Also known just as BAPE, this cult Japanese youth label is easily picked out by its big gorilla logo above the shop's entrance, opposite the Landmark, and by the queues that snake around the building on new-line delivery days.

Armani Chater House
Chater House, 11 Chater Road, Central; tel: 2532 7700; www.armani.com; daily 10am–7.30pm; MTR: Central; map p.137 D3
An Armani fiefdom has been created in the Chater Building, catering for every need: as well as the fashion lines for women, men and kids, the portfolio includes *Armani Fiori*, *Armani Casa* and *Armani Dolci*. When you have done shopping, there is the Armani Winebar and Lounge, a world first for anyone wishing to eat and drink a brand as well as wear it. There are also Armani stores in most big malls.

109

Joyce Boutique

Shop 334, Pacific Place, 88 Queensway, Admiralty; tel: 2523 8128; www.joyce.com; MTR: Admiralty; map p.137 E3

Joyce Ma's elegant stores have been among Hong Kong's foremost showcases for international fashion – especially European and Japanese labels – for over 20 years: upmarket, stylish and prestigious. Branches include 16 Queen's Road, Central, 106 Canton Road, Tsim Sha Tsui, and the Joyce Warehouse discount house in Aberdeen *(see p.105)*.

The Swank

103B, Ocean Centre, Harbour City, Tsim Sha Tsui, Kowloon; tel: 2736 1502; www.swank. com.hk; MTR: Tsim Sha Tsui; map p.134 B3

International labels and glamorous evening wear by local fashion king and self-proclaimed 'fag with faith', Barney Cheng. Branches in Harbour City and Pacific Place *(see p.101)*.

JEWELLERY, WATCHES AND GEMSTONES

Hong Kong has the world's largest jade market, the third largest diamond trading centre after New York and Antwerp, and one of the largest gold brokers. It is also a centre for trading in precious stones from all over Asia. Many finished jewellery items, from simple gold bangles to intricately designed diamond necklaces, are manufactured in Hong Kong.

Gold and jewellery factory outlets abound in **Hung Hom** in Kowloon, but prices here have risen steeply over the past few years. Better bargains can be had in the shops along **Queen's Road Central**. Top–flight hotel shopping arcades are another place to find quality jewellers, and there is a big choice on **Yee Wo Street** and **Hennessy Road** in Causeway Bay, and along **Nathan Road** in Tsim Sha Tsui.

For a professional gemmologist to certify authenticity before you buy diamonds, jade or gems, call the **Gemmological Association of Hong Kong** (tel: 2366 6006).

Larry Jewelry

Shop 319, The Landmark, Des Voeux Road Central, Central; tel: 2523 3880; www.larryjewelry. com; MTR: Central; map p.137 D3

One of Hong Kong's finest jewellers, with three more branches.

OPTICAL SERVICES

Hong Kong is a great place to buy eye-wear, whether it is prescription lenses or the latest designer sunglasses. Frames and contact lenses are bang up to date and excellent value; eye tests are free, and the service quick and efficient. There are hundreds of small opticians, as well as the major chains.

Bunn's Divers

188 Johnston Road, Wan Chai; tel: 3422 3322; http://bunns divers.com; MTR: Wan Chai; map p.138 B2

A specialist diving shop that stocks an exceptional range of prescription goggles and diving masks.

Fox Optical

12 Cochrane Street, Central; tel: 2541 3018; MTR: Central; map p.136 C3

A good-quality independent optician. Recommended.

Mandarin Optical

79 Queen's Road Central, Central; MTR: Central; map p.136 C3

Also a lens manufacturer, so service is especially fast.

Optical 88

65 Percival Street, Causeway Bay; tel: 2891 7316, www.optical88.com; daily 11am–10pm; MTR: Causeway Bay; map p.139 C3

Below: watch salesman, Cat Street.

Above: Chinese jewellery.

Largest of all Hong Kong's retail opticians, with scores of efficient outlets all around the Territory.

Optical Shop
G/F China Building, 29 Queen's Road Central, Central; tel: 2525 9861; www.theopticalshop.com; daily 10am–7.30pm; MTR: Central; map p.137 C3
Another reliable large-scale chain optician, with branches all over Hong Kong and the New Territories.

TAILORING
Hong Kong tailors are justifiably renowned for their skills, both in classic tailoring and in copying existing garments. Prices naturally vary according to the work involved, and the quality and quantity of cloth and trimmings, but you can get a good custom-tailored shirt for about HK$250, or a man's or woman's suit for HK$2,500.

Quality tailors usually require that you allow time for a couple of fittings; there are exceptions, but in general the days of the so-called 24-hour suit, at on-the-floor prices, are largely gone. Look for the

Hong Kong Tourism Board's membership logo when choosing a tailor. Remember too that Hong Kong cobblers can also make custom-made shoes; perfect for the complete outfit.

Tailor Kwan
Escalator Link Alley, 2/F Central Market, Central; MTR: Central; map p.136 C3

William Cheng & Son
8/F, 38 Hankow Road, Tsim Sha Tsui, Kowloon; MTR: Tsim Sha Tsui; map p.134 B2

Yuen's Tailors
Escalator Link Alley, 2/F Central Market, Central; MTR: Central; map p.136 C3

Pursue
2/F, 13 Lan Kwai Fong, Central; MTR: Central; map p.137 C2
For something different, try this modern store. Catering to men and women, it also has a lounge and bar area complete with entertainment system.

Sam's Tailor
G/F Burlington Arcade K, 94 Nathan Road, Tsim Sha Tsui, Kowloon; tel: 2367 9423; www.samstailor.com; Mon–Sat 10am–7.30pm, Sun 10am–midnight; MTR: Tsim Sha Tsui; map p.134 C2
Most famous of Hong Kong tailors, clothing celebrities from the Prince of Wales to Pavarotti. Nevertheless, it is still a modest little shop, and all customers are expertly and courteously catered for, at all kinds of prices.

Soong Salon de Mode
2/F, Flat A, Hangchung Mansions, 8–10 Hankow Road, Kowloon; MTR: Tsim Sha Tsui; map p.134 B2
Expat girls flock here for glamorous new creations and copies.

Left: dress sharp for the meetings.

Sport

Despite its relatively small population, Hong Kong packs a wealth of sport and activities into its territory, with options ranging from hiking and golf to rugby, tennis and horse racing. While events like the annual Dragon Boat championships are typical Hong Kong experiences, the sporting calendar is also packed with high-profile competitions in international sports that attract world-class sportsmen and women. And, with on-line booking to smooth the way, keeping up with your favourite kind of exercise and maybe seeing a major sporting event during your visit could not be easier.

Cricket

Great pitch action can be enjoyed at two annual events in Hong Kong: the **International Cricket Sixes** at Kowloon Cricket Club and the **Hong Kong International Cricket Festival** at Po Kong Village Road Cricket Ground. Both are held every November. The International Cricket Festival is the biggest club cricket sixes tournament in the world, with 35 male and female teams competing in an action-packed, six-a-side format. Best of all, it is free. Events aside, the Hong Kong Cricket Association website has details of all Hong Kong's clubs and the season's matches.

Hong Kong Cricket Association
tel: 2504 8102;
www.cricket.com.hk

Cycling

You would be very brave (or stupid) to take to Hong Kong's urban roads on a bike, but cyclists will find no shortage of cycling paths in the New Territories, particularly around Tolo Harbour, in the northeast beyond Sha Tin. Visitors can rent bikes in Sha Tin or Tai Po. Elsewhere, bikes can be rented in Shek O on Hong Kong Island, and on Cheung Chau, Lamma and especially Lantau islands. Bikes are in big demand at weekends – book, or hire early – and paths are very busy.

Not all trails in Hong Kong's country parks are open for mountain biking (check the signs), but a handful of parks do have trails; for details, contact the **HKMBA**.

Hong Kong Cycling Association
tel: 2504 8176;
www.cycling.org.hk
Mainly involved in competition cycling, with an annual race calendar.

Hong Kong Mountain Biking Association
www.hkmba.org
Essential source of information, particularly on authorised routes in nature parks, maps and other facilities.

Dragon Boat Racing

Dragon boat races are held throughout June, in the

Left: golfing with a view.

Left: Happy Valley racecourse.

Sport of Kings

You do not have to have any affinity with the gee-gees to imbibe the night-time buzz at Happy Valley racecourse. The evening is as much about Hong Kong's unique tightly-stacked cityscape and vertiginous tower blocks twinkling down over the packed stands as it is about thundering hooves. If you are a racing fan, though, do not miss the prestige international races such as the lucrative Hong Kong Derby (Mar), Queen Elizabeth II Cup (Apr) and Hong Kong International Races (Dec), when world-class horses and jockeys fly in to compete for the world's richest purses. All are held at the Sha Tin track. Race meetings are held every Wednesday night at Happy Valley, and every Saturday and Sunday at Sha Tin, from September to June. Alternatively, get a stylish introduction to Hong Kong racing with the HKTB's *Come Horseracing Tour*, which gives a day's racing at Sha Tin or an evening at Happy Valley in the comfort of the hallowed Hong Kong Jockey Club Members' Enclosure.

Dragon Boat Festival (*Tuen Ng*). Steeped in tradition – it commemorates a 3rd-century BC Chinese hero who threw himself into a river rather than bow to the orders of a tyrannical ruler – this is one of Hong Kong's most colourful 'sports'.

The **Hong Kong International Dragon Boat Races**, the main competitive event, with teams from many countries as well as Hong Kong, are held over two days towards the end of June, but there are local races throughout the month, and for weeks before the festival it is possible to catch crews in training before the big event. You can catch the action at various locations around Hong Kong including Aberdeen, Stanley, Sha Tin, Tai Po, Cheung Chau and Lantau Island; for each year's calendar, check www.discoverhongkong.com. SEE ALSO FESTIVALS, P.39

Football

Hong Kong only has an amateur football (soccer) league, but even so Hong Kongers are crazy about football, above all the English Premiership, which is shown in all the city's sports bars. Hunger for live football is slaked mainly by two tournaments, the **Lunar New Year Cup**, which pits the Chinese national side and/or a Hong Kong team against a mixed bag of other national teams around the time of Chinese New Year, and the **Barclays Asia Trophy** in late July, when English Premier clubs get some pre-season training (Liverpool, Chelsea and Newcastle have all taken part in different years) against teams from mainland China and the rest of Asia. Games are played at the Hong Kong Stadium. For more information, see www.hkfa.com/en.

Hong Kong Stadium
55 Eastern Hospital Road, So Kon Po, near Causeway Bay; tel: 2895 7895; www.lcsd.gov.hk/stadium; bus: 2, 5, 19, 25; map p.139 E1
Hong Kong's largest sports venue, seating 40,000, hosts a range of football competitions and the annual Rugby Sevens tournament.

Golf

Public courses are thin on the ground, but non-members are welcome from Monday to Friday at the **Hong Kong Golf Club**'s two courses at Deep Water Bay and Fanling. For sheer wow factor, head for the **Jockey Club Kau Sai Chau** public golf course: this Gary Player-designed course is set among rolling hills on Kau Sai Chau island, and affords stunning views of the South China Sea, Sai Kung hills and nearby islands. Plus, it is open to everyone at weekends.

A must-see for golf fans is the four-day **Hong Kong Open**, each November at the Hong Kong Golf Club in Fanling. For details see www.ubshongkongopen.com.
Hong Kong Golf Club
www.hkgolfclub.org
Jockey Club
Kau Sai Chau
www.kscgolf.com

Horse Racing

No-one loves a wager like the Hong Kong Chinese, but the only places gambling is actually legal in the Territory are its two race tracks. The racing season is the perfect marriage between the British affection for 'race day' and the Chinese obsession with numbers and fortune. It is not every day you get to bet on such auspicious dobbins as *Dragon* and *Gold*, *Tiger Storm* or *Hero of Abalone*.

The **Happy Valley** and **Sha Tin** racecourses are home to some of the richest races in the world (and Sha Tin's video screen is also the world's biggest). Entry to the stands costs from $10, which is also the cost of a minimum bet. Races are held every week from September to June, every Wednesday night at Happy Valley (usually beginning at 7.15pm), and on Saturdays and Sundays at Sha Tin (usually from 1–6pm). Check out the **Hong Kong Jockey Club** website (www.hkjc.com) for a full race calendar and all the latest information.
Happy Valley Racecourse
Happy Valley Stand, Happy Valley; tel: 2895 1523; www.hkjc.com; bus/tram: Happy Valley; map p.138 C1
Also home to the Hong Kong Racing Museum.

To really see the wild side of Hong Kong, contact **Kayak-and-Hike** (tel: 9300 5197; www.kayak-and-hike.com). Run by long-term HK resident Paul Etherington, this agency offers a big range of adventure trips – many by kayak – hikes and climbs, above all into the wild Sai Kung country park in the eastern New Territories.

SEE ALSO MUSEUMS AND GALLERIES, P.64
Sha Tin Racecourse
Sha Tin, New Territories; tel: 2696 6223; www.hkjc.com; KCR: East line to Sha Tin Racecourse

Rugby

The **Hong Kong Rugby Sevens** is one of Hong Kong's most popular annual events, and you do not have to be a rugby fan to enjoy it. The Sevens is basically one long fever-pitched party, held over three days in late March at the **Hong Kong Stadium** *(see p.113)*. Twenty-four seven-a-side teams compete to win the coveted Hong Kong Sevens championship, and, with the exception of the 20-minute Cup Final, each match lasts just 14 minutes. The atmosphere in the stands is electric. Tickets sell out quickly so book in advance (www.hksevens.com.hk). Look out for restaurant and entertainment outlets displaying the Rugby Sevens Offers: visitors just need to show a travel document to benefit.

Swimming

Public swimming pools are a Godsend when Hong Kong's humidity kicks in. The sports complex in **Kowloon Park** incorporates an Olympic-sized indoor and an outdoor

Left: waterskiing and sand castles.

pool, and there are smaller outdoor pools in **Victoria Park**. For a full list of public pools, see www.lcsd.gov.hk. Many hotels have good-sized pools for guest use and a limited number of spaces for non-guests (it is worth asking).

Then there are the beaches. About 41 of Hong Kong's shark-netted beaches have lifeguards, along with facilities including changing rooms, showers, swimming rafts and refreshments kiosks (from April to October). Popular swimming beaches include **Repulse Bay** and **Cheung Sha** beach on Lantau island.

Kowloon Park
Kowloon Park Drive, Tsim Sha Tsui, Kowloon; MTR: Tsim Sha Tsui, Jordan; map p.134 B2
Victoria Park
Between Victoria Park Road and Causeway Road, Causeway Bay; MTR: Causeway Bay, Tin Hau; map p.139 D/E 3-4

Tennis

Public tennis courts can be

Above: keeping the beaches safe.

found in **Victoria Park** and **Kowloon Park.** Some hotels also have courts, and can sometimes book spots for guests at private clubs.

In terms of competitions Victoria Park also has a well-equipped Tennis Stadium with a seating capacity of 3,611, which has hosted a number of international tournaments including the Davis Cup and the Champions Challenge, a premier women's tour tournament, held every January.
Victoria Park Tennis Stadium
Between Victoria Park Road and Causeway Road, Causeway Bay; MTR: Causeway Bay, Tin Hau
SEE ALSO PARKS AND GARDENS, P.85

Walking and Hiking

Hong Kong's 23 country parks offer endless opportunities for walking and hiking, and this is one of the most popular weekend pastimes. Significant trails include the 50km **Hong Kong Trail** that spans all of Hong Kong Island's five country parks, and the 70km **Lantau Trail** on Lantau Island.

Former governor and keen walker Sir Murray MacLehose opened up large tracts of local countryside to trekkers, and the famous 62km **MacLehose Trail** spans the New Territories. Shorter trails such as the various **Peak** trails and the cross-island trail on **Lamma** abound. Keen walkers should pick up a copy of *Exploring Hong Kong's Countryside: A Visitor's Companion*, available free from HKTB Visitor Information Centres. SEE ALSO WALKS AND VIEWS, P.128–31

Windsurfing

Windsurfing won Hong Kong its first Olympic gold medal in 1996, and the sport has steadily grown in popularity. Medallist Lee Lai-Shan trained off **Cheung Chau** island, which has become a popular spot for windsurfers. Boards are available for hire at Kwun Yam Beach on Cheung Chau, as well as in **Stanley** and a number of other locations. Check out the website www.windsurfing.org.hk for more details.

Marathon Running
The Hong Kong Marathon is Hong Kong's biggest outdoor sporting event. It is the last leg of 'The Greatest Race on Earth', an international series of marathons held in four different cities (the others are in Nairobi, Singapore and Mumbai). Held in late February or early March, it attracts around 40,000 runners, including many of the world's best. The event includes a half marathon and a 10km run as well as a full marathon, on a course that runs past some of Hong Kong's most dramatic scenery. The marathon course starts on Nathan Road in Tsim Sha Tsui, runs up to Tsing Yi island, then turns back south to finish at Golden Bauhinia Square in Wan Chai on Hong Kong Island.

115

Temples and Historic Sites

Hong Kong may feel new, but it has been inhabited for millennia, first by the Tanka boat dwellers, followed by the Manchus and Hakkas, and more latterly by the British. Each stage in Hong Kong's chequered past has left behind the remnants of different beliefs and ways of life. From Taoist temples and giant Buddhas to walled villages and an Anglican church, there is certainly a complex background of culture, history and belief to unearth if you know where to look.

Hong Kong Island

Government House
Upper Albert Road, Central; MTR: Central; map p.137 C2
The former residence of Britain's colonial governors was begun in Georgian neoclassical style in 1851, but considerably altered by the Japanese during World War II. The lush gardens are open to the public a few times a year, particularly when the azaleas are in bloom in March; check with the Hong Kong Tourist Board (see p.37) for details.
Man Mo Temple
126 Hollywood Road, Sheung Wan, Western; tel: 2540 0350;
daily 9am–6pm; free, donations welcome; MTR: Sheung Wan; map p.136 B3
Tourists regularly throng the atmospheric Man Mo, but this does not inhibit the temple's regular worshippers from filling it with clouds of smoke from joss sticks and incense spirals that dangle photogenically from the ceiling. Man is the god of civil servants and of literature, Mo is the god of martial arts and war. There are usually old men and women pottering around in the dark recesses of the temple, lighting incense sticks or laying out offerings.

Old Supreme Court – Legislative Council
Jackson Road, Central; check with tourist offices for visiting times; MTR: Central; map p.137 D3
Opened in 1912, the two-storey granite structure was built in grand Neoclassical style. It was converted in 1985 to house the Legislative Council (Legco).
St John's Cathedral
4–8 Garden Road, Central; tel: 2523 4157; www.stjohns cathedral.org.hk; daily 7am–6pm; free; MTR: Central, then bus/tram: Queensway; map p.137 D2

Below: a study in details.

Left: Tian Tin Buddha at Po Lin Monastery.

daily 8am–5pm; free, donations welcome; MTR: Yau Ma Tei; map p.132 B1

Over a century old, this temple complex is the main Tin Hau temple in Hong Kong city. The Taoist deity Tin Hau, goddess of the sea and protector of fisherfolk, has always been especially revered in Hong Kong, and there are scores of other temples to her throughout the Territory. Tin Hau's birthday in late April or May is a major festival, with colourful celebrations at all her temples, but especially in fishing villages around the coast.

Locals visit this city temple regularly, to leave offerings at an image of Tin Hau draped in intricately embroidered scarlet robes. To the right of the altar are 60 identical deities, which represent every year of the 60-year lunar calendar. Worshippers

Built in Victorian Gothic style in 1847–9, tranquil St John's is the oldest surviving Western religious building in Hong Kong, and the oldest Anglican church in East Asia.

Kowloon and New Kowloon

Chi Lin Nunnery

5 Chi Lin Drive, Diamond Hill, New Kowloon; tel: 2354 1604; daily 9am–5pm; free, donations welcome; MTR: Diamond Hill (exit C2)

Flanked by a lily pond and instantly recognisable by its beautifully embellished carved wooden roofs, the huge Buddhist Chi Lin complex was built between the 1930s and 1990s, but entirely in the classic style of the Tang dynasty (AD 618–907). Its seven wooden halls were even constructed using wooden tenons instead of nails. Nestled among the surrounding high-rise apartment blocks is the tranquil **Nan Lian Garden**, a relatively new public park also built in the Tang style. The scenic garden is meticulously landscaped over an area of 3.5 hectares,

in which every hill, rock, body of water, plant and timber structure has been placed according to specific rules and methods.

Hong Kong Observatory

134 Nathan Road, Tsim Sha Tsui, Kowloon; tel: 2926 8469; MTR: Tsim Sha Tsui; map p.136 C3

Built in 1883, the Observatory sits on a small hill amid a pretty garden, and continues to monitor Hong Kong's weather. There are occasional guided tours (in Cantonese).

Former Kowloon-Canton Railway Clock Tower

By Star Ferry Pier, Tsim Sha Tsui, Kowloon; MTR: Tsim Sha Tsui; map p.134 B1

This clock tower came into operation in 1915, as part of the main station of the Kowloon-Canton Railway. The rest of the station was knocked down in 1978, but, unusually for Hong Kong, it was decided to keep the local landmark of the tower.

Tin Hau Temple

Corner of Nathan Road and Public Square Street, Yau Ma Tei, Kowloon; tel: 2332 9240;

Monumental Hong Kong

Hectic Hong Kong does not give the impression of caring too much for its heritage, but it is surprising to find how much remains of 5,000 years of human settlement in the Territory, and it is a little-known fact that it has 80 officially-declared monuments. They include stone carvings that date back thousands of years, venerable Taoist temples, walled villages that still house living communities, and remnants of Hong Kong's colonial history, such as forts and even lighthouses. The handsome granite Western Market, the former Wan Chai Post Office (oldest surviving one in Hong Kong), the former Kowloon British School and St John's Cathedral all bear the hallmarks of British heritage.

Left: divination sticks and incense.

place 'Hell Bank' notes under the god dedicated to the years of their birth. The adjoining square has a very Chinese atmosphere, with elderly locals playing Chinese chess and chewing the fat.

Wong Tai Sin Temple
Wong Tai Sin Road, Wong Tai Sin, New Kowloon; tel: 2327 8141; www.siksikyuen.org.hk; daily 7am–5.30pm; free, entrance charge to some areas, donations welcome; MTR: Wong Tai Sin

You will know you have arrived at the Wong Tai Sin temple when you hear the sound of rattling *chim,* the bamboo fortune sticks used for fortune telling. Known as 'the fortune-tellers' temple', this Taoist temple complex in a natural setting at the heart of urban Kowloon is probably the liveliest and most colourful place of worship in the whole of Hong Kong. It is certainly one of the most rewarding for outsiders to visit, constantly bustling with worshippers. The rear of the main altar is carved to show the story of the god Wong Tai Sin, a simple shepherd who is said to have been given the formula for an elixir for

immortality by a heavenly spirit. There is a small entrance charge to some areas, such as the lovely **Good Wish Garden**, which may also be closed at some times.

New Territories

Temple of 10,000 Buddhas Monastery
Sha Tin; tel: 2691 1067; daily 9am–5pm; free, donations welcome; KCR: East line to Sha Tin (exit B)

There is a steep climb up to this monastery – dating only from the 1950s – but pilgrims are rewarded by the sight of actually well over 12,000 Buddha-statues, nearly all slightly different from the next, lining the walls and stairways. There is also a mellow vegetarian restaurant.

Kam Tin Walled Villages
Kam Tin, near Yuen Long; KCR: West line to Kam Sheung Road

Around the town of Kam Tim in the northwest of the Territories are two walled villages: **Kat Hing Wai** is the grandest of the remaining such villages in Hong Kong, a moated settlement built around 1600, and still lived in by the Hakka people. **Shui Tau Tsuen,**

further from Kam Tin, is smaller, but has well-restored temples.

Kun Lung Gate Tower
San Wai, near Fanling; KCR: East line to Fanling

Serving as the entrance to San Wai, a small, wonderfully preserved village of the Tang clan, this tower was built in 1744. It is the best surviving gate tower of a walled village in the New Territories.

Liu Man Shek Tong Ancestral Hall
Man Hau Tsuen, near Sheung Shui; Wed–Sun 9am–1pm, 2–5pm; free; KCR: East line to Sheung Shui

The key attraction of Sheung Shui, last town before the main crossing into mainland China, is this finely preserved hall, built in 1751 by the Liu clan as a meeting-place and to honour their ancestors.

Man Lun Fung Ancestral Hall and Tai Fu Tai Mansion
San Tin, between Yuen Long and Sheung Shui; daily 9am–1pm, 2–5pm; free; KCR: West line to Yuen Long, then bus: 75, 76, 76K

As part of its tour programme, the Hong Kong Tourism Board (HKTB) offers a convenient five-hour slice of Hong Kong's traditions – as well as a glimpse of the New Territories – on its Heritage Tour. This offers an opportunity to escape the frenzy of Kowloon and Central for unspoilt countryside, new towns and old villages, and see the relics of a far older China, including Tai Fu Tai mansion, ancestral halls and walled villages. For details, enquire at HKTB offices or check www.discoverhongkong.com.

Around the village of San Tin, are this **Ancestral Hall**, smaller than the Liu Man Shek, and thought to have been erected at the end of the 17th century in honour of a leading member of the Man clan, and **Tai Fu Tai Mansion**, a stately residence built in 1865 by a senior Man clan member who was bestowed the title of *Tai Fu* (mandarin) by the Qing emperor. It is the best-preserved traditional Chinese mansion in Hong Kong.

Man Mo Temple, Tai Po
Fu Shin Street, Tai Po; daily 9am–5pm; free, donations welcome; KCR: East line to Tai Wo
The Man Mo Temple in Tai Po was built about a century ago, and dedicated to the gods Man (literature) and Mo (martial arts). Built to mark the foundaton of Tai Po New Market, this market-town temple was constructed as a walled compound to emphasis seclusion.

Sam Tung Uk Village
Kwu Uk Lane, Tsuen Wan; Wed–Mon 9am–5pm; free; MTR: Tsuen Wan

No longer inhabited, this walled village was built by the Hakka Chan clan in the 1780s. Restored as a folk museum when its residents moved out, it has attractive displays on traditional Hakka life.

Tang Chung Ling Ancestral Hall
Lo Wai, near Fanling; Wed–Mon 9am–1pm, 2–5pm; free; KCR: East line to Fanling
Built in 1525, this hall dedicated to the ancestors of the local Tang clan was beautifully restored in 1922, and is still used for ceremonies. It boats exquisitely carved and colourful decorations.

Tsang Tai Uk
Near Sha Tin; KCR: East line to Sha Tin
Near the approach road to the Lion Rock tunnel, which carries the main road north from Kowloon, this is an outstanding example of a fortified village. The name means 'Tsang's big house'; built in 1848, it is a large, rectangular grey brick compound with high thick walls and tall corner towers.

Outer Islands

Po Lin Monastery and Tian Tan Buddha
Ngong Ping, Lantau Island; tel: 2985 5248; daily, monastery 9am–6pm, Buddha 10am–6pm; free, donations welcome; MTR: Tung Chung, then bus: 23, or ferry: Mui Wo, then bus: 2
Superlatives come thick and fast for the Tian Tan Buddha, the world's tallest seated outdoor bronze Buddha. Weighing 250 tonnes and perched at 34m high, the statue towers above the fascinating Po Lin Monastery, high on the slopes of Lantau Island.

The monastery was founded in 1906 as a religious retreat, and visitors can wander through its temple complexes and lovely gardens, often full of exuberant orchids. To get a further sense of the Po Lin experience, be sure to sample the delicious vegetarian food served in the monastery's giant, canteen-style restaurants (daily 11.30am–5pm; tickets from the office below the Buddha).

Below: ascending to the Buddha at Po Lin Monastery.

Transport

Hong Kong is one of the most easily navigable cities on earth. Apart from its clean, cheap and efficient Mass Transit Railway system (known as the MTR), it has ferry services, tramlines on Hong Kong Island, excellent airport connections, a huge fleet of minibuses and squadrons of larger, double-decked buses, and more taxis than you could shake a stick at. Wheels aside, the city is laced with overhead walkways to help get people off the busy streets, and boasts the world's longest mechanical stairway, the Mid-Levels Escalator, to ease the pain of Hong Kong Island's steep slopes.

Getting There by Air

Hong Kong is a major regional air-traffic hub, handling over 35 million passengers a year. Getting there from the UK has never been easier: 2006 saw the introduction of 17 new flights, giving travellers 77 non-stop flights each week from London to choose from. New options include the flights launched by the first-ever low-fare carrier to the Far East, **Oasis Hong Kong Airlines**, offering one-way travel to Hong Kong from London Gatwick from £75 plus tax,

A new Terminal 2 at Hong Kong International Airport opened in March 2007. Alongside the existing Terminal 1, it contains 130 shops and restaurants plus four entertainment zones, in the SkyPlaza. T2 is the centrepiece of a larger development, SkyCity, aimed at making HKIA an integrated 'airport city'. Other projects under development include a golf course, more hotels and – already in operation – the AsiaWorld-Expo site, with a giant-sized arena and exhibition spaces.

and daily services from Heathrow on **Air New Zealand**. Air NZ's new flight from London to Auckland via Hong Kong made a complete round-the-world service on one airline possible for the first time, giving the option of flying to New Zealand via Asia or the west coast of the United States, or vice-versa.

As the home and hub of **Cathay Pacific**, Hong Kong is also a primary gateway to China: the airline flies on to 21 destinations in mainland China, sometimes via its reputable sister airline, **Dragonair**. **Virgin** flies on from Hong Kong to Sydney, and passengers on **Qantas**'s through-flight from Hong Kong to Melbourne can change there for Perth, Brisbane or Sydney.

DIRECT FLIGHTS

These airlines fly direct to Hong Kong from the UK:
Air New Zealand
www.airnewzealand.co.uk
One flight a day from Heathrow.
British Airways
www.ba.com

Consider 'offsetting' the CO2 from your journey to and around Hong Kong through an organisation like **Climate Care** (www.climatecare.org). Their on-line calculator will tell you your carbon emissions for your trip and how much you should donate to the scheme.

Three flights per day from Heathrow.
Cathay Pacific
www.cathaypacific.com
Four flights per day from Heathrow.
Oasis Hong Kong Airlines
www.oasishongkong.com
One flight daily from Gatwick.
Qantas
www.qantas.co.uk
One flight daily from Heathrow.
Virgin Atlantic
www.virgin-atlantic.com
One flight every day from Heathrow.

INDIRECT FLIGHTS

Airlines below fly between the UK and Hong Kong with one stop en route, which may mean changing planes.

Left: know your Chinese road markings.

Audley Travel
Tel: 01993 838200;
www.audleytravel.com
Adventure trips in the whole of China, with Hong Kong as a base.

British Airways Holidays
Tel: 0870 243 3407;
www.baholidays.com
BA offers packages as well as flight and hotel combinations.

Cresta Holidays
Tel: 0871 664 7963;
www.crestaholidays.co.uk
A range of Hong Kong packages.

CTS Horizons
tel: 020 7836 4338;
www.ctshorizons.com
Varied tours and tailor-made itineraries across China and Hong Kong.

Hayes and Jarvis
Tel: 0870 200 4422;
www.hayesandjarvis.co.uk
Long-established company offering an ample range of Hong Kong and China tours.

Oriental Travel
Tel: 020 7632 4550;
www.china-tour.co.uk
China and Hong Kong specialists, for small-group tours and individual itineraries.

Thomas Cook Signature
Tel: 0870 443 4447;
www.tcsignature.com

Air France
www.airfrance.co.uk
Emirates
www.emirates.com
Finnair
www.finnair.co.uk
Lufthansa
www.lufthansa.com
Malaysia Airlines
www.malaysiaairlines.com
Singapore Airlines
www.singaporeair.com
Thai Airways
www.thaiairways.com

Getting There by Sea

Hong Kong is a starting-off or end-point to a great number of cruise itineraries, and its status as a global airline hub also makes it a natural springboard for Asian fly-cruise itineraries. Crystal, Cunard, Regent Seven Seas, Seabourn, Royal Caribbean International, Holland America, P&O, Silversea, Peter Deilmann and Swan Hellenic are among the cruise lines that use Hong Kong. Many itineraries use Hong Kong as a base before sailing on to beach and island destinations in the region.

Cruise ships dock at the **Ocean Terminal** at the southernmost tip of Kowloon, in Tsim Sha Tsui, right next to the Harbour City mall.

Hong Kong-based **Star Cruises** is one of the world's largest cruise companies, and in 2007 launched a range of 2–3-night mini-cruises to Xiamen and Hainan Island in China, a very easy way for travellers to dip a toe into the mainland. For information, contact tel: 2317 7711, www.starcruises.com.

Tour Operators

UK tour operators that feature Hong Kong include:

Below: rickshaws are a quick option in Central.

Above: taxis are available if their light is on.

Low-priced Hong Kong packages.

Thomson Worldwide
Tel: 0870 160 7438;
www.thomsonworldwide.co.uk
Packages and itineraries.

Tradewinds Worldwide Holidays
Tel: 0871 664 7964;
www.tradewinds.co.uk
Packages and made-to-measure itineraries, which can combine Hong Kong with other Asian destinations.

Travelmood
Tel: 0800 0111 945;
www.travelmood.com
Good for Hong Kong and Bali combinations, and stop-offs en route to Australia.

To and From the Airport

The impressive and highly efficient Norman Foster-designed Hong Kong International Airport (HKIA) is at Chek Lap Kok, on the northern shore of Lantau Island and about 34km from Central, which, as its name suggests, is the urban heart of Hong Kong Island. Immigration queues are dealt with swiftly, and suitcases are often circling the carousel by the time you reach the baggage hall.

The eight-level airport building is full of shops and restaurants, as well as ATMs

and the excellent **Hong Kong Tourist Board (HKTB)** information desks; be sure to collect the free welcome bag, with a map, vouchers and plenty of useful information.

All transport to the city leaves from the **Ground Transportation Centre**, which is well signposted from the Arrivals Hall. Details of all services can be found on the airport website.

SEE ALSO ESSENTIALS P.36–7
Airport Information
tel: 2181 0000;
www.hkairport.com

AIRPORT EXPRESS

The Airport Express railway, part of the MTR system (see p.123), runs from the Ground Transportation Centre in the terminal building, and is the

Street Signs
All street signs are in English and Chinese. Hong Kong street maps usually have both English and Chinese-language sections in the back, to make it easier to find your destination. Be aware that while at times the English name of a street or district is a transliteration of the Chinese, at others the Chinese name is totally different and may have no visible relation to the English one.

quickest and easiest, though also a relatively expensive, way to get into town. All trains run to and from the AsiaWorld-Expo exhibition site alongside the airport, as well as from the airport itself. Trains reach Central station on Hong Kong Island in just 23 min, with stops at Tsing Yi and Kowloon. Trains run in both directions daily from 5.50am–1.15am, at 12-min intervals. Single tickets to Kowloon and Central cost HK$90–100, returns HK$160–180; children aged under 11 travel for half the adult fare.

Free **shuttle buses** run between Central and Kowloon Airport Express stations and many nearby hotels, and the Hung Hom railway station. Many airlines also allow departing passengers to check in baggage at Airport Express stations, rather than at the airport.

BUSES
Airbus services, prefixed **A**, run at regular intervals to Hong Kong Island, Kowloon and the New Territories, and there are also slower and still cheaper 'commuter' buses (prefixed **E**).

A11 and A12 run through Central and the busiest areas

Octopus Cards and Tourist Transport Passes

Anyone using public transport more than a couple of times will find it better, and cheaper, to get a multi-journey card than buy tickets each time you travel. Octopus is a stored-value smart card, valid on all kinds of transport except taxis and some minibuses and ferries, which can be bought at MTR stations. You pay a deposit of HK$50 for the card, and then charge it up for however much you want to spend (minimum HK$150). You then swipe the card on special machines each time you board a train, bus, tram and so on, and the fare is deducted. Octopus fares are always lower than those for single tickets, and Octopus holders also get discounts at a growing number of shops in Hong Kong. For details, see www.octopuscards.com. Transport Passes are more limited, and specially designed for visitors. The MTR 1-day Tourist Pass gives you a day's unlimited travel on the MTR for HK$50; the 3-Day Transport Pass gives you 3 days travel on MTR and some bus routes, including one (HK$220) or two (HK$300) Airport Express trips.

on Hong Kong Island, A21 through the heart of Kowloon. Airbus fares to the main urban areas range between HK$33 and HK$45, E-route fares from around HK$14–HK$24. When you exit the Arrivals Hall, turn right for Airbuses or ordinary E-route buses. Route details are posted at the Transportation Centre, and on the airport website.

There are also night buses from the airport (prefixed N, which mostly run 0.20am–5am), and shuttle buses to Tung Chung station, on the main MTR network. Long-distance buses also run to Guanghzhou and other destinations in mainland China.

FERRIES

There are direct ferries between Tuen Mun in the New Territories and Tung Chung (daily, 6am–11.20pm), from where there are cheap shuttle buses to the airport. They are run by **New World Ferries** (www.nwff.com.hk).

TAXIS

Taxis are easy to find, at the rank outside the Ground Transportation Centre. Urban taxis are red; New Territories taxis are green; local Lantau taxis are blue. A taxi to Central on Hong Kong Island will cost around HK$340 or more, to Kowloon slightly less; all fares from the airport include HK$30 toll for the Lantau island road bridge.

Getting Around the City

Although the high-rise jungles of Hong Kong may look daunting to the visitor, this is actually an easy city to get around, thanks to a highly efficient and easy-to-use public transport system. Rush hours, though (Mon–Fri roughly 8–10am and 5–7pm), can prove unpleasant for the uninitiated. Travelling at this time of day

may make you feel less than charitable towards the local population as necessity has dictated that people push in without ceremony to get onto buses, trains and trams.

To make the most of the system, use an **Octopus** travel card or a **Transport Pass** *(see left)* rather than single tickets. Children aged under 11 travel half-fare on most transport in Hong Kong, and under-3s travel free.

MASS TRANSIT RAILWAY (MTR)

The fast, efficient, very clean and air conditioned MTR network operates daily from around 6am to 12.30–1am. As well as the Airport Express the MTR comprises six lines, covering 51 stations, with their hub at Central station on Hong Kong Island: the Island line (**blue** line, on maps and station signs) along the top of Hong Kong Island; the Tsuen Wan (**red**) line, from Central up through Kowloon to Tsuen Wan; the Tung Chung (**orange**) line, which flanks the Airport line out to Lantau; the Kwun Tong (**green**) line, from Yau Ma Tei in Kowloon out to East Kowloon; the Tseung Kwan O (**purple**) line between North Point on the island and East Kowloon; and the special Disneyland Resort

Below: MTR sign.

123

Above: the latest in commutertainment.

line (**pink**), connecting the orange line to the resort.

Travelling by MTR is quick, but a bit more expensive than going by bus or ferry. Adult single fares range from about HK$4–HK$26 (but, as with all public transport, fares are lower with an Octopus card or Transport Pass, see p.123).

MTR stations have several exits, identified by letters and numbers, so it is good to have an idea of which you want (there are also maps by each exit). The MTR has an interchange with the KCR rail line at Kowloon Tong, and you can walk between Mong Kok MTR and KCR stations, and the new East Tsim Sha Tsui KCR station and Tsim Sha Tsui MTR.

MTR Information
Tel: 2881 8888,
www.mtr.com.hk

BUSES
Six companies provide bus services in Hong Kong, but **Citybus** and the associated **New World First** have the most within the city. Buses cover every part of the Territory, but are most useful for areas not on the MTR or rail lines, such as the south side of Hong Kong Island and parts of the New Territories. Many routes start from or run through one of three termini, at Exchange Square, Central and the Admiralty Centre on Hong Kong Island, and by the Star Ferry Pier in Kowloon. Some routes run all night, with a less frequent service.

Most city buses are British-style double-deckers. Final destinations are marked in English and Chinese on the front. Drivers rarely speak much English, but timetables and route maps are posted at bus stops. Fares range from HK$1.20 for short journeys in the city to HK$45 for longer trips into the New Territories.

Note, though, that **drivers do not carry change**, so that if you do not have an Octopus Card or Transport Pass you must have the exact money.

Bus Information
Citybus; tel: 2873 0818,
www.citybus.com.hk
Discovery Bay Transportation Services
Tel: 2987 0208, www.hkri.com
Serves part of Lantau Island.

Taxi talk

Many taxi drivers can speak some English, and will know the main hotels and tourist spots, but exchanges can at times be challenging. Drivers will sometimes refuse a fare, usually if the journey will take them out of their way as they are about to finish work (rather than try to argue, it is probably better to walk off and find another taxi). Ask your hotel concierge to write your destinations down in Chinese. All cabs are equipped with a radio phone, and somebody at the control centre should be available to translate.

Below: Peak Tram.

Above: double decker bus.

Kowloon Motor Bus (KMB)
Tel: 2745 4466,
www.kmb.com.hk
Most Kowloon routes.
Long Win Bus Company
Tel: 2261 2791,
www.kmb.com.hk
Services to the airport.
New Lantao Bus Company
tel: 2984 9848
Serves all of Lantau island.
New World First Bus
tel: 2136 8888,
www.nwfb.com.hk
City routes and many to the New Territories.

TRAMS
Trams have been rattling an east–west path along the north side of Hong Kong Island since 1904, and the double-decked carriages still offer a picturesque ride as well as an extremely inexpensive means of getting across the city. Stops are frequent, and you can simply hop on and off as you please. The flat fare is HK$2, or HK$1 for under-12s and over 65s (exact change required, or use Octopus or Transport Pass); you get on at the back and get off at the front, paying as you get off. Tram routes operate between 6am and 1am. The top deck offers the best views.

The **Peak Tram** is actually a funicular railway, and has been running since 1888. It takes 8 min to reach the top from the terminus on Garden Road, Central (near Hong Kong Park). Trams run every 15 min, between 7am and midnight daily. The fare is $20 one-way, $30 return (Octopus and Transport Passes valid).
Hong Kong Tramways
tel: 2548 7102,
www.hktramways.com
Peak Tram
tel: 2522 0922,
www.thepeak.com.hk

MINIBUSES/MAXICABS
These 16-seater cream-coloured buses (with a red stripe) run on fixed routes, but stop anywhere except on double yellow lines. Once full they will not stop until requested to. They are usually faster than regular buses, but not as cheap. Destinations are usually written in English at the front of the van. Call out clearly when you want the driver to stop (try '*lee do*' in Cantonese). Fares vary from HK$1.50–HK$20. Drivers will give change for small notes only, but on some routes you can use Octopus Cards.

Green minibuses run to many small destinations, mainly in the New Territories.

TAXIS
Taxis are cheap, abundant and easy to hail on the street, although in rush hours you may need to join a queue at a rank or a hotel. Taxis in Hong Kong Island and Kowloon are red, and in theory can take you anywhere apart from non-airport destinations on Lantau. Sometimes you will come across taxis on Hong Kong Island which are so-called 'Kowloon taxis', and will only take passengers across to Kowloon. Green taxis run in the New Territories, blue ones on Lantau.

Minimum fare for red cabs is HK$15, and there are extra charges for luggage placed in the car boot, and tunnel and bridge tolls. Many, but not all, taxi drivers speak reasonable English; all fares are metered, and receipts given. By law all passengers must wear seat belts, and drivers will remind you if you do not buckle up straight away. If possible avoid taking taxis in rush hours, when journeys can take twice as long.

STAR FERRY
The traditional cross-harbour ferries are a Hong Kong institution, and a ride ranks as one of the best and cheapest sightseeing thrills. The 12-

Below: vintage tram in modern clothing.

Above: the Star Ferry faces a precarious future.

strong Star Ferry fleet of open-sided ferries still run between Central and Wan Chai on Hong Kong Island and Kowloon from 6.30am–11.30pm every day, although the historic Central ferry pier closed in 2006, to be replaced by a more anonymous modern quay. There are also routes from Hung Hom to Central and Wan Chai. Fares begin at just HK$1.70 (HK$2.20 on the upper deck) on the main Central to Tsim Sha Tsui route. Departures are every 6–12 minutes depending on the time of day, and the trip takes about 8 min.

More modern but less atmospheric New World Ferries also run across the harbour from North Point.

Star Ferry Information
tel: 2367 7065,
www.starferry.com.hk

Out of Town

Urban Hong Kong makes up only part of the Territory. Beyond the 24-hour bustle and intense cityscape extend dramatic scenery, traditional villages, serene monasteries,

beaches and hundreds of smaller, tranquil islands, all still easily accessible, thanks to the local transport system. The Pearl River also connects Hong Kong with the former Portuguese colony of Macau, and China's Guangdong province. Day trips to both are easy to do. For **bus information**, *see* p.125.

FERRIES TO OUTLYING ISLANDS

Ferries to Lamma, Lantau (including a 24-hour service to Discovery Bay), Cheung Chau and other islands leave from the **Outlying Island Ferry Piers**, just north of the Airport Express station in Central on Hong Kong Island.

Two types operate on most routes: **standard** ferries and the slightly more expensive **fast** ferries. New World First Ferry has the most routes.

Fares vary greatly but start from HK$11, and can be slightly more at weekends and holidays. Octopus Cards *(see p.123)* can be used on most ferries; otherwise, take correct change for the ticket

turnstile; change booths are only open at peak times. If visiting Lamma, be aware that there are two channels at the ferry terminal entrance, one for ferries to Yung Shue Wan (north), the other for Sok Kwu Wan (east).

FERRY INFORMATION
Discovery Bay Transportation Services
Tel: 2987 0208, www.hkri.com
Ferries to the south side of Lantau.
Hong Kong Kowloon Ferry
Tel: 2815 6063,
www.hkkf.com.hk
Ferries to Lamma.
New World First Ferry
Tel: 2131 8181,
www.nwff.com.hk
Ferries for most of the islands.

RAIL

The **Kowloon-Canton Railway** (**KCR**) has three lines in the New Territories: the **East Rail** line from East Tsim Sha Tsui station in Kowloon up to the mainland border at Lo Wu, with frequent stops including Sha Tin, Tai Po and Fanling, and a branch line east to Wu Kai Sha, near the Sai Kung Country Park, from Tai Wai; the **West Rail** line from Nam Cheong in New Kowloon (also an MTR stop, orange line) round to Yuen Long and Tuen Mun; and the separate **Light Rail** between Yuen Long and Tuen Mun.

Trains are fast and frequent: every 3–10 min, depending on the time of day, from 5.30am to 12.30–1am daily, and the full journey on East Rail takes 42 min, on West Rail 30 min. Fares cost HK$4.50–$36.50, and you can use Octopus Cards. KCR stations are hubs for local bus routes, notably at Sha Tin, Tai Po Market and Yuen Long.

KCR Rail Information
Tel: 2929 3399; www.kcrc.com

TO MACAU
There are very frequent ferry sailings every day between Hong Kong and Macau, 65km to the west, from two departure points: the **Macau Ferry Terminal** in Sheung Wan (Western), near the Outlying Islands Ferry Piers, and the **China Ferry Terminal** in Tsim Sha Tsui, Kowloon. Turbojet also runs direct ferry transfers from Hong Kong Airport.

It is wise to buy return tickets on Macau ferries in advance, especially at weekends or holidays, as seats can sell out. Fares vary between ferry services, and according to the class of ticket, which day and at what time you travel. For up-to-date information, check with individual companies, or the Macau Government Tourist Office, tel: 2857 2287, www.macautourism.gov.mo.

Turbojet offers the fastest, slightly more expensive service, from Macau Ferry Terminal. Ferries leave every 15 min

7am–1am, and roughly once an hour during the night, and the crossing takes 55–65 min. Tickets generally cost HK$135–$175, 'ordinary class', one-way.

New World First Ferry runs high-speed catamarans from the China Ferry Terminal, though most also pick up passengers in Sheung Wan. They leave every half-hour, 7am–midnight, and journey time is 65–75 min. Ordinary-class single fares are HK$137–$172.

Macau Ferry Information
New World First Ferry; tel: 2131 8181, www.nwff.com.hk
Turbojet; tel: 2859 3333, www.turbojet.com.hk

TO CHINA
Guangdong province has as its capital one of China's most vibrant cities, Guangzhou (formerly Canton), and the rural landscapes around Shenzhen lie only 45 min from Hong Kong by train or bus. Most travellers need a visa to enter mainland China *(see p.37)*.

The **KCR** railway operates **trains** roughly once an hour daily, 7.30am–7.15pm, from Hung Hom station in Kowloon, to Guangzhou via Shenzhen. Travelling time is just under 2hrs, and a single fare is HK$145–$190. There are also long-distance trains

to Beijing or Shanghai every two days. Tickets can be bought at KRC stations or online, at CTS (China Travel Service) branches or at many Hong Kong travel agents. Trains arrive at Guangzhou East station, a taxi ride from the city centre.

If direct tickets to Guangzhou are sold out, take the KCR to the border at Lo Wu (42 min). The Shenzhen station is just a short walk across the border.

Buses are a slower, even cheaper, alternative. CTS also has an extensive bus network, with daily departures from Hong Kong.

Ferries also ply between Hong Kong and several Guangdong cities including Zhuhai, Shekou and Fuyong (for Shenzhen airport). Most leave from China Ferry Terminal in Tsim Sha Tsui, and there is a direct ferry to Shenzhen from Hong Kong Airport; passengers on this route clear immigration into China, not Hong Kong. **Turbojet** has the most modern services.

China Transport Information
China Travel Service (CTS), tel: 2851 1700, www.ctshk.com
KCR Railway; tel: 2929 3399, www.kcrc.com
Turbojet; tel: 2859 3333, www.turbojet.com.hk

Below: all aboard, no frowns please.

Walks and Views

If there is one thing Hong Kong is not short of, it is stupendous views. Whether you are up at The Peak, sitting on the upper deck of a tram or exploring the outlying islands you are almost guaranteed a good view of a spectacular city set in a fantastic natural environment. Take the time to explore on foot and you will be justly rewarded. In parts of the New Territories and outlying islands it is possible to take long walks in dramatic mountain scenery, enjoy superb natural views and see barely a soul for hours and hours. It is difficult to believe that the hectic Central is only minutes away.

The Peak

Peak Tower, Lugard Road; www.thepeak.com.hk; Peak Tram: Garden Road, near Hong Kong Park; daily 7am–midnight

One of the main reasons people ascend the Peak – as well as the tram-ride to get there – is to marvel at some of the world's finest vistas. On one of Hong Kong's (increasingly rare) clear days there should be a view all the way to mainland China. Many find the nighttime views – a vast glittering swathe of electric light – even more spectacular. The **Peak Tower**, next to the top of the tramway, was renovated in 2006, adding new shops,

An ample supply of information is available to visitors aiming to explore Hong Kong's hiking possibilities. HKTB Tourist Offices provide advice, free maps and leaflets, and the excellent (and also free) *Exploring Hong Kong's Countryside: A Visitor's Companion*, by Edward Stokes. Anyone with a bit more time can also find a choice of good walking guides in bookshops, of which the *Hiker's Guide to Hong Kong*, by Pete Spurrier, is one of the best.

restaurants, and significantly more windows to make the most of the views. The viewing platform has been raised 30m to the top of the so-called 'wok' for a 360-degree panorama.

WALKS FROM THE PEAK
There is a variety of superb walks from the Peak. The **Peak Circle Walk** follows Lugard and Harlech roads from the Peak Tower, affording magnificent views across the harbour to Kowloon in the north; to Cheung Chau and Lantau to the west; and over the great mass of junks and sampans at Aberdeen to the south, with Lamma Island's telltale chimney stacks beyond. This gentle 3km walk, well signposted and shaded from the sun, takes about 45 min round-trip from the Tower.

The area around the Peak Tower is in fact **Victoria Gap**, whereas the summit of **Victoria Peak** itself (552m) looms up just to the west. Follow the Peak Circle Walk until you reach the **Governor's Walk**, which winds up to the attractive **Victoria Peak Garden**.

Left: view off the south side of Hong Kong Island.

Left: Dragon's Back trail is a walk for the brave.

Possession Street is also known as Shui Hang Hau. Its English name is due to the fact that it runs inland from the spot – initially called Possession Point – where the British first raised their flag and 'took possession' of Hong Kong in 1841. As the population grew a road was laid heading uphill, the present Possession Street.

In the run up to the 1997 Handover locals ruminated on whether such colonial names would be abolished in favour of more Chinese names, but Possession Street, along with many others, remains.

The summit itself is out of bounds.

It is also possible to walk back down to the city from the Peak, and enjoy some of the best views and footpaths around its wooded slopes. The **Central Green Trail** – marked by 14 bilingual signboards highlighting points of interest – meanders from Barker Road, a little below the Peak Tower, down across May Road and then via paths named Clovelly, Brewin and Tramway back to the Garden Road tram station. A popular longer walk continues westwards from the Peak Circle Walk through **Pok Fu Lam Country Park**. For the more ambitious, this path also joins up with the **Hong Kong Trail**, which curves around Pok Fu Lam before heading east along the ridges above Aberdeen to wind right across Hong Kong Island all the way to Tai Tam and Shek O, a full distance of 50km. Nature-lovers can wander through forests of bamboo and fern, stunted Chinese pines, hibiscus and a jumble of vines, with a good amount of shade.

If you do not want to take on the whole trail, there are various points where you can cut off and find buses back to the city.

Western District

MTR Sheung Wan; map p.136 B4.
The western districts of Sheung Wan and around Hollywood Road are among the most characterful – and the oldest – parts of Hong Kong city, and so some of the most popular areas for exploratory urban walks. You will be so mesmerised by the street life, you will barely notice your legs moving.

Sheung Wan

Begin at **Western Market** *(see p.103)*, a large red-brick Edwardian building a short way west of Sheung Wan MTR. Turn left (away from the harbour) into **Morrison Street**, and immediately right into **Wing Lok Street**, where you will find numerous speciality shops selling ginseng and the so-called, much-prized 'bird's nest' used in soup, gathered from the sides of caves. At the end of this street turn left into **Des Voeux Road West** – home to little shops displaying huge

Below: an unexpected guest.

Above: a trail through Tai Tam Country Park.

varieties of exotic dried seafood – and then left again into **Ko Shing Street**, the wholesale centre for Hong Kong's thriving herbal medicine trade. It is easy to wander for hours, trying to figure exactly what the wares on show – rare plants, dried animal organs – could be.

Hollywood Road

To compare Sheung Wan with its less pungent but still atmospheric neighbour, walk back to Des Voeux Road West, and turn right into

---

If you try any walking in the summer months, when Hong Kong is at its most humid, be sure you have sufficient water with you before you set off. With humidity levels peaking around 90 per cent, you will need all the re-hydration you can get. However fit you are, Hong Kong's humidity can be extremely debilitating, especially to the uninitiated, so you should build more time in to your schedule to allow for this and wear light, cotton, breathable clothes.

Bonham Strand West (parallel to Wing Lok) and then right again into **Possession Street**. From here the road slopes upwards to meet **Hollywood Road**, famous for its curios and antiques shops. Head left, and when you have done browsing continue on to the famous **Man Mo Temple**, with maybe a detour left into **Upper Lascar Row** (Cat Street Bazaar) for more browsing among traditional Chinese carvings, antiques and oddities, rejoining Hollywood Road at **Ladder Street**.

Inside Man Mo *(see p.116)* the air is thick with aromatic smoke from the incense coils dangling from its roof. Carry on along Hollywood Road to reach the **Mid-Levels Escalator**. From here you can explore SoHo, or wind down into Central.

Tai Tam Country Park

Bus: 6, 66 from Central; map p.137 D3

The Tai Tam reservoirs that lie in the southeast of Hong Kong Island offer an oasis of calm for walkers. This is a relatively easy downhill walk, which passes many good picnic stops, beautiful surroundings and the calm, still waters of the reservoirs.

Set off from **Park View**, above Causeway Bay on the **Wong Nai Chung Gap** road to Repulse Bay and Stanley (if you take the 6 or 66 bus from Exchange Square, get off at the Wong Nai Chung Reservoir). Follow the road that turns east off the main road downhill past **Hong Kong Parkview**, down past a picnic area, cross the dam and turn right. The stream leaving the first reservoir is hidden in a wooded ravine.

Cross the bridge below the **Tai Tam Intermediate** reservoir, and pause at the pavilion on the left for a view over the bigger **Tai Tam Tuk** reservoir. Keep to the road beside this reservoir and walk its length before crossing over a picturesque bridge. Within 10 min or so you will arrive at **Tai Tam Road**. From here you can catch a bus (14, 314) back to the city.

Lantau

Ferries from Outlying Islands Ferry Terminal, *see p.126*, or MTR: Tung Ching, then local buses

The centre of Lantau island is dominated by lofty mountains, the most notable of these being Lantau Peak and Sunset Peak. These peaks are criss-crossed with winding pathways and trails, linking several Buddhist monasteries. From the **Po Lin Monastery**, follow the sign to the **Tea Garden**, and at the entrance follow the hiking trail for about 15 min. If you have time, pause at the **Wisdom Path** on your left. Otherwise, look for the entrance gate leading to **Lantau Peak**. Much of the route wanders through substantial natural woodland, with hillside streams crossing the trail. The peak is on your right, and this trail winds around its northern slopes.

SEE ALSO OUTER ISLANDS, P.20, TEMPLES AND HISTORIC SITES, P.119

Lamma

Hong Kong Kowloon Ferry services from Outlying Islands Ferry Terminal; tel: 2815 6063, www.hkkf.com.hk

The gently rolling, north-to-south walk between Lamma's ferry piers takes a couple of hours and will give you a flavour of both sides of the island, as well as rewarding you with some of its most beautiful views. Take the ferry to **Yung Shue Wan** on the north side, and, after strolling through the village (10 min), follow signs indicating a left turn to **Hung Shing Ye**. As the concentration of low-rise houses gradually thins, the path begins to wind past small vegetable plots and dotted hamlets, with the three chimneys of Lamma Power Station looming ever-present on your right.

Hung Shing Ye Beach is relatively clean, with changing rooms, snack stalls and a small café. At the far end of the beach the narrow concrete path starts to climb more steeply towards a hill with an observation pavilion. This is a good halfway point if you want to head back.

The reward for carrying on to **Sok Kwu Wan** on the east side of Lamma becomes immediately apparent as the path winds around the mountain, opening up fabulous sea views to your right. The walking is not strenuous, and before long the path begins to descend into **Lo So Shing**, a sleepy hamlet of traditional Chinese houses. Enjoy a wander through the narrow alleyways between these characterful old homes.

From the village, either follow the signs to the pretty (and relatively secluded) **Lo So Shing Beach** or continue directly to **Sok Kwu Wan** (Picnic Bay). Stop for lunch or dinner at one of the string of waterfront Chinese restaurants, before catching a ferry back to Central (check times before leaving the ferry pier).

Be aware that, although Lamma is famous for not having any conventional motor vehicles, locals are allowed to have small tractors and trucks adapted from tractors, which they may sometimes drive along footpaths pretty aggressively. You will hear them coming.

Below: climbing ivy.

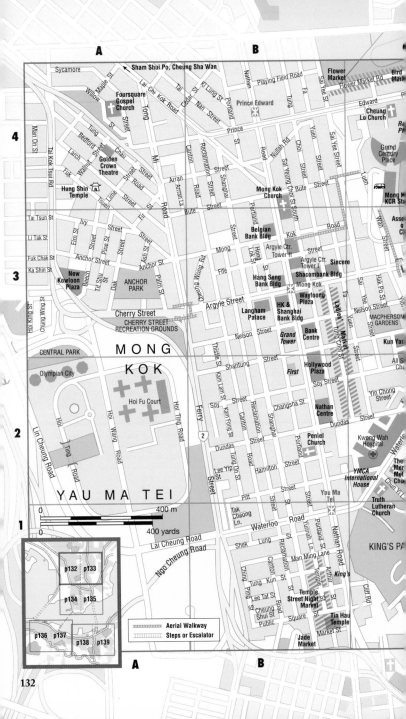

Sycamore

Sham Shui Po, Cheung Sha Wan

Maple St
Willow
Lai Chi Kok Road
Tai
Kok
Cedar St
Nan Street
Portland
KY Lung St
Playing Field Road
Nathan

Flower
Market
Fa
Sai Yee St
Flower Market Rd
Bird
Mark

Foursquare
Gospel
Church ✝

Tong
Street

Prince Edward

Prince Edward ✝

Edward

Cheung
Lo Church ✝

Re
Pl

Man On St

Tai Kok Tsui Rd

Tung St
Bedford St
Larch St
Walnut St
Fuk St
Chui
Street

Canton

Reclamation Street

Shanghai

Road

Nullah Rd

Choi

Prince

Sai Yeung Choi St South

Yuen

Street

Street

Street

Street

Luen

Grand
Century
Place

Golden
Crown
Theatre

Mi Street

Arran
Arran La

Bute
Street

Portland

Mong Kok
Church ✝

Bute
Street

Mong Kok
KCR Sta

Hung Shin
Temple ⛩

Lime Street
Tsuen St
Ash St
Palm St

Wan Street

Asse
o
Ch

Tai Tsun St

Li Tak St

Fuk Chak St

Ka Shin St

Ivy Street
Elm St
Pine St

Anchor Street

Beech

Tit Shu St
Oak St

Anchor St

Portland

Mong Kok Road
Hong Lok St

Belgian
Bank Bldg

Kok

Street

Argyle Ctr.
Tower II

Road

Sincere

Sai Yee Street

Hak Po St

New
Kowloon
Plaza

ANCHOR
PARK

Fife

Argyle Ctr.
Tower I

Hang Seng
Bank Bldg

Shacombank Bldg

Mong Kok

Fa Yuen Street

Nelson Street

MACPHERSON
GARDENS

Cheung Wing St

Hoi Kung St

Cherry Street

Argyle Street

Langham
Palace

Wayfoong
Plaza

HK &
Shanghai
Bank Bldg

Ladies' Market
Tung Choi St

Kun Yar

CHERRY STREET
RECREATION GROUNDS

Nelson Street

Grand
Tower

Bank
Centre

CENTRAL PARK

Lin Cheung Road

Olympian City

MONG

KOK

Hoi Fu Court

Hoi Ting Road

Hoi Wang Road

Hoi
Ting
Road

Thistle St

Shantung Street

Kam Lam St

First

Soy St

Kam Fong St

Hollywood
Plaza

Soy Street

All S
Ch

Yin Chong
Street

Ferry
Street

Canton

Reclamation Street

Shanghai

Changsha St

Nathan
Centre

Dundas
Street

Kwong Wah
Hospital

Wate

YAU MA TEI

Dundas
Street

Lee Ying Lo St

Portland
Street

Hamilton
Street

Lee Yip St

Peniel
Church

YMCA
International
House

The
Mer
Met
Chu
Chun Yi

0   400 m
0   400 yards

Pitt
Street

Tak
Cheong
Ln.

Yau Ma
Tei

Truth
Lutheran
Church

Lai Cheung Road

Ngo Cheung Road

Waterloo

Road

Shek
Lung

Reclamation St

Nathan Road

Portland St
Tunnah Ln

KING'S PA

p132 p133

p134 p135

p136 p137 p138 p139

Man Ming Lane

Ching Ping St

Tung Kun St

Canton St

Lee Tat St

Cheung Shui St
Public

Temple
Street Night
Market

King's

Arthur

Jade
Market

Temple

Square

Tin Hau
Temple

Market St

Cliff Rd

〰〰〰〰〰 Aerial Walkway
▥▥▥▥▥ Steps or Escalator

A   B

D   E

↑ Wong Tai Sin Temple

Kowloon Hospital

Lomond Rd

Walled City Park

Argyle   Street

Baptist Church

MA TAU WAI

Kowloon Rehabilitation Centre

Kadoorie Ave

Braga

Circuit

san Boys chool

St John's Ln.

Tin

Kwong Road

4

Gillies Rd

Tweed Rd

Street

Farm Road

Kadoorie Avenue

Street

Dunbar   Road

Perth

Shek Ku St

St Mark's Church

Sheung Hong St

Sheung Shing St

Tin Kwong Road

Argyle

Hop Yat Church

Kau Pui Lung Rd

Staics Ave

Julia Ave

Metropole

Man Fuk Rd

King Tak St

Mormon Church

Sheung Wo St

3

Emma Ave

YWCA

Man Wan Rd

Princess

Pentecostal Tabernacle

Kowloon Central Library

Sheung Shing Street

Ho Man Tin Estate

Sheung Lok Street

Chinese Church of Christ

loon Chamber ommerce

Pui Ching Road

Fok St

Ho Man

Tin Hill Rd

Hill

Rd

Fat   Kwong

Sheung

Good

Chung

Hau

Shepherd St

Street

2

Wylie

Ho Man Tin Street

Ho Man

Tin

Hill

HO   MAN

Chung Man St

Village St

Carmel

TIN

Sheung Lok Street

KO SHAN ROAD PARK

Ko Shan Theatre

Ko Shan Rd

Hau

Man

St

Margaret

Road

King's Park Rise

Chu Man St

Oi Man Shopping Centre

Sports Centre

Chung Yee St

Fat Kwong Street

Hau

Street

Shun Yung St

East Kowloon Corridor

1

ARK

Wylie Road

Queen Elizabeth Hospital

Road

Chung

Yan Fung St

Valley Rd

Wo Chung St

D   E

133

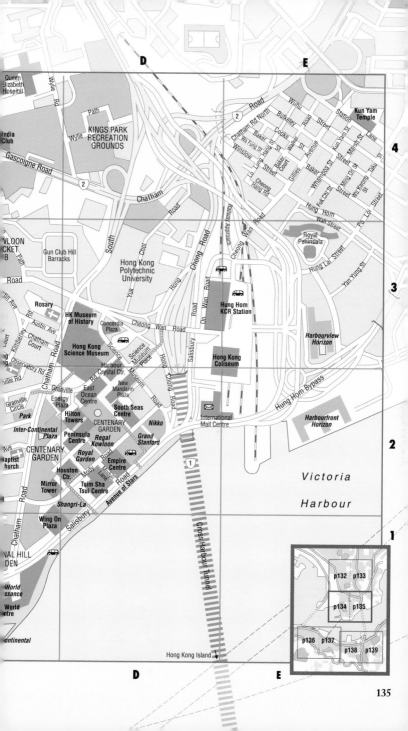

Queen Elizabeth Hospital

India Club

KINGS PARK RECREATION GROUNDS

Gascoigne Road

Wylie Rd

Path

Wylie

Path

Road

Kun Yam Temple

Wuhu

Bulkeley

Wa Fung St

Baker St

Cooke

Walker

Station

Kun Yam St

Marsh St

Lane

St

Chatham Rd North

Winslow

Ling Nga

Street

Cheong

Court

Baker

Court

Gillies

Avenue

Baker Street

Whampoa St

Ching On St

Wing Kwong St

Tak U

St

Hung Hom

Wah Street

Chatham

Road

South

Road

Choi

Yuk

Hong

Wan

Road

Cheong

Wan Road

Railway Road

On

Wan

Road

Hung Lai Street

Yan Yung St

Po Loi St

Royal Peninsula

KOWLOON
CRICKET
CLUB

Path

Road

Gun Club Hill Barracks

Hong Kong Polytechnic University

Hung Hom KCR Station

Harbourview Horizon

Rosary

HK Museum of History

Concordia Plaza

Cheong Wan Road

Salisbury

Road

Hong Kong Coliseum

Austin Ave

Kimberley

Chatham Court

Observatory Rd

ville Rd

Granville Circle

Park

Inter-Continental Plaza

CENTENARY GARDEN

Baptist Church

Ave

Hong Kong Science Museum

Science

Science Museum Place

Harbour Crystal Ctr.

East Ocean Centre

Enetgy Plaza

Hilton Towers

Peninsula Centre

Houston Ctr.

Mirror Tower

Mody

New Mandarin Plaza

South Seas Centre

Nikko

Grand Stanford

Empire Centre

CENTENARY GARDEN

Regal Kowloon

Royal Garden

Tsim Sha Tsui Centre

Shangri-La

Wing On Plaza

NAL HILL
DEN

World
ssance

World
ntre

ontinental

Chatham

Road

Salisbury

Mody

Lane

Avenue of Stars

Road

International Mail Centre

Hung Hom Bypass

Harbourfront Horizon

Victoria

Harbour

Cross Harbour Tunnel

Hong Kong Island

p132 p133

p134 p135

p136 p137

p138 p139

135

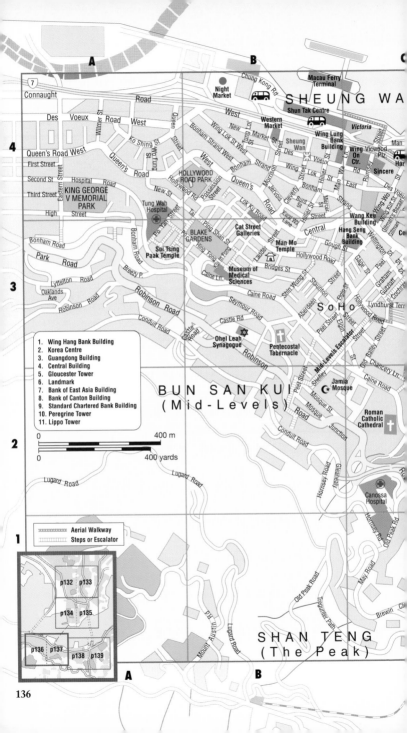

Map labels

7
Connaught Road

SHEUNG WA

Des Voeux Road West

Macau Ferry Terminal

Chung Kong Rd

Night Market

Western Market

Shun Tak Centre

Queen's Road West

First Street

Second St

Third Street

High Street

Hospital Road

KING GEORGE V MEMORIAL PARK

Eastern Street

William St

Ko Shing St

Queen's Road

Wong Fung St

Queen's Road West

Bonham Strand West

New Market St

Wing Lok St West

Des Voeux

Bonham Strand

Wing Lok

Queen's Road

Jervois St

Bonham

Mercer St

Bonham Strand

Sheung Wan

Des

Voeux

Wing Lok

St

Burd St

Hillier St

Cleverly St

Kwai Wa St

Victoria

Wing Lung Bank Building

Wing On Ctr.

Viewbod Rd

Man

Har

Sincere

Des Voeux

Kennedy's Beach

Hollywood Road Park

New St

Hollywood Rd

Possession Street

Queen's Rd

Lok Ku St

Central

Bonham Rd

Tung Wah Hospital

Po Yan St

Tai Ping Shan St

BLAKE GARDENS

Ping Fong In Fong

Cat Street Galleries

Ladder St

Man Mo Temple

Hollywood Road

Gough St

Wang Kee Building

Hang Seng Bank Building

Wellington St

Gage St

Peel St

Ce

Sui Tsing Paak Temple

Caine Ln.

Museum of Medical Sciences

Bridges St

Shin Wong St

Caine Road

Aberdeen St

Staunton

Square Street

Elgin St

Graham St

Gutzlaff St

Cochrane

Park Road

Bonham Road

Breezy P.

Lyttelton Road

Oaklands Ave

Robinson Road

Robinson Road

Conduit Road

Castle Road

Castle Rd

Seymour Road

Peel Street

SoHo

Lyndhurst Terr

Hollywood Rd

Bridges St

Shelley St

Mid-Levels Escalator

Bartley St

Chancery Ln.

Ohel Leah Synagogue

Pentecostal Tabernacle

Robinson

Mid-Levels Escalator

Caine Road

BUN SAN KUI
(Mid-Levels)

Peel Street

Mosque St

Jamia Mosque

Mosque

Junction

Road

Roman Catholic Cathedral

0   400 m

0   400 yards

Conduit Road

Gleanealy

Hornsey

Canossa Hospital

Lugard Road

Lugard Road

Building index

1. Wing Hang Bank Building
2. Korea Centre
3. Guangdong Building
4. Central Building
5. Gloucester Tower
6. Landmark
7. Bank of East Asia Building
8. Bank of Canton Building
9. Standard Chartered Bank Building
10. Peregrine Tower
11. Lippo Tower

Legend

Aerial Walkway

Steps or Escalator

p132 p133

p134 p135

p136 p137 p138 p139

Old Peak Road

Mount Austin Rd.

Lugard Road

Tregunter Path

May Road

Old Peak Rd

Brewin Cl

SHAN TENG
(The Peak)

A   B

D   E

← Kowloon

Pier 1
Pier 2
Pier 3
Pier 4
Pier 5
Pier 6
Pier 7
Pier 8

Outlying Islands
Ferry Piers

Man
Man
Kwong
Man
Kwong
Street
Man
Po
Street
Street
Finance Street

Star Ferry
Pier

Victoria

Harbour

4

Four
Seasons
Hotel

International
Building

IFC Mall

IFC One
IFC Two

Central
Station
The
Forum

Hong
Kong

Harbour View Street

Hang Seng
Bank
Building

Connaught
Road

Exchange
Square

General
Post
Office

Jardine
House

Area under
Reclamation

3

Pottinger
St.

Douglas
St.

China
Travel
Service

Queen's
Theatre

King's
Theatre

Theatre Lane

Chiu Lung St.

Central

St George's
Building

Mandarin
Orient

STATUE

City
Hall

Edinburgh

Place

CHUNG WAN
(Central District)

Former
Prince of
Wales Bldg

Lung Wui Road

Tim Wa Avenue

Citic
Building

Tim Mei Avenue

3

Shell
House

New
World
Tower

Peddar
St.

Chater

Road

Prince's
Building

Ice House
St.

Des Voeux
Road C.

Chater
Club

Ritz
Carlton

Legislative
Council
Building

CHATER
GARDEN

Lambeth
Walk

Bank of
America
Tower

Fairmont
House

Cotton Tree Drive

Murray

Far East
Finance
Centre

Admiralty
Centre

Harcourt

HARCOURT
PARK

Road

7

May
House

Wyndham Street

Zetland St.

Duddell St.

Queen's Rd C.

HSBC
Bldg

Bank of
China

Battery Path

Albert

St John's
Cathedral

Road

City Bank
Plaza

Bank of
China
Tower

Admiralty

Queensway
Plaza

Tamar

Street

Rodney St.

United
Centre

2

St Paul's

HK Central
Hospital

Lower

HK Diamond
Exchange
Building

Government
House

American
Embassy

Albany Road

Albert

Ice
Garden

St Joseph's
Cathedral

Hilton

Peak Tram
Terminus

Cotton Tree Drive

Flagstaff
House
Museum of
Tea Ware

Supreme
Court

Supreme Court Rd

Government
Offices

Island
Shangri-La

Queensway

Pacific
Place

Conrad

Marriott

Justic Drive

Monmouth
Path

Star
Street

2

ZOOLOGICAL &
BOTANICAL
GDNS

Cotton Tree Dr.

Garden

Kennedy Road

Visual Arts
Gallery

HONG KONG
PARK

Aviary

Regent on
the Park

Borrett Road

Kennedy Rd

Bowen Drive

Union

First Church of
Christ Scientist

Macdonnell Road

Bowen

Road

Bowen

Road

Borrett Road

1

Peak Tram Funicular

Magazine Gap Rd

May Road

Magazine
Gap Rd

Magazine Gap

Peak Tower

D   E

137

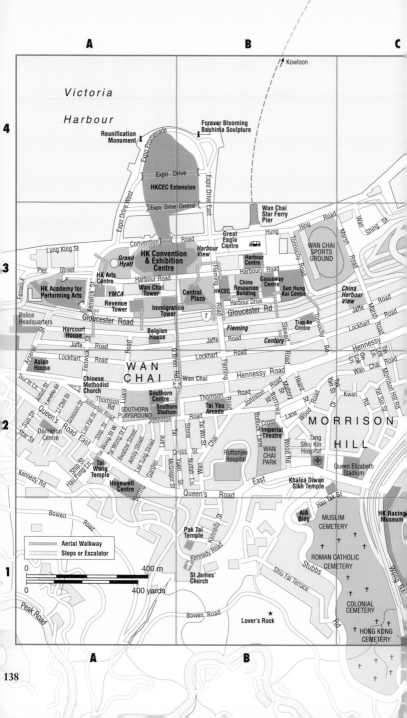

Kowloon ↑ Cross Harbour Tunnel

Causeway Bay
Typhoon Shelter

Victoria Ctr.

Whitf. Road

Electric Rd

Jupiter St

Hing Fat St

Gordon Rd

Mercury St

8

Wing Hing St

Electric

Tsing Fung St

Kellet Island

Royal HK Yacht Club

Hung Hing Road

Park Road

Victoria

Lau Li Road

Ngan Mok St

Tung Lo Wan Rd

Dragon Rd

Temple St

Tin Hau

4

Lau Sin St.

Hing Fat St.

Noon-Day Gun ★

Police Officers' Club

Tin Hau Temple

Tin Hau

CAUSEWAY BAY

Gloucester Rd

Cleveland St

VICTORIA

Queen's College

Chinese Rhenish

Cannon St.

Houston St

Kingston St.

PARK

Lin Fa Kung Temple

Jaffe Road

Paterson St

Causeway Road

3

Percival Street

Lockhart Road

World Trade Centre

Excelsior

Daimaru

SOGO

Gt. George St.

Causeway Bay Road

Sugar St.

Park Lane

Windsor House

Central Library

Lo Wan Road

Rd East

Matsuzakaya

Jardine's Bazaar

Yee Wo Street

Road

Moreton Terrace

Shelter St

Lo Wan Rd

Soohoo Street

King Street

Lily St

Road

Jardine's Cres.

Lee Kai Chiu Rd

Tang Lung

Pak Sha Rd

Yun Ping Rd

Irving St.

Tang

Lee Garden Rd

Lee Gardens

Lan Fong Rd

Kung Lee

Shepherd St

Sun Chun St

Russell St

Hysan Ave.

Sunning Rd

Leighton

Tang

St Paul's Hospital

Cotton Path

St Mary's Church

Tai Hang Road

Times Square

Sharpe St

Hoi Ping Rd

Haven St.

Ka Ning Path

Shing Kwong

Eastern Hospital Road

Yiu Wa St

Leighton Road

Matheson Street

Canal Road East

Leighton Ln.

Caroline Hill Road

Tai Hang Road

2

LEIGHTON HILL

Leighton Hill

C & W Sports Club

Caroline Hill Road

South China Athletic Stadium

CAROLINE HILL

Tung Wah Eastern Hospital

Craigengower Cricket Club

Sports Road

Wong Nai Chung Road

Leighton Hill

St Margaret's

Happy View Ter.

Confucius Hall

Stadium Path

HK Football Club Stadium

Broadwood Road

Broadwood Road

Ventris Road

SO KON PO

HK Stadium

1

Happy Valley Racecourse and Recreation Ground

Seventh Day Adventist Pioneer Memorial

ames Hall

Chung Road

PARSI CEMETERY

† HINDU CEMETERY

Hindu Temple

PAU MA TEI (Happy Valley)

Tai Wong Temple

p132 | p133

p134 | p135

p136 | p137

p138 | p139

141

Index

Insight Smart Guide: Hong Kong

Text by: Teresa Machan and Ryan Levitt
Edited by: Nick Rider and Jason Mitchell

Photography by: Alex Havret/apa, except Corbis 34, 41B; Getty 37T, 48BL&BR; 48/49T, 49C, 51BC&B, 69B; Government Information Services 51T; Harbour Plaza Hotel 55, 56B; Intercontinental Hong Kong 56T; Island Shangri-La 53BL&BR; Gerhard Joren 51TC; Mary Evans Picture Library 50CB; Mandarin Oriental Hotel 52/53T; Manfred Morgenstern 50TC& B, 51TC

Picture Manager: Hilary Genin
Maps: James Macdonald and Neal Jordan-Caws
Series Editor: Maria Lord

First Edition 2008
© 2008 Apa Publications GmbH & Co. Verlag KG Singapore Branch, Singapore.
Printed in Canada

Worldwide distribution enquiries:
Apa Publications GmbH & Co. Verlag KG (Singapore Branch) 38 Joo Koon Road, Singapore 628990; tel: (65) 6865 1600; fax: (65) 6861 6438
Distributed in the UK and Ireland by:
GeoCenter International Ltd
Meridian House, Churchill Way West, Basingstoke, Hampshire RG21 6YR; tel: (44 1256) 817 987; fax: (44 1256) 817 988
Distributed in the United States by:
Langenscheidt Publishers, Inc.
36–36 33rd Street 4th Floor, Long Island City, New York 11106; tel: (1 718) 784

0055; fax: (1 718) 784 0640l
Contacting the Editors
We would appreciate it if readers would alert us to outdated information by writing to:
Apa Publications, PO Box 7910, London SE1 1WE, UK; fax: (44 20) 7403 0290; e-mail: insight@apaguide.co.uk